In the thick of the fight

JAMES McCLURE

In the thick
of the fight

York County, Pa. counters the Axis threat in WWII

YORK DAILY RECORD/SUNDAY NEWS ∎ YORK COUNTY HERITAGE TRUST

World Wide Web:
Part of this work, plus a wealth of other information on York County history, can be accessed at the York Daily Record/Sunday News' Web site, www.ydr.com.

To order:
Copies of this work are available through the York County Heritage Trust, 250 E. Market St., York, Pa. 17405, 717-848-1587, www.yorkheritage.org and other regional booksellers. James McClure's "Never to be Forgotten, A Year-By-Year Look at York County's Past," "Nine Months in York Town, American Revolutionaries Labor on Pennsylvania's Frontier," "Almost Forgotten, A Glimpse at Black History in York County, Pa." and "East of Gettysburg, A Gray Shadow Crosses York County, Pa." can be obtained through these outlets. Videos, "Never to be Forgotten" and "Nine Months in York Town," based on the books, are available through the Heritage Trust.

Copyright ©2005.
James McClure.

ISBN Number 978-0-9710416-6-0

Library of Congress Control number: 2005923230

McClure, James
In the Thick of the Fight/York County, Pa., Counters The Axis Threat in WWII / [Researched and written by James McClure; Edited by Kim Strong; Design, visuals by Ted Sickler]. [York, Pa.]: York Daily Record/Sunday News, [2005].

On the cover

This World War II poster, found in the York County Heritage Trust files, shows three arms raised, two with fists gripping tools and one grasping a rifle. The illustration suggests that the Allies can achieve victory through the cooperation of men and women working in defense plants and fighters in the field. An enlarged version of this poster, dated 1942, hung from the ceiling of Union Station in Washington, D.C. At its top, an inspirational quote from U.S. Vice President Henry Wallace appears: 'Strong in the strength of the Lord/we who fight in the people's cause/ will never stop until that cause is won.' This is one of hundreds of U.S. government wartime posters that used the power of advertising to promote ideas: increase production and unity and sell bonds and stamps. These signs, sometimes called propaganda posters, appeared in York County and across America in high-traffic areas — schools, factories, offices and store windows. In short, these posters reminded Americans why they were fighting and what the fight was for.

On the back cover

York Corporation, York Safe and Lock and A.B. Farquhar Co., venerable York County companies, threw their might behind the war effort and received large defense contracts and coveted Army-Navy 'E' production awards in return. They were among 19 York County plants that did this despite losing thousands of employees to the Armed Forces. This illustration comes from an A.B. Farquhar Co.-produced booklet issued as part of its reception of the production award in early 1943. Inside the booklet, the company praised its workers on the war front and home front: 'Now you men are in the thick of the fight for Freedom. We cannot but feel the great responsibility that we in the shops have, to give you everything we can to speed Victory.'

Contents

'Do these things temporarily so that democracy may continue permanently. Help now, so that peace, happiness and prosperity shall not be abolished forever. Aid the "Arsenal of Democracy." It is America's war effort for the common welfare of future generations.'

— Donald Epstein, Grade 12, The York-High Weekly, 1942.

'The war will be lost even though we win the battles if our boys come back to an empty shell and not to the thriving life they left. It is the duty of those at home not to let that happen. We must not forget that it is just as patriotic to work for our high standards as it is to fight for them.'

— The Barker, P.H. Glatfelter Co., 1943

'Regarding the troops, there was hardly a family in the county that did not have a direct connection with someone serving in the armed forces. We all felt united in a way which I still find difficult to explain to those who did not experience it. Our common goal to win the war permeated our daily life beyond any other subject.'

— Orin Stambaugh, High Speed Radio Operator, U.S. Army, Pacific Theater, World War II Writing in 2003

Credits and acknowledgments

Author: James McClure
Editor: Kim Strong
Photo/layout coordinator: Ted Sickler
Layout artists: Tracey Bisher Cullen, Samantha K. Dellinger
Copy editor: Deborah L. Hummel

Giving due credit

The author thanks those listed above for their patient and above-and-beyond work on this project — the fifth book-length, York County history venture most members of this team have worked on.

Thanks, too, to York Daily Record/Sunday News editorial assistant Loretta Martin and receptionist Donna Hollinger for helping to prepare the manuscript and Joanne Althoff and Cheryl Spilman for preparing the photographs.

Thanks to Carroll County Times copy editor Joseph McClure for preparing the index and editing the manuscript.

Michael Newsome continues to be an indispensable encourager on all these works.

Thanks to Della McClure and Joe, Regina and Tony for their forbearance and support.

Much of this work's research came from the York County Heritage Trust's Historical Society Library. Thanks to June Lloyd and Lila Fourhman-Shaull for their review of the manuscript. The Heritage Trust has been a helpful partner on this project, as on past coordinated projects.

Thanks to James Rudisill, Luther B. Sowers and Barre Shepp, director of the York County Veterans Affairs Office, for reviewing the manuscript.

Much appreciation to Fred Uffelman and Thomas Norton, York Newspaper Co., for their support and assistance.

Photo credits:
York County Heritage Trust, York Daily Record/Sunday News, The Gazette and Daily, Farm Security Administration/Office of War Information, National Archives and Records Administration, Enoch Pratt Free Library, Northwestern University Library, Museum of American History, University of Minnesota Libraries, Hanover Public Library, Hanover Evening Sun, York Corporation/York International, Pennsylvania Historical and Museum Commission, Robert N. and Ethel Senft collection, Robert Frutiger collection, Spring Grove Bi-Centennial Commission, Deborah L. Hummel collection.

Foreword

'I believe the Lord had a hand in this'

Today, many in York County know the names of Devers and Goode only as identifiers of elementary schools. Both York schools honor true World War II heroes from the city.

Gen. Jacob Loucks Devers led the Invasion of Southern France in August 1944, just a few months after D-Day. His move through France to the Rhine meant Germany had to resist the Allies at two points on its western front.

And Rabbi Alexander D. Goode of York gave up his life vest — and his life — so that others might live. Goode was one of four chaplains who went down with the transport ship Dorchester in 1943.

But the names of thousands of county World War II heroes aren't on the side of buildings — names like Frutiger and Senft, both workers before the war at major military contractor York Ice Machinery Corporation, later York Corporation.

Red Lion's Lt. Thomas W. Frutiger marched with thousands of other American captives up the Bataan Peninsula in the Philippines. He survived that unrelieved horror — the Bataan Death March. But as his captors transported him away from invading Americans, friendly fire sank his ship. He was among the 571 or more county residents who did not come home.

Conewago Township's Robert N. Senft did return, as did more than 20,000 other York County fighting men and women.

On his way to the planned invasion of Japan in 1945, the Army clerk arrived in Okinawa just as the war ended, in time to see bulldozers covering mass graves of the island's Japanese defenders.

Fighting with his typing fingers, Senft supported those on the front line, both at Yorkco before he was drafted and in his military duties.

This is a tale of York County war heroes and unsung soldiers, great industrialists and lathe operators.

This is a story of soldiers maneuvering howitzers overseas, sailors on submarine lookout aboard zigzagging ships on the seas and Army Air Forces pilots dogfighting with Zeroes above the seas.

• • •

This is also a story of the men and women who made, in full or in part, the big guns, ships and planes that contributed to the Allied victory.

In this way, workers at York Corporation played a prominent role in the intriguing York County story of World War II. They worked at a company that was such a part of York that people referred to its two massive plants as "The Yorks."

The company's principals — men like P.H. Glatfelter and Thomas Shipley — caught refrigeration on its way up. Refrigeration and cooling equipment manufacturing stood as a leading American high-technology industry at the turn of the 20th century.

HELLO, WASHINGTON–YORK, PA., CALLING

The cover story of an October 1941 edition of the Saturday Evening Post points to York. The story told how York County industries cooperated to aid the military.

This poster promotes the Saturday Evening Post's story that identifies York County's prowess in mobilizing for defense purposes, even before America's official entrance in the war.

By World War II, York Corporation had gained international leadership in refrigeration and air conditioning and employed about 5,000 people at its York plants and field offices.

Many York County companies supported their people on the home front and war front. But probably no other company sent as many men and women to war — 1,200 — or lost more men in uniform — 25.

The company's chairman, William S. Shipley, is credited as prime promoter and organizer of the internationally recognized York Plan. The plan called for companies to share lists of equipment and skilled laborers to score massive contracts that couldn't otherwise be handled locally.

It took thousands of committed people to make the York Plan work, and many of their stories are reflected in this book.

The story of a single horizontal boring machine sitting in Yorkco's red-brick factory illustrates how the York Plan worked.

York Corporation typically used the machine about 350 hours a year before World War II.

But in February 1941 — just days after President Franklin D. Roosevelt's fireside speech calling for America to become the "Arsenal of Democracy" — it had been running continuously for four months and had enough work ahead to keep it humming until summer.

Yorkco's boring equipment machined parts for powder presses. Another York plant had the contract to make the presses, necessary for the manufacture of gunpowder. But that company did not have a boring machine. If this second York plant were to try to purchase such a machine, the equipment wouldn't be delivered for months.

Fortunately, the underused boring machine at Yorkco could handle the work. The cooperation of the two companies meant that the then-current gunpowder shortage could be mitigated. A shortage of gunpowder could mean a lapse in firepower.

York County would play a small role to ensure Americans entered the war with full cartridge belts and thus added to the life expectancy of countless fighting men.

That's no boring tale.

• • •

The teenage Pennsylvania soldier dug a foxhole in the backside of a hill on Okinawa in April 1945. His mission as a member of a mortar squad in Co. E, 307th Infantry, 77th Infantry Division was to provide cover fire for riflemen as they advanced over the rise to force Japanese foes off the next hill.

Early the next day, the offensive began. But something clearly went wrong. White phosphorous shells began landing in the soldier's position — from the rear.

Friendly fire.

Those shells were intended for the next hill, to set up a smoke screen for the infantry. The semi-solid white phosphorous sprayed over the soldier, immediately burning and smoking on contact. It covered the soldier's face, hands, legs and back. Somehow, his helmet protected his hair and eyes.

The soldier and the rest of his squad, all burned, were evacuated to a field hospital, five miles behind the lines. That night, "kamicraze" pilots, as soldiers called them, targeted ships in the harbor. Some were shot down; others found their marks.

At times, the soldier took cover in caves that served as tombs for the Okinawans.

Less than a year before, the young man had sat at his desk in a Pennsylvania high school. Now, on the other

These York Corporation workers labor on what appears to be a steel gun barrel. They actually are working on another tool of war, a heavy machine tool used to finish off crankcases and high-pressure cylinders for engines and compressors that are part of refrigeration units, vital to the Allied war effort.

side of the earth, the badly burned 18-year-old lay in a cave listening to suicide bombers screeching toward floating targets.

The wounds healed slowly, but he recovered enough to return to his unit at Cebu in the Philippines. It was August, and the war was just over. Atomic bombs on Hiroshima and Nagasaki took care of that.

Only about 20 percent of his original company was there in Cebu. Most had been killed in action on Okinawa.

Friendly fire had probably saved the soldier's life.

"I believe the Lord had a hand in this," he later wrote, "and I have thanked him many times since."

The soldier returned home and married. That soldier is my father, Robert E. McClure III. It is to him and my mother, Betty Pebley McClure, that I dedicate this work. Like many of his fellow fighting men, he seldom talked about those horrid experiences 60 years ago. Now thousands know.

But most importantly, my prayer is that this soldier's grandchildren would understand the faith and sacrifices of their grandparents.

And my hope is that readers of this work would better understand what it meant to be in the thick of the fight.

— James McClure

Prelude

— 1917-1919 —

The Little Courthouse, a replica of the Colonial Court House, stands on York's Centre Square, later Continental Square, during World War I. The courthouse served as a center for war bond sales. An effigy of Kaiser Wilhelm II is seen in the left foreground. For a small sum, donors could drive nails into the German leader's head. Walter G. McBlain, D.W. Heinekamp and O. Roland Read are seen in front. The building was put back into service in World War II, when it operated as Victory House.

Gallery

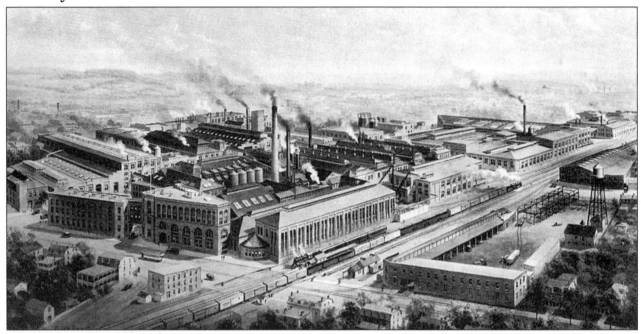

This 1921 image shows the York Manufacturing Company plant, along West York Avenue, later Roosevelt Avenue, in York. The facility, known as the West York plant, produced refrigeration equipment for the military in World War I. By World War II, the company was a symbol of York's industrial might. It had built a second factory on a Grantley Avenue site, the Grantley plant. The plants covered 96 acres, with 1.36 million square feet of working and storage space.

This flier conveys the destitution of those in Europe, devastated by World War I. The York War Chest used this image as a means to raise funds.

This newspaper clipping from 1906 shows officers of the York Manufacturers' Association: from left, John C. Schmidt, president of Standard Chain Co. and Schmidt and Ault Paper Co.; Thomas Shipley, York Manufacturing Company; S. Forry Laucks, York Safe and Lock Co.; and Francis Farquhar, A.B. Farquhar Co. Their companies would operate through World War I and would contribute leadership and know-how toward bringing defense work to York County during World War II. The Manufacturers' Association became a leader in coordinating and promoting the York Plan.

The Gazette and Daily received word of the German surrender at 2:50 a.m., Nov. 11, 1918, early enough to get the news in that day's edition. A Gazette and Daily representative gave York Mayor E.S. Hugentugler the news, and he ordered the ringing of sirens and bells to alert townspeople that an armistice had been reached. World War I was over.

'The greatest victory of all time'

The news clattered across The Associated Press wire into The Gazette and Daily's newsroom.

The Germans had signed an armistice. Their forces would disarm and retire from France, Belgium and other occupied areas at the 11th hour of the 11th day of the 11th month in 1918.

The newsroom and composing department feverishly reset the front page of York's morning newspaper. It was 2:50 a.m., and the southcentral Pennsylvania daily's front page would carry the big story on the noted date, Nov. 11, 1918.

By pre-arrangement, someone at the East King Street newspaper had gained a special assignment to deliver the news to York Mayor E.S. Hugentugler. So the messenger scurried to the mayor's house, six blocks west on the same street.

The knock on his door marked the last sleep Hugentugler and his town would enjoy that night.

"He at once issued orders for a general announcement through the fire alarm and the factory and locomotive whistles, and the people were so awakened from their slumber by the gladsome news of the greatest victory of all time," The Gazette and Daily reported in that day's paper.

The commotion so startled Melvin Wilt at the Royal Firehouse that he lost his hold on the sliding pole from the firefighters' bedroom to the apparatus room. His cut head,

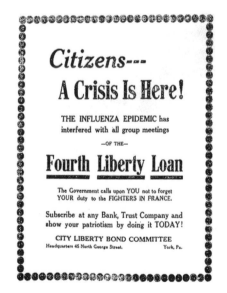

The government financed World War I, in part, through the sale of bonds. When the Spanish flu epidemic threatened the Fourth Liberty Loan drive, organizers placed advertisements in county newspapers to remind residents of those fighting against the Germans in France.

bruised hip and sprained back were among the most serious injuries reported during the spirited celebration.

The mayor set a meeting at 10 a.m. in York County's East Market Street courthouse to prepare for a grand celebration and parade on Saturday.

But this was Monday. York's residents couldn't wait. They grabbed anything at home that would make a noise — kettles, pans, motor horns, trumpets, gongs and rattles.

The crowd banged and hollered on York's streets for nearly 24 hours — tagged as the greatest impromptu celebration in city history.

From left, George Wood, William A. Myers, and Jeannette Zinn died in the service of their country in World War I. The deaths of two brothers, Harry and John Withers, sons of Daniel H. Withers of York, also added to the death toll. The brothers were killed by the explosion of a single German shell in France.

'This is a Loyalty Bond'

History had ensured York County was well practiced in its celebrations.

An occasion in 1834 was one such example. That year, the citizenry lined the town's streets to observe the death of the Marquis de Lafayette.

The charismatic, young Frenchman had soothed unrest toward Commander in Chief George Washington during a visit to the Continental Congress, then meeting in York. This was the American Revolution's Valley Forge winter, the bitter cold months of 1777-78.

And local folks credited Lafayette with the French support that helped spell victory for Americans in their quest for independence in that war against Britain.

Fifty-six years later with Lafayette long buried in France, York residents paid their respects with a solemn funeral procession honoring the marquis, complete with empty hearse.

In the years leading up to World War I, York's long memories of Lafayette's support helped ease the county's conscience for its considerable contributions toward France's and Britain's war against Kaiser Wilhelm II's German forces.

Some in York County had held a low view of America's buildup to the war.

People of Pennsylvania Dutch stock — actually German in background — dominated the hills and valleys of this rich agricultural county of about 140,000 people. Parishioners still heard sermons in the German language, and many spoke German in their homes. A German-language newspaper had stopped its presses only 20 years earlier.

Many residents had close relatives fighting for the German army. One citizen learned that his brother earned Kaiser Wilhelm's Iron Cross for bravery. Another was notified that his two sons had been killed in fighting.

But after America entered the war in 1917, Mayor Hugentugler bristled at the contention of some that German-American counties could not be trusted. He headed a patriotic town that sent troops early and often to fight in the American Revolution and Civil War, even amid

Tablets listing the 195 York County residents who died in World War I grace the lower façade of the York County Courthouse soon after the war's end. The tablets bear the names of those in uniform who died in battle or from influenza and other illnesses between April 7, 1917 and Nov. 11, 1919.

ambivalence over the politics fueling those conflicts.

The mayor reacted with dispatch to this clear and present rumor that York wouldn't deliver against the Germans. He banned anti-war meetings, organized anti-spy groups, assigned guards to county industrial plants and prosecuted distributors of anti-war literature.

At the same time, he called for York residents to back a loyalty pledge showing support for the war. Three-quarters of city men eligible to vote signed the pledge, and Hugentugler promptly sent the signatures to President Woodrow Wilson.

Others in town showed their patriotic colors. As their name suggests, a squad of Four Minute Men briefly spoke on patriotic themes at movie theaters and other places of amusement.

Their talks were laced with slogans: "Earn the right to say, I helped to win the war," "This is a Loyalty Bond as well as a Liberty Bond" or "A cause that is worth living for is worth dying for, and a cause that is worth dying for is worth fighting for."

As popular gathering places, theaters represented a ready spot for such talks. The movie houses specialized in

THEY KEPT THE
SEA LANES
OPEN

INVEST IN THE VICTORY LIBERTY LOAN

The U.S. government found informational posters useful in World War I. Here, the poster promotes the sales of Liberty Bonds to finance the war.

This cover of Steel Horizons shows World War II soldiers marching to war, as soldiers from past American wars — Revolutionary, Civil, Spanish-American and World War I — are shown in the background. York County residents willingly volunteered — and shed blood — in these conflicts.

propaganda films and patriotic fare. Residents particularly connected with Mary Pickford's films. The actress had once traveled with Charlie Chaplin to York to promote Liberty Loans to help finance the war.

York County industries geared up to support America's forces and their allies in France. York Manufacturing Company, for one, received a contract to construct a huge refrigeration plant to preserve food for Gen. John J. Pershing's men over there.

'One of the many hammers'

During the brief war, York residents backed five Liberty Loan drives. Residents pledged $2 million in the first drive and more than quadrupled that amount by the fourth campaign, waged amid a raging Spanish influenza epidemic.

Some overzealous campaign workers constructed a "Yellow Streak Monument" in York's square to name resi-

dents who were not yet holders of bonds.

The 150 residents of Cross Roads, in southeastern York County, raised eight times their allotment to buy bonds to finance the war. York Haven, in the county's northeast, garnered 20 times its allotment.

To cover Liberty Loan drive expenses, local patriots set up a wooden carving of the kaiser's helmeted dome in York's main square and put a 10-cent-a-nail price on it. Donors lifted a hammer with a red, white and blue handle to drive the spikes into the German emperor's head. At one point, eight pounds of nails protruded from the wooden figure's noggin.

"This is one of the many hammers in the land that is helping to nail kaiserism," The York Dispatch, The Gazette and Daily's evening competitor, reported.

Those financial sacrifices were meager compared to the human cost. More than 6,000 county residents served in the American military. Between April 7, 1917 and Nov. 11, 1919, 195 residents in the Armed Forces or working in military support roles died from battle casualties, the influenza epidemic or other illnesses.

Pvt. William A. Myers, who entered the service at 16, was perhaps the youngest of those who did not return to the farm from Paree. The teenager, killed in front-line fighting, received a posthumous Distinguished Service Cross for valor under fire.

"He was just a boy in years, but he played a man's part," a historian wrote.

German farm boys were not the only ones to lose their lives.

Jeannette Zinn, valedictorian of her York High School class seven years before, died from pneumonia in Britain while on her way to do YMCA war relief supervision in France. Pvt. George Wood, a black serviceman from York County, died in France serving in a machine gun unit.

'Last Cross' did not last

So when the gaped-mouth whistles and swaying bells came alive in the dead of night in November 1918, county residents had paid for the privilege of parading, both stepping spontaneously and marching in scheduled formation.

As the sun rose that morning, firefighters from the Vigilant assembled a figure of the kaiser, dressed in brass helmet and black uniform. They nailed the effigy to a cross and hung the figure and his new wooden mount to a streetlight standard in front of their firehouse. They scrawled "The Last Cross" on the wooden crossbeam.

But the Vigilant firefighters' "Last Cross" notation did not last.

For a solitary lance corporal in the defeated German army would soon emerge to put forth a vastly different cross — a broken cross sewn onto a flag.

Scarcely more than two decades after this Armistice Day end to The Great War, York County residents would again head to battle by the thousands — and die by the hundreds — to throw down Adolf Hitler's forces and the Nazis' despised swastika.

Then service members fighting overseas and those working at home in factories would help to pull down another banner.

That one bore a Rising Sun.

I

'Pretty heavy stuff for a Sunday morning'

— 1941 —

Students at Edgar Fahs Smith Junior High School in York man an airplane spotting post on school grounds. Within weeks of the Japanese attack on Pearl Harbor, thousands of York County residents stood guard 24 hours a day. This vigil lasted until manpower shortages late in 1943 limited watches to once a week. Spotters spent hours studying silhouette cards of all types of aircraft so they could detect friend from foe.

Gallery

> *1st Pres. Church*
>
> *part 3 serv* · *Used each Sunday during World War II as*
>
> ## Prayer for Those in the National Service
>
> ✠   ✠
>
> ALMIGHTY GOD, who art a strong tower of defense to them that fear thee, we bow in earnest prayer for all those in the service of this nation, who are facing danger on land or sea. We thank Thee that they are encircled by Thy loving care. Keep them strong to resist all dangers to heart or soul; protect them against the perils of the sea or air or land; guard them from the violence of enemies; and enable them so to do the duty that may fall to them that for the inhabitants of this land and of all lands there may be peace and freedom to serve Thee. In the longing of great love we pray this for our own who have gone out from this congregation. In deep sincerity we pray this for all who are serving this nation. And we pray it in the name of Him who is the Captain of our Salvation, Jesus Christ our Lord. Amen.
>
> *Written by The Rev. T. S. Dickson*

The handwritten note suggests the Rev. T.S. Dickson's prayer was read every Sunday at York's First Presbyterian Church.

This group of selectees is among the 500,000 Pennsylvanians who got their first taste of Army life at the New Cumberland Reception Center in northern York County. New Cumberland also played host to a special training unit, which schooled 13,000 men, previously unable to read and write.

This poster shows Dorie Miller on board the U.S.S. West Virginia during the Pearl Harbor attack. A messman with no gunnery training, he worked a gun, fighting back. He received the Navy Cross for his heroism.

The Gazette and Daily reports the tragic news from Pearl Harbor on Dec. 8, 1941, a day after Japan's attack on America's strategic naval base. Dozens of county men were stationed in Hawaii at the time of the bombing.

'Those are war clouds'

It was just another Sunday for Robert N. and Ethel Senft of Zion View.

Bob Senft was looking forward to a day away from town after a long week at York Ice Machinery Corporation. Ethel would get a day of rest from cooking, washing, ironing and other chores at the Conewago Township home the young couple shared with her widowed mother and grandfather.

That morning, they attended services at nearby Quickel's Church. After that, the couple followed a York County Sunday afternoon custom — visiting family and friends. They drove north on the winding Susquehanna Trail to Harrisburg. There, they called on Ethel's mother's cousins.

Sometime that afternoon, a newsboy's pitch of an "extra" interrupted the Sunday quiet:

Pearl Harbor bombed!

This attack on the U.S. Pacific Fleet's Hawaii base was all the Senfts — and most people in America — would talk about that day. And for the next four years.

" ... (T)hat Sunday, December 7, 1941, 'change' was about to infest everyone's thinking," Bob Senft later wrote.

• • •

If only the Senfts had heard a hauntingly accurate forecast issued the previous night, they would not have been surprised at the news.

An elderly West York seer became inspired after observing beautiful clouds moving across the Saturday evening sky.

"Those are war clouds," he prophesied, "I've seen them before, and I know what they mean. The war is at our back door right now, and it's going to move in very shortly."

According to a newspaper account, those hearing his words smiled tolerantly.

• • •

Hostilities bringing America into World War II began unofficially at 7:53 a.m.

That's when the first wave of 181 attacking Japanese planes struck much of America's Pacific fleet anchored at Pearl Harbor.

The two-hour attack killed 2,403 servicemen and civilians, demolished 164 planes and damaged or destroyed eight battleships.

When word of the surprise attack crossed multiple time zones and reached York County that Sunday, it decided the long, testy debate about whether Americans should join Britain and Soviet Union in their war against German and Italian aggression.

From that point, York County would do what it could with what it had to add to Allied firepower in a world war against Axis aggression.

• • •

For Ethel Senft and other young wives, the Pearl Harbor attack brought a particularly deep anxiety.

It could mean only one thing. Her high school sweetheart and husband of 18 months would be summoned to serve his country.

"I knew he would be going," she said.

'We had made our decisions'

When the bombs fell, York County residents were just settling into a calm holiday season after a wearying battle against a deadly polio epidemic.

In late June, Dr. John D. Yeagley, York's public health director, noticed an increase in polio reports. Health officials acted quickly, closing swimming pools, banning children from attending meetings and eventually canceling gatherings. Children were isolated in the city, and visitors were discouraged from coming to town.

Before the outbreak subsided, nine were dead and about 100 inflicted with the paralyzing disease.

With the epidemic over, county residents were particularly primed to celebrate.

As in the past, York's marquee department stores — Bear's, Wiest's and The Bon-Ton — tried to outdo their competitors with window displays and decorations.

The Bon-Ton's main window at Market and Beaver streets featured a St. Nick bearing a shaking stomach, oversized even for Santa Claus. His "Ho, Ho, Ho" could be heard more than a block away in Continental Square.

Twenty thousand evergreens had arrived in York on Saturday, Dec. 6, ready for Christmas use.

But as if a bomb had hit Continental Square instead of a remote Hawaiian naval base, people became instantly drawn to the news.

Residents sat around their blaring radios, gobbled up local and out-of-town newspapers or stood outside The Gazette and Daily's East King Street building to read wire reports on a board. Meanwhile, they threw flags to the breeze, dressing towns throughout the county in red, white and blue.

A vexing question in many discussions was how the Japanese could pull off such a sneak attack.

Charles Small of West York, who had served a seven-year military hitch in Hawaii, said he "couldn't understand how the Japanese got close enough to spring such a surprise attack — especially at Pearl Harbor, most strongly defended of the Pacific outposts."

Those who hazarded thoughts about Christmas faced the sad probability of celebrating without sons, brothers, husbands and other loved ones in the military.

"There will be no furloughs now," a West York correspondent wrote in The York Dispatch, "or at best only a scattered few."

• • •

People retained exactly where they were and what they were doing when they first heard about the attack. These frozen-in-time moments became part of countless conversations.

Nineteen-year-old Elwood W. "Bill" Gates was pumping gas at an Esso Station on North George Street in York when he heard the news. He was there to meet friends to go to the month-old Playland Roller Rink, already a popular Sunday activity.

The group made the trip to the east York hangout in a somber mood.

"How would this country react? What would be our way of retaliating?" Gates wrote years later. "By the end of the evening of skating, we had made our decisions."

The next morning, Gates and two other skating buddies stood in line at the Recruiting Station at the York's South George Street Post Office. Before the war's end, Gates, a Marine medic, was retrieving and treating wounded men from the assault on Iwo Jima in the Pacific.

Sunday afternoon, Jim Hubley walked up to his friend, Larry Douglas, at the entrance of the North York Playground building.

"Hi, Larry. What's cooking?

The trolleys are gone, but bus service is in full gear for those seeking to save rationed gasoline in this look at York's Continental Square in the 1940s. After the war, the city implemented one-way traffic patterns.

A photograph from a similar angle shows York at Christmas in the early 1940s. Later in the war, the square was less festive during the holidays. The government banned outside Christmas lighting to save electricity.

His response baffled Hubley: "What do you think of Pearl Harbor?"

With sincerity, Hubley replied, "Who's she?"

Hubley, acting sports editor for The Gazette and Daily, proceeded into the building to cover a basketball game. The meaning of Pearl Harbor soon became clear.

"Quickly, news of the attack spread among the athletes, youthful fans and followers, all of whom would be affected the rest of their lives by what had just occurred, far removed from the North York playgrounds," Hubley wrote years later.

Elsewhere in the county, Sheilavay Spangler Doll's family gathered around the radio with a major concern. Her brother was a Pan-Am pilot flying between the United States and Hawaii.

Finally, in the evening, a call came from a family member on the West Coast. The brother was at home — sick in bed. He hadn't made the flight that day.

Vesta Frigm and her date had stopped at a cigar store for an ice cream soda. The atmosphere lacked the usual light-hearted buzz.

"It was then and there that we heard," she later wrote, "Air Raids! Sinking Ships! Death! Destruction!"

Mary Smith Yinger awaited her mother's discharge

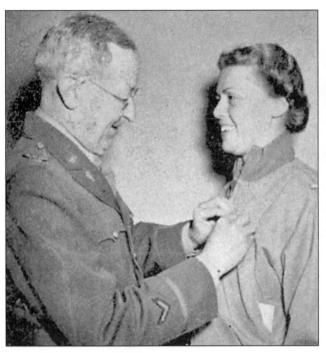

Hundreds of York County residents went into the military, even before Pearl Harbor officially brought America into the war. Mr. and Mrs. George Trout saw a daughter and son go off to war. Grace E. Trout, far left, joined the Army Nurse Corps in 1941 and served for 55 months. She did medical work after engagements in Africa, Italy, Germany and France. Harry S. Trout, left, served 40 months in the Pacific, seeing action with the Navy on Okinawa, Iwo Jima, Saipan, Tinian and the Marshalls. The brother and sister lived in Glen Rock after the war.

from the hospital. The news of the Pearl Harbor attack took away from the celebration.

Later, the young woman made an intriguing link: Her mother had been admitted to the hospital on Nov. 11 — the Armistice Day anniversary ending World War I — and discharged on Dec. 7 — the date of the attack that drew America into World War II.

Sixteen-year-old baby sitter Donna Shermeyer was listening to big band music on the radio when an announcer broke in with the news.

"I was scared," she said. "I was hoping the folks I was baby-sitting for would come home soon."

Isaac Payne was working in Washington, D.C., in December 1941. He knew he would be drafted, as did many men.

"I was old enough for them to grab me," he said.

Payne was right. He later served in Europe.

Other county residents were miles from home when they heard the news.

Collegian Mary Skold was riding a train to Boston. The news of the Pearl Harbor bombing was shouted through the train.

Richard Fry was visiting a sister-in-law in Maryland when he heard it on the radio.

"My first reaction was, where's Pearl Harbor?" he recalled. "… We all got very patriotic and felt we should do something right away."

R. Elizabeth Koontz heard the news leaving her college dining room. She had a special friend serving at Hickam Field, targeted by the Japanese pilots.

"Fortunately, his life was spared," she later wrote, "and even though I was planning to write him a 'Dear John' letter in the future, I was, nonetheless, concerned for his safety."

Rabbi Alexander D. Goode sat in his living room in York when he heard the radio news. After more than four years, he had just resigned his position with Temple Beth Israel.

He might become a military chaplain.

His thinking upset his wife, Theresa.

"The night of Pearl Harbor, I nearly fell apart," she said later. "Alex, the great patriot that he was, wanted to enlist immediately. I just looked at him and didn't say a word."

• • •

The attack meant that 96-year-old Caroline Schlosser of York would witness four wars. Her late husband, James Brown Schlosser, had fought for the North in the Civil War.

She could not quite comprehend the immensity of the Japanese assault but took an opportunity to dispense some advice to a newspaper reporter.

"No nation without God as their guide," she stated, "can hope to win."

• • •

On Monday — the day after the attack — The Gazette and Daily reported at least 26 county men might be stationed in Hawaii.

Publishing later that day, The York Dispatch upped the total of county men possibly in Hawaii to more than 200.

Neither newspaper could confirm servicemen actually on duty there. The best the War Department could do was say no word had been received about casualties, and families would be notified promptly as soon as anything definite was received.

All residents could do was wait and pray.

'Guys started getting hit'

Far from home at Pearl Harbor, servicemen with past or future York County links were reliving a frightful Sunday.

Charles Gilbert of York was standing on the deck of

Three York Boys Wounded In Pearl Harbor Battle

First Of Kin Of Private Richard S. Garrety, Private William L. Kellar And Sergeant James S. Minnich Advised By U. S. War Department

Extent Of Injuries Not Told

Three York boys stationed with the U. S. Army in Hawaii were wounded in action in defense of their country Sunday, their relatives learned yesterday by wire from the war department at Washington, D. C. They are Sergeant James S. Minnich, 23 years of age, grandson of Mrs. Sarah E. Sechrist, 133 South Queen street; Private William L. Kellar, 19 years old, son of Mr. and Mrs. P. L. Kellar, 465 West Princess street, and Private Richard S. Garrety, a nephew of Mrs. Isabel Ritz, 823 South Pershing avenue. The telegram did not disclose the nature of the wounds nor in what condition the York boys are.

The Gazette and Daily informed county residents about wounds sustained by three young soldiers in the Japanese attack on Pearl Harbor.

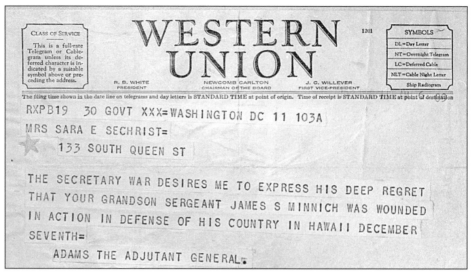

Sara E. Sechrist of York learned via telegram that her grandson, James S. Minnich, was wounded at Pearl Harbor.

HEADQUARTERS 17TH AIR BASE GROUP (REINFORCED)
Office of the Group Commander
Hickam Field, T. H.

12 December 1941.

SUBJECT: Commendation.

TO: The Officers and Men of the 17th Air Base Group (Reinforced).

THIS COPY FOR: Sgt James S. Minnich

1. You have just experienced what was for practically all of you a first baptism of fire when we were so treacherously raided on Sunday, 7 December 1941, by units of the Japanese Air Force. Certainly no troops in the world have ever been placed at more disadvantage than were you on this occasion. With no warning and with very few weapons available you were attacked vigorously and relentlessly by a determined foe.

2. Your actions at that time and at all times since has been highly commendable. You fought valiantly against a foe who had superiority

Sgt. James S. Minnich of York received this commendation from his commanding officers after the Pearl Harbor attack.

the U.S.S. California, the southernmost ship in Battleship Row, when he saw the Japanese planes approach.

"It was pretty heavy stuff for a Sunday morning," he later said.

The attack left Gilbert with second- and third-degree burns and a concussion.

Darrell Allen was aboard the submarine Cachalot, then undergoing repairs, when the attack began.

Gunners took over the sub's .30- and .50-caliber guns and fired back. A Japanese bomb came within 20 yards of the sub, one of four in the harbor that day. It did not explode.

Allen rushed to repair leaks in the sub's hull. Strafing from attacking planes caused bullet holes of all sizes. Sometimes, Allen deployed toothpicks to plug leaks.

Harold Heffner was on kitchen patrol at Schofield Barracks when he saw planes with Rising Sun insignias on their wings. The dishes were rattling in the mess hall. The planes strafed some barracks.

"Guys started getting hit," he recalled, "you could see the bullets. I didn't know they were Japanese."

After the attack, Heffner's unit headed to the beach. They would defend against an anticipated enemy landing.

Blain Cutler, a bugler, was in the chow line at Schofield when the low-flying planes roared overhead. When the bullets started hitting, he blew the alert call.

Wives and children of officers ran to the mess hall.

"We put them in there so they wouldn't get hit," he recalled.

Later, patrols went out to check on enemy planes that

had been shot down.

"They sent the guys out to smash the planes and kill or get the pilots or whatever was left of them," he said.

For weeks, the buddies of Woodrow Thoman, stationed at Fort Kamehameha, part of the harbor defenses, had expected an attack.

"I kept insisting the Japanese were too smart to attack us," he later wrote.

Even when he heard explosions at Pearl Harbor, he figured it was the Navy doing maneuvers — albeit a dumb time to do so.

But when the planes moved closer, he changed his mind about who was in the cockpits. They were flying so low that soldiers could see the faces of the Japanese pilots. The Americans had to duck to avoid the bullets.

A guy on KP peeling potatoes outdoors did all he could. He threw the spuds at the attackers.

John Main, a private stationed at Fort Armstrong, observed attacking planes passing over at 10,000 feet. Someone handed him a Browning automatic rifle. He fired some bursts at the planes, certain he did no damage.

Someone dispatched his squad to nearby Hickam Field to pick up a firetruck — crash trucks, as the Army called them. The airstrip was still under attack.

Their mission was unsuccessful. All the crash trucks were burned, their tires melted.

He and two other soldiers scurried beneath a tow truck to avoid the line of fire.

But the cover didn't work.

Main felt pain in his leg. He had sustained a minor wound, perhaps from a ricocheting bullet.

"I don't know how I got it," he recalled, "but I got a small slug in my leg, between the skin and the bone, lower part of my leg."

Sgt. James S. Minnich, Army Air Forces, was also in a hangar at Hickam Field.

When he first heard the bombs, he thought the Navy was practicing.

But this was no drill.

He ran for cover, but the strafing fire caught him in the arm.

If the bullet had gone a quarter of an inch deeper, he would have lost his arm. Instead, he was laid up in the hospital for six months.

• • •

News of Minnich's wounds reached York within a week of the attack. So did word of wounds sustained by hometown boys Richard S. Garrety and William L. Kellar.

The military's notice of Charles Gilbert's wounds reached York about 10 days after the assault.

Such telegrams seldom told the extent of the wounds, leaving loved ones to think the worst.

• • •

The dreaded news of a York County serviceman's death reached home by week's end.

The military listed Pvt. Eugene B. Bubb, 19, as killed in action but did not release details about his death at Hickam Field.

His late father, John E. Bubb, who served in World War I, had died earlier in 1941. Eugene Bubb's 15-year-old sister, Fern, received the telegram.

"We didn't have the radio on that Sunday (Dec. 7). We

LET US HAVE FAITH!

It has happened. American possessions in the Pacific have been attacked by a mad aggressor . . . Japan. The day we all hoped could be avoided has come. But even though it has come, the hands and hearts of Americans are clean. We did not strike the first blow. We were attacked . . . and we shall answer that attack with all our strength and might.

These are hours for every American . . . man, woman, and child . . . to consult the recesses of his soul. We are at war. What is the first thing each of us can do? We humbly submit that it is this: TO HAVE FAITH. Faith in our God, faith in our Country, and faith in our President. Faith in our constituted authorities, and in our armed forces.

Let there be no doubting or dissension. Rather, let us UNITE with resolute hearts to see this thing through to the end. At this moment, America stands as the hope of all decent mankind for a tomorrow when justice and honesty will replace injustice and deceit. Each one of us is part of that hope. We must not and shall not fail.

York and York County have set an example to the Nation for the way in which we have quickly produced defense materials. Just as we are an arsenal of defense, let us also be a fortress of American Faith. Our countrymen have died and are dying that we might remain free. Their memories shall remain sacred to us unto the end of Time. LET US HAVE FAITH!

WITH THE HELP OF ALMIGHTY GOD
THE RIGHT WILL PREVAIL

H. E. GOODLING ELECTRIC CO.
309 W. Market St. York, Penna.

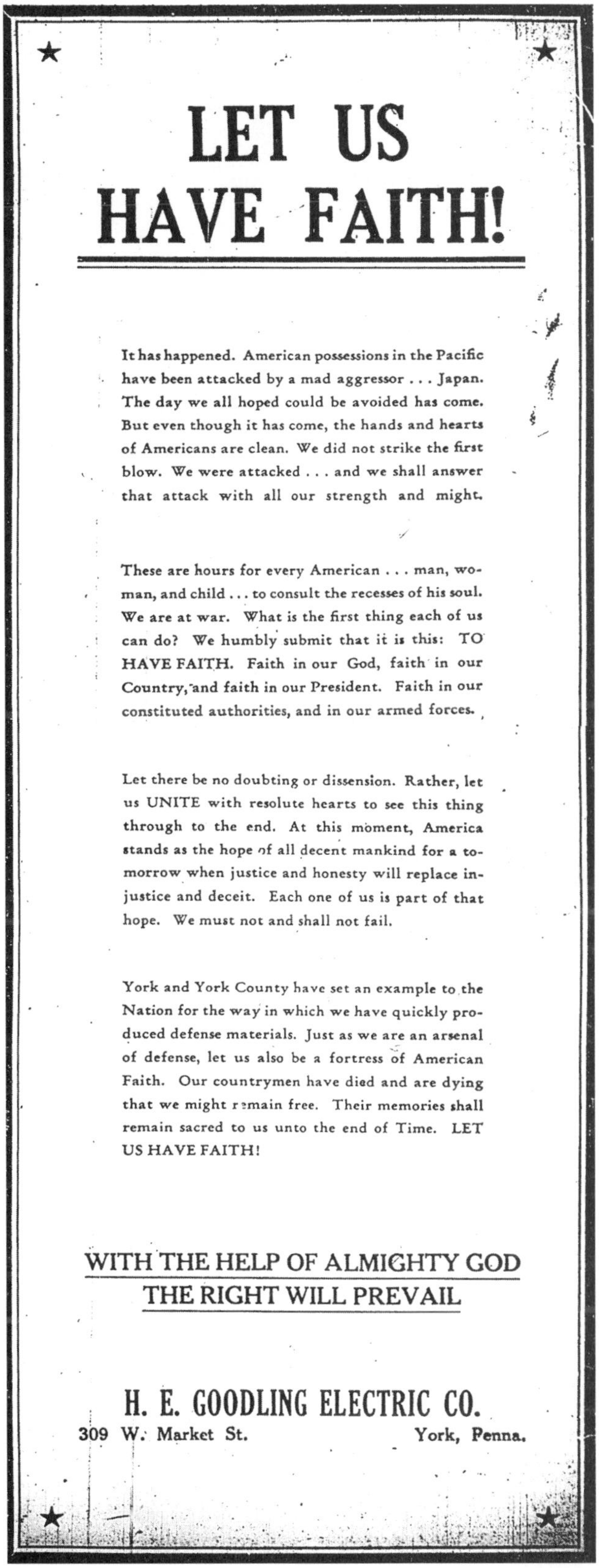

Immediately after the attack on Pearl Harbor, local businesses paid for advertisements in York County newspapers, seeking to reassure readers and to encourage fighting men and their families.

were visiting relatives in Gettysburg," she said years later. "By Thursday we hadn't heard anything, and I thought he would be all right."

Eugene Bubb was the first known York County serviceman to die in the war.

• • •

The Pearl Harbor attack stranded civilians in faraway places.

A York Ice Machinery Corporation engineer was floating in the Pacific when the Japanese assaulted his ship's Hawaiian base.

The civilian, working for the successor to York Manufacturing Company, was aboard a destroyer. His job was to test the ship's Yorkco refrigeration unit during a shakedown cruise.

The big ship would fire its guns, and engineers would check to see if the action caused leaks in pipes.

Before entering active duty, Thomas W. Frutiger instructed engineers at York Ice Machinery Corporation. This image, printed in reverse, would not have pleased Frutiger. A photography enthusiast, he had joined the York Camera Club and operated a Red Lion photography store before his call-up as a reserve officer in 1941, months before Pearl Harbor. A Camera Club newsletter from 1945 described Frutiger: 'Quiet, earnest, self-effacing, well liked by those in the Club fortunate enough to know him.'

After the attack, the destroyer was called into action.

The engineer would board another ship on its way back home, and that ship would gain a new assignment.

"It took 14 months for him to get home," another Yorkco engineer, Austin Diehl, recalled years later.

On the other side of the world, Rebecca Little Singer was caught in Germany.

The former York resident spent much of the war in Leipzig, a city that later staggered under torrid British bombing.

Rebecca Singer experienced an array of emotions. Her twin sister, Mrs. John Y. Burgard, lived in York.

Singer was married to a German soldier of two wars. Her son, Peter, a German soldier, later fought on the Russian front and was listed as missing in action. An American son, Herman, was stationed as a civilian employee at the Middletown Air Depot, across the Susquehanna River from York County.

" ... (S)he was torn between family love," a newspaper later reported, "and loyalty to her country."

'York is a target'

In four hours on Monday — the day after the attack — a month's worth of enlistees volunteered at York's military recruiting station on the second floor of the U.S. Post Office.

Sgt. Joseph Novotney was so busy administering exams and answering questions that he lost count of those seeking enlistments, saying, "it was useless."

Some in line were 16 years old.

Other grizzled veterans considered a return to active service. West York Fire Chief Joseph G. Spahr, with 18 months duty in World War I, said he'd go again.

George L. Leas, quartermaster corps; Richard C. Kleffman, coast artillery; and Robert L. Doyle, infantry parachute group, were among the first to be accepted.

For some time, recruiting offices opened early and kept evening hours to sign up enthusiastic enlistees.

• • •

Those enlistments added to the thousands of York County residents already in the field.

For patriotic or practical reasons, county residents had been inclined toward the service almost since the county's founding in 1749.

With about 285 one-room schools in the county and no four-year college, formal education ended for many at a young age. Factories and farms in this southcentral Pennsylvania county of 178,022 beckoned before or after a hitch in the service.

County newspapers regularly told about current military assignments. Most were stationed in safe places — at least for the moment — compared to the scores in and around Pearl Harbor.

In the days following the Pearl Harbor bombing, newspaper readers learned that Daniel K. Medill joined fellow young attorneys Palmer C. Bortner and William S. Eisenhart Jr. in the service. Medill was assigned to a coast artillery unit at Fort Monroe, Va.

Sterling M. Wantz served at Fort Belvoir, Va.

Emanuel G. Shull Jr. and Morgan Smith Whiteley gained assignments to Fort Knox, Ky.

There, they would serve under a fellow county native and the U.S. Army's Armored Force chief, Gen. Jacob Loucks Devers.

Red Lion's Thomas W. Frutiger was stationed with the

A William Penn High School teacher instructs about the war from a headline-covered blackboard. The war reinvigorated the teaching of history and geography. 'A new vocabulary was gleaned from the airways,' a city schools report stated. 'Boys and girls were alert as never before to the world about them, a world that crowded in upon their consciousness.'

These York City elementary students compose a song for a bond campaign. The blackboard, left, shows how students contributed toward building a tank and a rifle by giving up candy and gum.

454th Ordnance Company at Fort William McKinley in the Philippines.

Frutiger, a 30-year-old Lehigh graduate, was commissioned a second lieutenant in the Reserve Officers Training Corps. While working as an engineer for York Ice Machinery, the now-1st lieutenant was called to active duty on May 1, 1941, and ordered to the Philippines on Nov. 1.

He was one of the first Yorkco employees to be called up, assigned to ordnance duty in the Army Air Forces. His department supplied the airmen with weapons, ammunition and combat vehicles.

He arrived in the Philippines on Nov. 23, joining thousands of American soldiers on a group of islands under Allied control about 1,500 miles south of Japan.

The GIs braced for an attack. The assault on Pearl Harbor meant enemy forces would be coming their way.

Japan struck the Philippines the next day.
And the enemy would persist for five months.

• • •

Some men avoided recruiting stations and Selective Service offices, to their detriment.

Authorities arrested a 29-year-old Hanover truck driver after he failed to return a Selective Service questionnaire.

The man had given the draft board his Baltimore Street address. The papers came back to the Selective Service officials two times, prompting authorities to go looking for the man.

• • •

For the first time since 1918, York residents on the Monday and Tuesday after the Pearl Harbor bombing greeted their hometown boys in uniform during wartime.

Two companies of local National Guardsmen, part of the 28th Infantry Division, passed through on their way to Fort Indiantown Gap. New Jersey's 44th Division also rolled along York's streets en route to Fort Dix.

Both units had just ended maneuvers in the South.

Section after section of military vehicles invaded the town. In East York and other refreshment stations along the convoy routes, women handed out apples, oranges, cookies, cigarettes and magazines in chilling weather.

A call went out by mid-day on Tuesday. Anyone wanting to replenish the station, at the corner of East Market and Marshall streets, was encouraged to step forward.

• • •

Monday morning, York city and county officials acted quickly to implement emergency civilian defense plans.

Col. William H. Beckner, local Civilian Defense director, emerged from a closed-door meeting with a call for voluntary service on the home front. The World War I officer would hold a litany of official-sounding titles during the long war, but he would serve as the point person on most local defense programs.

"This is an 'all out' program for the defense of York," he said, "and every citizen will be required to do his or her duty."

He released a list of assignments in the event of an attack on York and its extensive factories engaged in military production.

Bomb squads would be organized to dispose of time bombs and duds, and rescue squads would be responsible to free injured people from debris.

First-aid parties and stretcher squads would be developed to bring injured residents to casualty clearing stations.

Boy Scouts and Girl Scouts would act as messengers.

Demolition crews would be assigned to clear rubble, damaged walls or parts of bombed-out buildings.

City hall would serve as headquarters for all defense services. A system of signals would be established. The New York Wire Cloth whistle, equipped with a valve that permitted it to blow varying tones, would be deployed to make the first call. Whistles at a dozen manufacturing plants would follow.

Officials believed that York and its 56,172 residents — a population earning it a spot in the top 200 U.S. cities — could expect an attack, considering the length and breadth of plants undertaking defense work within its borders.

"York is a target to the new type of warfare. For the

This meeting of local industrial leaders at the Yorktowne Hotel suggests the high level of cooperation that marked York County's defense work on the home front. Civilian Defense officials feared this industrial might would attract enemy air strikes and urged vigilance against enemy attacks.

present, we do not expect long, sustained repeated attacks," he said. "This is a war not so much of armies and navies as of production. We can get out of this mess only if we can produce. There must be no retarding of our national production."

He listed multiple challenges facing county residents: They must prepare for the devastation of modern war. They must learn to remove injured people from ruined buildings and transport them to hospitals. They must know how to extinguish incendiary bombs, control broken gas and water mains and patch damaged sewers.

The government had proclaimed York as a vital defense area, Beckner said. Its factories must continue to produce for the military, regardless of hardship.

"Therefore, it is our job to deprive ourselves of leisure moments," he said, "and devote our time and thought to make sure the wheels of industry are kept moving."

• • •

Spokesmen for other government agencies added steady voices to this newly composed wartime chorus.

Capt. Joseph A. Kling, a company commander in the Pennsylvania Reserve Defense Corps, reassured the public that his men were fully mobilized.

The 60 members of Company 1, Kling's York unit, would spend their nights at home and report at 8 a.m. sharp each day to the North George Street armory.

Kling's men initially would be responsible for the safety of bridges, dams, communication lines and other presumed targets of saboteurs.

His men were subject to call-up at any time of day or night.

The State Council of Defense placed York County and other air warning districts under its jurisdiction on alert until further notice.

The council instructed county air raid wardens to place watchers on duty 24 hours a day until further notice.

Soon thereafter, boys at York's Edgar Fahs Smith school responded to the challenge. During daytime hours, they staffed an airplane spotting post on school grounds, located atop a hill in the city. Students from other city schools and adults from the community stood guard at night.

Spotting stations started sprouting up through the county — on top of the Hotel McAllister in Hanover, at the baseball field in York New Salem and near Christ Lutheran Church in Jackson Township.

The prime spot atop the Hanover hotel became necessary because the remote nature of spotting points at Smith's Station and Hanover Municipal Water Works taxed scarce gasoline supplies and wore out irreplaceable car tires.

The Jackson Township post illustrated community support for the aircraft spotting program.

Glatfelter Paper Co. provided a building for the around-the-clock operation and the post's mascot, a stray dog that

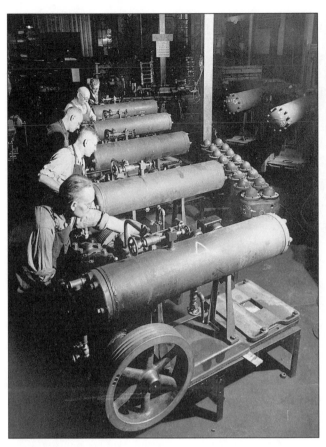

This bank of water-cooled condensers for industrial refrigeration equipment stands like a battery of heavy machine guns as York Ice Machinery Corporation workers, fighting the war on the home front, test their operating efficiency.

This defense worker at York Safe and Lock listens for defects during the grinding of a powder chamber for a 37 mm gun.

had found a new home. The Spring Grove PTA provided raincoats and hats. A school loaned a telescope, made from the periscope of a World War I submarine. The War Department provided blue armbands for the on-duty spotters.

Dillsburg Civilian Defense officials first placed the borough's station at the high school athletic field but later constructed a shack on the Charles Mumper farm, in the borough's east end.

The 10-foot-square building, with windows on all four sides, was equipped with a stove, desk, cot and phone.

The Dillsburg spotters, working in pairs, pulled two-hour shifts. When spotters sighted an aircraft, they would call with code words, "Army Flash 84."

The reply would come: "Army, go head, please."

The spotters would state the plane's description, its direction and whether its altitude was low, high or very high.

A screening center would pass on the information to a Long Island airfield.

After only a short time in use, a spotting post in a former schoolhouse on Prospect Road near Longstown went up in flames.

Dedicated spotters kept up their 24-hour-a-day vigil without shelter, running to a phone in Luther P. Marks' nearby garage.

• • •

York defense officials began to study the 10-foot-by-10-foot Poorhouse Run tube as a shelter in case of air raids.

The culvert, running three to four blocks from Market to Chestnut Street, directed the stream under the city. Engineers considered diverting the waterway and closing off storm drains.

They questioned whether the reinforced concrete tube was far enough underground to provide bomb protection. Further, a railroad running along its roof would provide a tempting target for enemy pilots.

'You had eight years ...'

Minutes after Col. Beckner's admonitions about preparedness, students in York County classrooms listened to President Franklin D. Roosevelt's address to Congress on radios.

Principals in York's schools made sure students had returned from lunch at 12:30 p.m. sharp, 30 minutes early.

"Yesterday," the president said, "December 7, 1941 — a date which will live in infamy — the United States of America was suddenly and deliberately attacked by naval and air forces of the Empire of Japan."

Roosevelt asked for a declaration of war, and the Senate responded with a unanimous vote. The House came through with all in agreement except one, Montana pacifist Jeanette Rankin.

Harry L. Haines, York County's congressman, later explained his aye vote:

Japan drew America into the war. The American people are not cowards and responded appropriately. The war was brought to them.

"We must be united," the congressman said. "There must be no other issue."

At 4 p.m., Roosevelt signed the declaration of war.

• • •

In the days following the attack, York's rival newspapers were in rare agreement that the nation must respond to Japan's despicable act.

In editorials, The Gazette and Daily, coming from the Democrat side, and The York Dispatch, sympathetic to Republican positions, struggled to find words strong

Employees assigned heavy work schedules at York Safe and Lock, holder of millions of dollars in military contracts, placed posters in the windows of their homes to ensure proper shuteye.

Some retailers refused to display posters with gruesome battle scenes in their windows. One grocery company opted to post this image — 'Dear God, keep them safe!' — showing students in gas masks suggesting, 'It could happen here.'

enough to adequately decry the sneak assault.

The Dispatch called for the extermination of Japan: Smite that nation so hard with one big blow so that it would not be able to take the offensive again.

"There are many problems to be worked out in a war of this type in which one side is a cunning savage without principle, without morals, without a touch of civilization to the cause of slaughter and destruction," the newspaper stated.

The Gazette and Daily lamented that America should have known better than to negotiate with the Japanese, and the result was an attack in Nazi fashion by the Nazis' partner.

"We should have known that we were dealing with highwaymen," the newspaper chided, "who would abuse any courtesy and consideration extended them and use it against us."

For too long, America had been making automobiles instead of warplanes.

From this point on, America should use its incomparable industrial resources to confront the Axis foes, the newspaper stated.

• • •

The newspapers weren't alone in viewing the German-Italian threat as insidious as that of their Axis partner Japan.

Members of York's Rotary Club heard a midweek speech from former German jurist Dr. Hans Hirschberg, who considered the survival of Christianity at stake along with the attack on democracy.

"This war is a struggle for the possession of the soul between two philosophies involved in a deadly fight," stated Hirschberg, who had broken away from Adolf Hitler's regime.

"The true aim of Nazism is the destruction of Christianity," he said. "It is a war of extermination."

According to Hirschberg, a high-ranking minister of religion in Germany had declared Hitler a deity by stating, "Hitler is the Jesus Christ as well as the Holy Ghost of the Father."

Hirschberg gave Rotarians a history lesson:

The Versailles Treaty at the end of World War I left Germany crushed and without leadership. Anyone offering hope for the future could gain an audience. This gave Hitler his opportunity.

At first, the Protestant Church did not oppose Hitler's views. Historically, the church and state in Germany did not oppose each other. Now, Martin Niemoller and fellow clergymen speaking against the Third Reich had ended up in concentration camps.

Further, Propaganda Minister Joseph Goebbels demeaned the Apostle Paul by saying, "He was nothing but a drunken, dirty syphilitic old Shepherd."

Hirschberg focused his remarks on Hitler's policy toward Christians, but the initial stages of the Fuehrer's deadly "Final Solution" toward Jews in German-occupied Europe were then under way. News about the systematic execution of Jews in concentration camps would reach America in fragments later in the war.

The judge challenged Rotarians to read Hitler's "Mein Kampf," an outline of the campaigns that were to come.

"You had eight years to read it, and most of you have not done so," he lectured. "If you had, you would not have been surprised when Japan attacked you."

• • •

Such speeches heightened county citizenry's concerns about sabotage and the likely saboteurs — those of foreign birth.

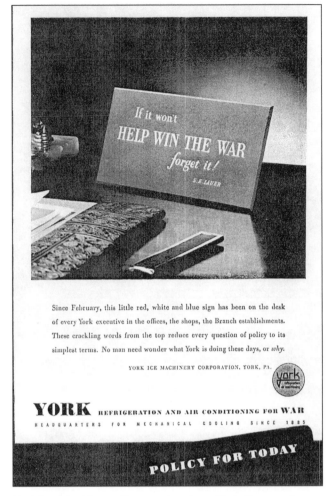

Since February, this little red, white and blue sign has been on the desk of every York executive in the offices, the shops, the Branch establishments. These crackling words from the top reduce every question of policy to its simplest terms. No man need wonder what York is doing these days, or *why*.

YORK ICE MACHINERY CORPORATION, YORK, PA.

YORK REFRIGERATION AND AIR CONDITIONING FOR **WAR**

HEADQUARTERS FOR MECHANICAL COOLING SINCE 1885

POLICY FOR TODAY

York Ice Machinery Corporation, later York Corporation, established the motto 'If it won't help win the war, forget it!' as a way to focus its workers on its challenges in equipping the military and to promote its commitment to defense production. This advertisement highlights the sentiments of Stewart E. Lauer, the company's president.

Residents had already gained the scent of subversion.

Just months before the attack, nine influential citizens petitioned York County Court against a charter by the Jehovah's Witnesses. The court papers claimed the religious group was an un-American body and would represent a subversive influence. It would bring about disrespect for the American flag.

Later in the war, the Fawn Township School Board removed three children from school because they refused to salute the flag.

The action had precedent because Congress had ruled that civilians must always show respect to the flag during the pledge.

The children, Jehovah's Witnesses, believed that saluting the banner was contrary to the Ten Commandments, particularly "You shall have no other gods before me" and "You shall not make for yourself a graven image."

Further, newspapers regularly reported the number of county residents who were born in Axis countries.

Shortly after the attack, government officials stated that

822 of the county's 178,022 county residents were born in Italy, Japan and Germany — the primary Axis powers.

In early 1942, the government required aliens — unnaturalized natives of foreign countries at war with the United States — to apply for identification cards at post offices.

In the days after the requirement went into effect, 12 Italians stepped forward, and no Germans or Japanese signed up.

As early as 1940, York's Italian community had urged its members to seek naturalization, and 80 percent had done so.

John Lucia, an officer in the local Sons of Italy chapter, opposed Italy's pact with Germany. He said Italians of York, whether citizens or not, would pledge allegiance to the United States.

Lucia, a World War I veteran, said 25 Italians from York County had served in the Army or Navy during that war.

• • •

Not only was the county's guard up, authorities had their handcuffs ready.

The day after the Pearl Harbor attack, law enforcement officials in southcentral Pennsylvania rounded up several German aliens and checked their paperwork. One arrest came in York County.

Home defense guards from Lancaster County gained the 24-hour-a-day assignment of picketing the two Susquehanna River bridges between Wrightsville and Columbia.

They kept busy. A trucker was assessed a $25 fine for carrying dynamite without marking his rig as a carrier of high explosives.

The trucker was transporting the explosives to a construction job.

On two occasions, pickets questioned trios of Japanese at the Columbia-Wrightsville toll bridge.

Maj. B.F. Charles, in charge of the bridge guards, was not satisfied that the first group of Japanese was crossing with any real business purpose.

The second threesome, residents of York's North George Street, claimed they were itinerant "chicken sexers," helping farmers determine the sex of young chickens. This was a family tradition, handed down from father to son.

FBI agent George Franklin released the young men after lengthy questioning. He applauded the guards' alertness and said the questioning was time well spent.

From that point on, guards questioned every Japanese man and woman who crossed the bridge. If those apprehended could not produce the proper papers, they would be arrested.

The alert guards kept up the lookout for Germans and strangers, too.

They stopped three men riding in an auto with a New York tag and turned them over to state police for questioning.

Another time, federal agents raided the homes of 100 residents with alien status in York County. About 20 FBI agents perused the houses for subversive printed material and contraband items.

Local police called the raid an "honest to goodness fine-tooth-comb hunt."

The agents, accompanied by local authorities, searched

from roofs to cellars, poring through closets, bureau drawers and trunks.

"Personal papers, letters, and documents of all sorts which came into the hands of agents in their search were closely read for evidence of subversive activity on the part of the subject," The Dispatch reported.

Authorities netted a set of high-powered binoculars, a Japanese dictionary, 20 short-wave radio sets, expensive cameras, maps and literature considered subversive. They also snagged automatic pistols, shotguns and rifles.

Those detained gained hearings in a makeshift courtroom at the York Post Office. Those considered a threat to national safety faced internment for the rest of the war.

The suspects mostly cooperated. Agents said they were interested in protecting innocent aliens as well as apprehending those who might be dangerous.

• • •

Marcelo P. Bueno was fortunate that The Dispatch informed the public he was a Filipino, not Japanese.

A holder of a University of California engineering degree, the state Department of Labor employee was touring county industrial plants to learn about safety.

"People who see the Filipino on the streets are prone to mistake him for Japanese, which he most emphatically is not," the newspaper stated. "He is a full-blooded Filipino and as such is an American and 100 percent for America."

'We have places for them all'

After the Pearl Harbor news, S. Forry Laucks, president of York Safe and Lock, interrupted a New York vacation to return to his business.

He wanted to be close to the action at York Safe, an employer of 2,000 workers busily filling military contracts with equipment formerly used to make safes.

"We are working night and day and Sunday on defense work," he wrote President Roosevelt, "and I am sure I can speak for all our workers' complete loyalty to you and our country and will make renewed efforts to speed up production to the utmost limit."

• • •

Within 48 hours of the bombing, York residents stopped by the North Duke Street office of the American Red Cross to donate money and volunteer their services.

"Tell them to call up," Minnie P. Hatton, Red Cross executive secretary, told a newspaperman. "We have places for them all, work for them all to do."

This activity preceded the call for $125,000 to be raised as the York community's part of the $50 million national Red Cross war fund.

The local chapter's board asked William S. Shipley, chairman of York Ice Machinery, to head the drive.

Shipley's campaign lieutenants included William J. Fisher of A.B. Farquhar Co. and Beauchamp E. Smith of S. Morgan Smith Co. These names would appear repeatedly in the war years as leaders in industrial and community activities.

At the same time, Mrs. James P. Paul of the Red Cross sought additional women to produce surgical dressings and attend first-aid classes, home nursing courses and

'Something new in tank camouflage!', York Ice Machinery Corporation's Shop News reported early in the war. Workers keep from public view an example of war materiel produced at the plant, a unit other than the company's traditional refrigerator and air conditioning machinery. Welders pictured top row, from left, Donald Phillips, Ralph Longe, Fred Sprenkle, Harvey Isby, Reuben Zeager and Paul Walker. Bottow row, from left: Meredith Haupt, Allan Duffy, Arthur Klinedinst, Milton Wishard, Curtis Harbold, Charles Chester Stine, Jacob Menges and Michael Meyer.

knitting and sewing groups.

Twenty-eight thousand surgical dressings were due by Christmas.

• • •

The press on already-busy manufacturers picked up noticeably in the days after the attack.

About 60 York Ice Machinery employees had previously committed to sing at the community Christmas tree-lighting ceremony in front of the York County Courthouse.

But the men of the Yorkco chorus, who had performed at the ceremony the previous seven years, canceled their appearance.

They had defense work to do.

• • •

Bob Senft did not rush to enlist in the Army.

His job with York Ice Machinery, with its growing list of defense jobs, meant he was contributing to the war effort. He had his wife to support.

And he helped watch his mother-in-law, Bertha Bear, and her father, Adam Grim, in the Zion View home the three-generation family shared.

Still, the 22-year-old knew he would get his draft notice some day. Until then, he would do what he could on the home front.

"He'd wait," Ethel said years later, "until they'd come and get them."

II

'We are in it with both feet'

— 1942 —

'Before you say, "I wish I was with them," stop and think,' York Ice Machinery Corporation's Shop News stated in July 1942. 'You are with them ... every minute you work at York.' The newsletter reminded employees that refrigeration and air conditioning helped to speed the manufacture of powder, shells, ships, gasoline and blood plasma. The jobs the workers were doing, the newsletter advised, made their war service as vital as that of any man who carried a rifle.

Gallery

Robert Scott of the Edgewood Arsenal holds a little 'bundle for Berlin,' according to a caption with this 1942 Farm Security Administration-Office of War Information photograph. These 75 mm shells were mass-produced in around-the-clock shifts at the arsenal, located in Harford County, Md., across the Mason-Dixon Line from York County.

This father and son from the Stewartstown area served in World War II. Plural A. Davis, left, entered the U.S. Army Air Forces in November 1942 and served in the China-Burma-India Theater. John M. Davis entered the Navy in May 1943.

This Farm Security Administration photograph at Maryland Avenue's Floorola Products captures Kay Busser, one of scores of women at work in York's factories in 1942. 'A modern Molly Pitcher of the machine, this secretary-treasurer of a small Eastern manufacturing company knows as much about drills and lathes as the oldest employee around the place. And it was in part through her foresight and initiative that this floor waxer plant was converted to war production. She's shown here with a youthful worker who is operating one of the recently converted machines,' the caption states.

'He's watching you,' drawn circa 1942, is part of a series of posters warning against loose talk that defense officials feared could equip enemy spies with information concerning troop movements and defense work.

Stewart E. Lauer, president of York Ice Machinery Corporation, stands on the bed of a truck to inform employees of their role in the Allied war effort shortly after the attack on Pearl Harbor. 'The first vicious onslaught of the treacherous Japanese left us gasping for an instant,' he wrote in the company's Cold Magic newsletter, 'but America is now aroused, and united as never before!' The newsletter gave a concise summary of the scene: 'The Boss explains a few things, tells us we're on the front line of war industry ... what our daily work means in fighting terms.'

'A war of ships and machines'

The devastation at Pearl Harbor left some workers at York Ice Machinery Corporation wondering if they were doing enough for the war effort.

For months before Japan's attack, machinists had been spending extra hours producing refrigeration equipment and air conditioning for Navy and Army bases, ships of all sizes and manufacturing plants operating under blackout conditions.

But questions traveled around the company's West York and Grantley plants about the possibility of retooling lathes, grinders and boring machines to make bullets and guns and military tanks.

The company's top executive stepped up one cold day to provide answers.

President Stewart E. Lauer mounted the flatbed of a truck parked on a shop floor. With American flags hanging as a backdrop and overhead, he stood solidly behind a lectern on his makeshift stage. Hundreds of Yorkco workers clad in coveralls, execs with ties and women in office garb formed his audience.

The 31-year Yorkco exec began by putting the company's role in perspective as the country engaged in its toughest war.

"We are in it with both feet," he said.

He went right to the question: tanks or refrigeration?

"Bullets and guns are most important to win a war but are a small part of any war machine. Soldiers, sailors and marines can't fight on empty stomachs. They can't eat bullets and gunpowder."

A fighting man simply cannot survive the rigors of a world war on canned or dried food, he said.

Gunpowder launches bullets. Steam turbines power ships. Bulletproof glass protects tank operators. Fine engines run tanks and planes. Hundreds of manufacturers must work together to outfit complete military operations.

"And a modern war machine can't get going and keep going without refrigeration," he said.

For months, government officials had clearly stated they wanted defense work done where it could be done best.

Yorkco, with its 4,500-some county workers and 1,000 sales and service people in the field, was in the refrigera-

Workers brought Depression-era projects to conclusion, before turning their attention to serving in the military or working defense jobs to equip and supply the Allies. Here, laborers stand behind a coffer dam to work on the foundation of the Pennsylvania Railroad bridge in York. Their work was part of the U.S. Army Corps of Engineers' Codorus Creek Channel improvements in 1942. These improvements, which included construction of Indian Rock Dam, came after high water flooded York in 1933 and 1936. The construction of a new city hall in York, which opened on West King Street in 1942, was another high-profile public project from the war years.

tion business. That is where the bulk of its defense work would remain.

"The need for refrigeration in this war will be much greater than in the last World War," he said. "This is a war of ships and machines."

With the constant concern about attacks on American soil, most defense industries worked in windowless buildings. Modern war machines — airplanes and tanks — required sophisticated equipment.

"These instruments are made in blackout buildings that must have refrigeration and air conditioning to make them accurately," he said, "and even to make them at all."

Yorkco was exercising 60 percent of its industrial strength on war work and expected that number to increase to 80 percent. Remaining resources would be used for repairs, other food industry purposes and essentials for civilian homes.

"I know we are all so 'burned up' at the Japs and so keen for revenge, that we would like to think of 100 percent industrial capacity for war purposes," he said. "When we approach anything like that, we will have Naziism ... and the next thing we would have is starvation."

At that moment, York refrigeration was preserving food supplies at Navy bases in Hawaii, Midway, Wake, Manila and other points in the Pacific. Cold storage systems operated in Camp Robinson in Arkansas, Camp Edwards in Massachusetts, March Field in California, Fort Huachuca in Arizona and in numerous other Army camps.

In a recent 18-month period, Yorkco provided the Navy with 1,064 compressors, condensers and other machinery for battleships, aircraft carriers and submarines.

Yorkco refrigeration was being used to make bullet-proof glass, high-octane gasoline, aircraft radios and high altitude simulation chambers to test aircraft.

And yes, he said, the company was engaged in direct

war work. For example, it had landed a $2 million contract to make 35, 6-foot gun carriages. Workers were machining parts for 3,500 British tank guns; 2,000 Navy 50 mm machine guns; 1,200, 81 mm trench mortars; and 4,000 torpedoes.

He reminded the assembly that America didn't start or want this war but was determined to win it.

"We'll have to make sacrifices, pull our belts tighter, give of our time and our money to the righteous cause of freedom," he said.

He urged the employees to speed up their work. If they saw an opportunity for efficiency, they should tell their foremen.

"Now men, let's get back to work and work together!" he said, stepping down to the shop floor.

After Pearl Harbor, such sentiments were expressed repeatedly in shops around York County.

Companies and their workers would do what they could with what they had.

And what they had was considerable.

• • •

In these years, York County consistently hit the list of top counties in the United States in value of farm products sold.

The county, drained by numerous streams flowing into the Susquehanna River on its eastern border, received a healthy 40 inches of rain a year. It boasted a soil naturally fertilized by a limestone base and a moderate climate that delivered an annual average temperature of 55 degrees.

And the county was near everything. Farmers could efficiently ship agricultural goods to market, even across the sea.

Rail service had connected the town with the Port of Baltimore, 50 miles to the south, since 1838.

This bird's-eye view of York in 1942 provides an indication of the city's industrial might when defense production was still on the upswing. East Prospect Street is seen in foreground. The large industrial site, upper center, is American Chain and Cable. ACCO was among 30 or more York-area companies that cooperated in the York Plan to secure large defense contracts. ACCO and other defense contractors attracted temporary and permanent workers to the city. York's population topped out just short of 60,000 by the end of the decade.

That same railroad helped York serve as a staging area for tens of thousands of blue-clad troops early in the Civil War. That railroad brought in raw materials by the carload and shipped away finished products by the ton during the subsequent Industrial Revolution.

• • •

Before the railroads came wagons.

Immigrants had passed through the county's well-worn roads to points south and west since the first permanent settlers moved west of the Susquehanna River in about 1730. To reach North Carolina, many German and Scotch-Irish immigrants passed through York and the southwestern York County town of Hanover as they made their way along the Great Wagon Road to the Shenandoah Valley.

Early on, the Southern-oriented county developed into a market center, an agricultural and transportation hub.

In the early 1940s, this agricultural base that had fed York County's development since its founding was grudgingly conceding its dominance to manufacturing.

An incident in 1887 suggested that, even then, manufacturing was growing deep roots.

Outdoor market sheds had stood in York's Centre Square since its earliest days. There, farmers sold the work of their hands. Post-Civil War industrial growth came, but these busy sheds still benefited the county's agricultural community.

The sheds should stay, many argued.

But these dilapidated sheds clogged transportation to factories and the movement of finished goods to market. It was 1887, not 1787. York was no longer a borough but a city. And massive covered markets dotted the city.

The sheds had to go, others argued.

A middle-of-the-night raid on the sheds decided the matter. Someone tied ropes to the corners of the outdoor markets and pulled them down.

When the deed was discovered the next morning, it was too late. The forces of industrialization had carried the day.

• • •

The same location and transportation advantages that aided county agriculture worked for industry, too. As a city directory from the 1940s stated, York was within a night's train ride from 20 million people.

The town, which celebrated its 200th anniversary in 1941, sat on the east-west Lincoln Highway, connecting Atlantic City, N.J., and San Francisco. The Lincoln Highway intersected with the Susquehanna Trail, running from the Canadian border to Baltimore and Washington, D.C. That nexus occurred in York's Continental Square, former site of the ill-fated market sheds.

During the World War II years, three railroads served York County: Pennsylvania, Western Maryland and Maryland and Pennsylvania.

The Susquehanna River ensured the availability of ample electricity to power factories. Three power stations — Safe Harbor, Holtwood and York Haven — operated on the river. A large steam plant in Middletown, upriver from York Haven, ran electricity to York as did a smaller steam plant in York.

In the county seat of York, about 225 manufacturers represented about 100 kinds of industry — makers of shoes and shoe polish, candy and false teeth, neckties and shirts, cigars and beer, baskets and caskets.

• • •

Oblivious to this industrial bustle, a runaway steer, trotting around Continental Square in the heart of York early in the war, sought to remind residents of their agricultural roots.

Two men in a truck pursued the cow.

"The steer," Police Chief C.P. Gerber told The York Dispatch, "obeyed the traffic rules."

It circled the square in the proper traffic lanes.

That was post-Depression York County. Its people did their work simply, ably and followed the rules.

• • •

Before the war, those plentiful farms and factories lured young people to their employ. High schools sometimes weren't accessible in the rolling rural areas of this 900-square-mile county.

Many boys and girls ended their formal education in the sixth or eighth grade in the county's 285 one-room schools, more than any county in the state. City educators encouraged boys to take the York industrial course, alternating two weeks in school and two in city shops.

"The industries cooperate fully and are anxious to employ these boys with pay," the city directory stated.

The lure of agricultural and industrial jobs often eclipsed higher education. The county did not play host to a junior college until 1941, later expanded into the four-year York College in 1968.

This meant people were most adept at working with their hands, and father often passed such skills down to son.

S. Forry Laucks, York Safe and Lock's president, always said, "When you want a job thoroughly done, you can't beat the Pennsylvania Dutch for doing it."

The city directory said the county sported habits of clean living and fidelity to American ideals. And the directory explained that the county had avoided the influx of a troublemaking European element that plagued other cities.

The writer overlooked the fact that the earliest settlers in York County came from Europe. The Scotch-Irish concentrated in the hilly southeastern portion. The Germans lined up their plows in the fertile central valley carved by Kreutz, Codorus and Conewago creeks. York and Hanover, the county's two population centers, sat in this valley. English Quakers founded a band of settlements in the northern angle of the triangular-shaped county.

Marylanders, some German, others Irish, often of the Catholic faith, moved into the southwestern angle, the Hanover area.

Further, York County's industrial growth early in the 20th century beckoned blacks from the deep South to move north. They would board railroads to Baltimore and proceed north on the Northern Central Railroad, later the Pennsylvania Railroad, across the Mason-Dixon Line into York County. There, they would primarily find service or domestic jobs in a county that doubled in size between 1880 and 1940.

By 1942, York County was one of the largest, most populous counties in a state that was second only to New York in population.

• • •

York County presented a quirky juxtaposition of progressiveness on the industrial front with a sometimes-primitive bearing on the domestic front.

Residents regularly went to powwowers to seek cures for minor ailments. Those lay doctors would prescribe remedies laced with white magic and home remedies.

York powwower Charles W. Rice specialized in treating blindness. His prescription went like this: Sea-monster tears at $2.50 per drop, plus incantations, the sign of the cross and a Himmels-brief.

Indeed, the county's infatuation with white magic ran amok in an incident that spawned the Hex Murder trial of 1929, sometimes identified as the nation's most notorious witchcraft trial since Salem, Mass.

Three defendants were found guilty that year in the death of a suspected witch. The superstitious trio sought a lock of hair and a Bible from Nelson Rehmeyer, a purported witch who lived in southern York County. They needed these items to break a spell that they believed was cast by Rehmeyer.

In the process of obtaining the hair and Bible, they killed Rehmeyer.

Then, a year after the verdict, a 71-year-old man died in a farm machinery accident on Rehmeyer's property.

"Tragedy seems to haunt the Rehmeyer farm ... ," a newspaper reported.

John Curry, a teenage defendant in the slaying, demonstrated artistic skills in prison. After a 10-year prison stint, he joined the Army and was assigned to Gen. Dwight D. Eisenhower's staff as a cartographer. He helped draft maps

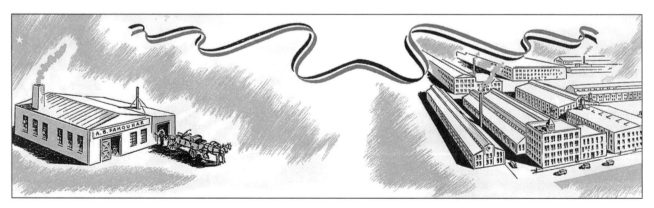

These pages came from the commemorative program observing A.B. Farquhar Co.'s reception of the Army-Navy 'E' award for excellence in 1943. At the time of this award, only 2 percent of American industrial plants had won the 'E' pennant. This drawing shows the evolution of Farquhar's York plant from its early years in the Civil War era to its multi-block size in the World War II years. The Farquhar story was typical of many county industries spurting ahead during the Industrial Revolution, founded by entrepreneurs with big visions, quality ideas and high energy.

Curtis E. and Mary Dean Stermer of Glen Rock both entered the Armed Forces. Curtis served 40 months in the Army starting in 1942, including a stint in the European Theater. He taught science after the war. Mary Stermer served 24 months on medical duty in the Women's Auxiliary Army Corps (WAAC), later Women's Army Corps (WAC).

Thomas Shipley joined York Manufacturing in 1897. When he died as head of the company in 1930, York Ice Machinery Corporation was the largest refrigeration equipment manufacturer in the nation. The entrepreneurial Shipley also founded Thomas Shipley Inc., which sold York Ice Machinery air conditioning units worldwide. The company later entered the heating field, purchasing York Oil Burner Co. Thomas Shipley Inc. later evolved into Shipley Energy.

William S. Shipley, Thomas Shipley's youngest brother, led Yorkco through the World War II years. He died in 1951. A company history said Yorkco was Shipley's life: 'I must keep in touch,' he once said. 'If I didn't, it would be just like lying down in a hole and piling the dirt in on top of my head.'

S. Forry Laucks led York Safe and Lock for more than 50 years, landing defense contracts early in the military buildup leading to World War II.

for the Invasion of Normandy in 1944 and designed a shoulder patch for Operation Overlord, the code name for the D-Day assault.

• • •

Even in 1942, only 35 miles of York's 90-mile road system were paved. Despite 100 miles of sewage mains, outhouses were still common within city limits, even downtown.

In rural parts of the county, residents operated stills by the hundreds. In one raid in 1940, Liquor Control Board officials uncovered 3,100 gallons of mash and 85 gallons of finished product. One sample of the home brew came in at a blinding 42.8 percent alcohol.

But a bit of backwardness amid the roar of machinery was perhaps understandable.

Many county residents could still remember the days before the Industrial Revolution, even the Civil War when an entire rebel division overwhelmed the county in the days before the Battle of Gettysburg. York's last Civil War veteran would die in 1944.

And a 77-year-old laborer at the York Fairgrounds, Bentz Heilman, liked to tell how he saved Calamity Jane from freezing one 40-degree-below-zero night in Deadwood, S.D.

Further, John M. Hyson, a Red Lion physician who had died only 10 years before, had treated a former Revolutionary War drummer boy as a young medical school student.

This respected doctor who had delivered hundreds of York County residents into the 20th-century world had also treated a 100-year-old soldier from the America's 18th-century fight for independence.

'You can count us in'

York County's agricultural past helped fertilize the red brick industrial buildings that joined the tall steeples of

hearty churches in York's skyline.

Savvy wagon-makers, longtime equippers of farmers, for example, evolved into automakers. In the first quarter of the century, about 15 automakers operated out of York County. Pullman Motor Cars became the most celebrated, producing more than 12,000 vehicles.

Before the war, York-Hoover Body Co., with roots in the carriage-making business, produced a prototype for a military vehicle that could navigate the most rugged terrain. It received and successfully completed orders for 69 more vehicles.

York-Hoover turned down another order for 4,500 sturdy vehicles because it had pledged its resources elsewhere. Future work on the Jeep, bearing the York-made design with minor modifications, went to Willys Co. and the Ford Motor Co.

A.B. Farquhar started as a York-based farm implement maker and introduced an array of machinery and engines used internationally.

P.H. Glatfelter harvested lumber to make paper in his Spring Grove plant. That paper, when pressed with inked type, provided a record of great industrial achievements in York County and nationally.

Often, these manufacturers, so well-prepared to grab World War II defense work, were products of the lifework of a great man or small group of men.

The Rev. Stephen Morgan Smith had been one such industrial pioneer.

York's Moravian minister served as a chaplain for a Pennsylvania volunteer infantry unit in the Civil War. He left town for another pastorate in 1866, but a throat condition soon impaired his ability to preach.

An often-told story suggests his recuperation afforded him the opportunity to observe his wife, the former Emma Fahs, as she ran the household.

This led him to successfully gain a patent for a mechanical clothes washer.

He returned to York, secured another patent and convinced five other men to invest in his Success Clothes wringer and related washing devices.

The York Manufacturing Company, thus, was born in 1874.

Jacob Loucks, one of Smith's partners, was himself an industrial pioneer in York County.

It was Loucks who sold a small paper mill in Spring Grove to his brother-in-law, Philip Henry Glatfelter, in 1863.

Glatfelter turned to papermaking. Loucks invested in Smith's company.

York Manufacturing struggled along for several years. Smith left to develop another patent, a turbine water wheel, and formed his own business, the S. Morgan Smith Co., in 1890.

Jacob Loucks, meanwhile, became president of York Manufacturing, adding steam engines and boilers to its product line. In 1883, Loucks started focusing on a line of ice-making machines, and the company produced its first unit two years later.

But his company struggled until a white papermaking knight reappeared in 1888.

P.H. Glatfelter, by then an investor in varied financial interests in York County, paid off York Manufacturing's $15,000 debt and assumed control of the company and its ice-making line. For the second time in 25 years, Glatfelter had purchased a struggling company from his brother-in-law.

But Jacob Loucks was not through contributing to York County.

In 1887, Loucks' daughter, Ella, married to watchmaker/repairman Philip Devers, gave birth to a son and named him Jacob Loucks Devers.

Devers became the highest-ranking military officer the county ever produced.

• • •

Meanwhile, P.H. Glatfelter turned York Manufacturing around, too, with aid from unseasonable weather and Thomas Shipley.

A warm winter of 1890 meant that ice, stored in large sheds insulated with sawdust, was scarce that summer. Scarce ice meant spoiled food. Spoiled food meant thousands of food poisoning cases.

The public became convinced that ice-making machines were more reliable than the whims of nature. Glatfelter positioned his company to meet this new demand by recruiting Shipley from competitor Frick Co. in 1897. He doubled Shipley's salary and offered him a 4 percent ownership share.

This started a relationship between York Manufacturing, Shipley and, later, his two brothers, William and Samuel, that lasted more than 50 years.

Shipley focused the company on ice-making and refrigeration equipment. By World War I, the company employed 5,000 at its 19-acre West York plant on Roosevelt Avenue.

And it was ready to provide refrigeration for military

This poster reminded workers that they were fighting the war, too, in their jobs at war production plants and using part of their wages to buy bonds to finance the war.

uses — in Army camps and munitions plants. Its refrigeration coils chilled air aboard fighting and supply ships. Its equipment cooled a $1 million meat and ice plant in France.

In the 1920s, the company changed its name to York Ice Machinery Corporation to highlight its major product line and added a second plant on Grantley Avenue. "The Yorks," as local folks called the company, now covered 96 acres.

So when the Great Depression buffeted the company's fortunes and the winds of another world war started blowing in the late 1930s, the company knew how to garner government and military work. And it had ample machinery and facilities.

By that decade, it had also reached the rank of the nation's top refrigeration equipment manufacturer.

• • •

York Safe and Lock's S. Forry Laucks also learned a bit about procuring government defense contracts during World War I.

His company was a maker of safes — large and small — used worldwide. York Safe's fireproof door guarded the tomb of Sun Yat-sen, founder of modern China, in Nanking, and it had produced the largest bank vault in the world, guarding the Emperor's nest egg in Tokyo.

The company particularly struggled during the Depression when scores of banks failed. Plenty of second-hand vaults were on the market. In the late 1930s, Laucks' work force had dwindled to 350 employees, and his company had sustained losses of $2 million.

In 1938, he toured Army arsenals around Washington, D.C., and found them depleted of ordnance equipment — guns and ammunition — the type of machinery his specialty company could build.

"If the workers in your plant can make something so massive as a bank vault, and yet so delicate and precise as the lock on a safety-deposit box — well, I guess they can turn out not only a gun carriage but the breechblock of the gun and the firing mechanism as well," he later explained.

Laucks presented his case to the War Department. In 1938, Laucks' company received a $1.55 million contract to build 138 mounts for new 3-inch anti-aircraft guns.

Representatives of the Manufacturers' Association of York recreate a meeting from July 1, 1940, at which the York Plan was conceived. The 1941 re-enactment at William Penn High School was broadcast on NBC radio. Robert E. Gephart, secretary/treasurer of the manufacturers group, left, substitutes for Brandt-Warner Manufacturing Co.'s Warren C. Bulette. Others pictured, from left, William S. Shipley, chairman, York Ice Machinery Corporation; William J. Fisher, vice-president, A.B. Farquhar Co.; Robert P. Turner, vice president, New York Wire Cloth Co.; and Milo Boulton, NBC announcer.

National defense officials later noted this was the first defense contract awarded to private industry since the last world war.

• • •

As his closely held ownership neared its 50th anniversary in 1940, Forry Laucks had overseen the shifting of his facilities to armament production and positioned himself to land large contracts. He sped up his company's production lines as global unrest increased.

But he didn't do it alone.

He farmed out more than 45 percent of the 6,000 individual parts found in the anti-aircraft mounts to York Ice Machinery, S. Morgan Smith, A.B. Farquhar and dozens of other nearby companies.

Small businesses secured subcontracts with Laucks as well.

In Gettysburg, Barge Donmoyer set up a machine shop in a new, but never-used, tourist cabin. He finished metal parts for a 37 mm anti-tank gun.

Floorola Products in York converted its machining from making floor-waxers to manufacturing parts for gun carriages and breechloading guns.

Kay Busser, assistant to owner Ernest Newcomer, sought the business from Safe and Lock. The shop became so busy that Busser, herself, gained an assistant to ease the workload.

Harry Dusman, former harnessmaker in York, turned out leather pads for shoulder guards on anti-aircraft and anti-tank gun mounts.

And Charles Coffey's business bridged county industry and agriculture.

Factory space was so scarce in York that he set up a machine shop in the end of City Market, one of five large, covered market houses in York where farmers still sold their wares. He crafted parts for Safe and Lock machines that, in turn, made armor plates.

• • •

Laucks did not live to see all the defense products his thousands of employees would turn out or the Army-Navy "E" award his company garnered for excellence in war production. At the age of 72, he died of a liver ailment at his Lauxmont estate, overlooking the Susquehanna River.

After his death in April 1942, poor labor relations, unsatisfactory management practices and other factors led to the U.S. Navy, followed by Blaw-Knox Co., taking over the company's special ordnance plant.

This plant had an orders backlog of $100 million at the time of the Navy takeover, and the military deemed every penny vital to the Allied fight.

The York Safe assembly line included critical 40 mm Bofors anti-aircraft guns for land and sea use. These Swedish-designed guns became so widely known and used that anti-aircraft guns generally came to be called Bofors.

• • •

Going to the public trough was not in the nature of independent-minded, Republican-oriented York County businessmen, who abhorred government spending.

J.W. Gitt, owner of The Gazette and Daily, served on the York Ice Machinery board of directors at the time the company started to gain Depression-era government contracts.

One contract to provide heating and cooling for a federal building in Washington, D.C., came at a particularly opportune time. It was new business, and Yorkco would actually get paid for it, unlike other work the company had done where customers couldn't afford to pay.

After rejoicing, the board discussed signing a Manufacturers' Association of York resolution against government spending during bad economic times.

As Gitt recalled years later, the board was about to approve it when he spoke up.

"Here you just got a government contract which is going to save you," he said, "and now you want to con-

'The more Women at work ...' was part of a series of U.S. government posters designed to recruit female factory workers. Here, a woman assembles what appears to be part of an airplane cockpit.

demn government spending. Are you crazy?"

The board deferred action.

• • •

The autocratic and Democratic Forry Laucks was not the type of person to work within a community to promote sharing underused tools and lists of available workers through a long war.

That job would fall to William S. Shipley and the Manufacturers' Association.

By the summer of 1940, "W.S.," youngest brother of the late Thomas Shipley, served as Yorkco chairman. At a meeting of the Manufacturers' Association that summer, a formalized cooperative plan — the York Plan — came together.

An NBC radio broadcast in 1941 convened the principals to re-enact this meeting. The replay before a national audience went this way:

Robert P. Turner, vice president of New York Wire Cloth Co., presiding: The meeting will come to order. Gentlemen, we are here to discuss the problems that have arisen in our industries in behalf of the national defense effort.

William S. Shipley: I have a suggestion, Mr. Turner.

Turner: What is it, Mr. Shipley?

Shipley: If the rest of the directors agree, I think we should take an inventory of all the resources of York's industrial community, and look at national defense from the community standpoint. For instance, in our factory we have machine tools that are idle part of the time. Now Mr. Bulette, in your plant, you have machine tools that are idle, too, don't you?

Warren C. Bulette, president of Brandt-Warner Manufacturing Co.: Yes, we have machine tools that we use only part time.

Shipley: And Mr. Fisher, over at your company, do you have machine tools that may be used on defense work?

William J. Fisher, vice-president of A.B. Farquhar Co.: That's right. We've been making agricultural implements and doing defense work.

Shipley: Fine! Now — the idea is this. With the machine tools in all the factories in York, we can help the government more than ever! We can take contracts — and then by letting our subcontracts to the other factories — by pooling all our resources — we can raise production and cut out bottlenecks!

All: That's a great idea — you can count us in.

• • •

The committee organized the York Plan around 15 points. The first two points were indispensable for the plan to work: "To make use of our present facilities in regards to tools," and "To get idle tools and idle men working."

Communities across America seeking to emulate the York success story called on William Shipley to tell about the York Plan. So did intrigued congressional committees in Washington, D.C.

Shipley's stump speech explained how a community could position itself where the men, machines and material in almost every plant worked for virtually every other plant.

And he brought with him the York Plan's slogan: "To Do What We Can With What We Have."

To safeguard American cities against enemy use of poisonous gas and other contingencies, these workers at Maryland's Edgewood Arsenal sew hand harness tabs on gas masks. Many York County residents worked at the nearby arsenal and other Maryland defense plants.

'It is not carelessness'

While defense work aided many companies, some businesses struggled during the war because of unavailable products and labor or high prices required to purchase scarce goods.

York County auto dealers, for example, faced ruin when a federal ban on automobile sales went into effect in early 1942. Automakers were converting their product lines to make military vehicles.

W. F. Grove, Marvin Schaffer, Ammon R. Smith and Henry Fritz traveled to Washington, D.C., to implore Congress to permit dealers to sell cars on hand as well as used cars.

Congressmen learned that 500,000 salesmen would be out of work nationally. The auto industry argued that many salesmen were too old to work in industry, a contention that later proved to be incorrect.

Even if such arguments had been persuasive, scarcity of gasoline and tires in subsequent months took motorists off the road.

With their case denied, car dealers repaired cars to make ends meet, if parts could be found.

• • •

The war had a direct or indirect effect on every county resident.

For one thing, it caused people to adjust their clocks and watches to war time.

Congress authorized Americans to turn their timepieces ahead one hour, effective Feb. 9, to save electricity.

York County residents traveled to work in the dark. The Dispatch noted that some people cheered themselves with the thought that they would regain the hour's sleep when war time ceased six months after the end of the conflict.

On the morning of Feb. 9, the county commissioners gave Paul Messerly, county clock winder, the nod to change the clocks in the courthouse tower.

George Anderson emerges from behind the devil mask.

That's York Corporation's George Anderson working behind the devil mask. The image appeared in about 700 U.S. newspapers. 'When I painted that face on my hood, I never expected that it would get so much publicity,' Anderson said.

Eight 'Weldettes,' newly minted York Ice Machinery welders, shroud a tank hull they would finish that day.

Messerly climbed the tower's many steps and made the change at 9:45 a.m.

War time then became official in York County.

• • •

Francis K. Minch, Henry C. Hanna and six other men, sporting volunteer police commissions, provided an around-the-clock guard on Lake Williams, near Jacobus, and York Water Co. reservoirs, on the hill south of town. Concerned about sabotage, the water company closed the lake to boaters and other recreational users who had enjoyed access to York City's water supply for years.

The water company entered into a pact with counterparts in Lancaster, Adams and Franklin counties for mutual aid if service was disrupted by air raids or sabotage.

Members of the United Association of Journeymen Plumbers and Steam Fitters vowed to assist water company employees if an invasion or saboteurs damaged pipes.

• • •

Soon after the Pearl Harbor attack, shoppers could no longer find Japanese-made goods on most shelves in York County.

Storeowners intentionally cleared their inventories of merchandise made by the enemy across the Pacific. They posted appropriate goods with signs stating "Made in America."

The York Retail Merchants also restricted deliveries to save irreplaceable vehicles and tires. They placed fliers in wrapped packages stating: "We are at war! We must save, not waste!"

The merchants urged customers to shop carefully. That would reduce refunds and exchanges, generators of waste paper and additional trips.

"Paper, string and paste are all going into national defense," the merchants stated. "If your package is not wrapped so well as is our usual custom, it is not carelessness. It is because these articles are needed to help win the war."

• • •

Each day, York County's newspapers were packed with war news from home and abroad.

The March 4, 1942, editions of county newspapers tell the story of a community at war.

In an attempt to aid the energy shortage, S. Morgan Smith Co. had manufactured a windmill designed to produce enough electricity to light a town of 2,000 inhabitants. Developers were testing the 18-story mill in Vermont's Green Mountains.

York's American Legion Post 127 accepted Gen. Devers, the Army's chief of armored forces, into its membership.

Devers had filled out a membership application during a visit to York only days before. Post members promptly added the general's name to their roster.

A.L. Troutman, a YMCA instructor, addressed the topic of "Rubber and Its Importance to the National Defense."

America used 90 percent of the world's rubber and produced none of its own, he warned. Residents would notice the seriousness of the shortage within the next two years. Japanese movements in southeast Asia had choked

These eight women were among the early enlistees from York County in the Women's Army Corps. Front row, from left, Virginia Frutiger, Beatrice Runk and Jane Miller; back row, from left, June Reed, Ruth Needles, Esther Seitz, Emily Brenner and Margaret Gable. E.J. Wagner, Army recruiting officer, is in the back row, right.

Nellie Scott, a York Hospital nursing school graduate, became an Army nurse because of shortages of military medical workers. 'There was a war going on, and everyone was involved,' she said years later. 'You know, it was the biggest war ever, and they needed nurses.' Here, the newly minted lieutenant, left, waits for a train with six other nurses in 1943. She served with a nursing unit in Italy that followed the front-line troops as they advanced against Nazi resistance. The Army later transferred her to the Philippines, where she cared for wounded and ill soldiers late in the war.

off America's primary rubber source.

America has started rubber plantations, he said, but it would take a decade for domestic production to reach full capacity.

Photographs or stories of young county men bound for the service were printed nearly every day. This day, Ray F. Leppo and Arthur S. Young were set to join Uncle Sam.

The Dispatch published a photograph of Eugene A. Wise performing an experiment in York's engineering defense training center. Penn State offered the night school course to train technical workers for needed positions in war industries. During the day, Wise worked as a tester in McKay chain company laboratories.

Harvey A. Baublitz was back in town after surviving the sinking of his ship off the Atlantic coast. A German sub torpedoed Baublitz's ship, the Marone, and the Merchant Marine jumped into a lifeboat. Forty-two hours later, naval patrol planes came to his rescue.

A visiting National Education Association representative detailed how York's educators and school children were involved in the war effort.

"York teachers have been teaching in terms of community life and current problems," the article stated. "In time of war, they are going right on with this policy."

As part of a home economics course, William Penn High School girls cared for the children of working mothers. Junior high students rolled bandages, and others made first-aid cases in woodshop.

Madison Avenue Elementary School students salvaged paper and tin foil. Instead of giving money directly to the Red Cross, students purchased yarn and knit afghans for the relief organization.

Students also sold defense bonds and stamps through the school.

About half of the 360 teachers in York had completed the Red Cross first-aid course.

The newspaper also reported a speech by the Rev. T. Samluk of York's St. Mary's parish.

If women of American have courage and strength of character and a willingness to do more than is expected of them, he said, then the men will go forward with a knowledge that their sacrifice is not in vain.

"There, on you depends the success or failure of the war," the Rev. Samluk contended, "even more than the men."

Prof. Henry S. Keith, supervising principal of New Freedom schools, lectured a large gathering of air raid wardens on "Bombs, Their Composition and How to Combat Them."

His talk at Hanover Junior High School included experiments with chemicals used to make bombs. He showed how they burned or exploded.

The educator explained the different types of bombs, how they're made and how to handle them.

"Bombs of a large size, he said, need not be worried about if they land close by," a newspaper reported. "In that case, he said, you won't be around to worry."

• • •

Later in March, York's newspapers told about the death of John E. Fauth, 25, reportedly the war's second victim from the county.

The Red Lion High School graduate, an airplane mechanic working in Burma, died of wounds sustained in an air raid.

Despite the heart-rending news of her son's death, delivered via a cablegram, Lizzie Fauth was holding up remarkably well, The Dispatch reported.

Words had not yet reached York County about the death of Chief Petty Officer Paul A. Sowers of York aboard the USS Pecos.

The ship changed course to pick up survivors from the USS Langley when Japanese dive bombers attacked.

The Pecos went down, and Sowers was among the 50 killed.

• • •

The military joined a Higher Power in calling ministers to a different kind of active duty.

Rabbi Alexander D. Goode, who had decided after the Pearl Harbor attack that he would serve, received a mid-summer commission as first lieutenant in the Army Air Forces.

This ended a long, discouraging wait for his assignment. He immediately put in for overseas duty. He was summoned to Harvard Chaplain School, leaving his wife, Theresa, and young daughter, Rosalie, behind in York.

'Well, somebody should represent us'

In May, Mary Louise Deisinger of York became the first local applicant for enlistment in the Women's Army Auxiliary Corps officer candidates' school.

She was a high school graduate and had attended a military school for two years.

Six others declined to give their names to reporters, fearing their bosses might object to their applications.

Before year's end, other York-area women had left for basic training. Their names were no secret. Beatrice Runk, Jane Miller, June Reed, Ruth Needles, Esther Seitz, Emily Brenner, Margaret Poet, Margaret Gable, among others, joined the military.

Esther Orpin shared her interest about enlisting in the Navy auxiliary with her parents.

She met resistance at first.

"You have a home," her parents said. "That's for people who don't have a home."

Orpin soon learned from her sisters that her parents actually would be proud if she signed up. The next day, she visited the recruiting office.

"There were no men in my family in the service," she said years later, "and I thought, 'Well, somebody should represent (us).' "

Within a year, Anna Wise became the first county grandmother to enlist in the WAACs. Women enrolling in the service agreed to serve through the end of the war. By then, 100,000 were serving in non-combat roles — technicians, secretaries, supply clerks and mechanics.

Women soon served in auxiliary services for other military branches — Women Accepted for Voluntary Emergency Service (WAVEs), the women's Navy reserves; Women's Air Force Service Pilots (WASPs) and others. The auxiliary for female Marines never gained a catchy acronym.

The WASPs ferried aircraft domestically and also flew between the United States and Europe.

Some WASPs died towing practice targets for gunners to sharpen their skills. Errant bullets took down their planes.

• • •

1. KEEP COOL

This panel from a newspaper advertisement counseled York County residents to 'Keep Cool' before, during and after air raids.

The U.S. Public Health Service issued a series of posters geared toward women workers, many of them newcomers to the shop floor. The posters focused on Jenny, a female factory worker. Many companies doing defense work, seeking to avoid loss of valuable labor, emphasized safety, sanitation and healthy practices. Polio, for example, remained a concern in York County during warm weather months. York Ice Machinery Corporation addressed three cases of epidemic meningitis at its Grantley plant in 1942. At least one of the three men afflicted died. Throat and nasal cultures were taken of company employees associated with the workers.

As men enlisted or were drafted, more York County women began entering the work force.

By one accounting, one in four women helped form the American work force before the war. It was more than one in three in 1944.

This migration to the workplace was expected.

In 1940, a local Women's Home Defense committee

had asked York County women to sign up for defense
work. These women — whether employed or not —
showed interest in teaching, assisting nurses, driving and
mechanics and taking shorthand and typing. In the first
day of sign-ups, 20 percent of available city women
stepped forward for training.

With men away in the service, many women worked
outside the home to support themselves, their children and
their extended families. A private in the Army earned only
$50 a month to support himself and his family back home.

• • •

Lillian E. Garrett of York worked as a junior clerk
stenographer with the agricultural marketing service in
Washington, D.C.

A job change created news.

She gained a new stenography position with the
Selective Service in 1942, said to be the first federal
employee to switch from civilian work to war work under
a just-imposed executive order.

"Five feet three inches and 115 pounds, Miss Garrett ...
admitted the idea of being the first transferee left her
somewhat breathless," The Dispatch reported.

• • •

Educators streamlined course work at the Atreus
Wanner Vocational School in York to hasten the training of
women for the work force.

For senior girls, the district eliminated certain subjects
so they could spend half of a day in shop class. Girls were
drawn to the course by the claim that women were receiving the same wages as men. Recent draft calls had
crimped the supply of male workers.

Harry B. Herr, Wanner defense training course coordinator, said the employment of women was no longer an
experiment. Sixteen local industries had accepted trained
women workers to operate machinery.

The P.H. Glatfelter Co. was one of them.

"We are faced more and more with employing women
on jobs which we have always thought only men could
do," The Barker, Glatfelter's newsletter, stated.

Women were working capably in the Spring Grove mill.

"Considering that men are not available," The Barker
said, "we could hardly keep operating without the women."

• • •

Actress Hedy Lamarr urges York County residents to buy
war bonds at York Safe and Lock's Ordnance Plant during
a visit in 1942. Those pledging to purchase bonds got a
chance to meet Miss Lamarr. In another attempt to aid
the military, Lamarr shared a patent for a concept called
'frequency hopping,' a method to control torpedoes without enemy detection or jamming. The patent was not
developed during the war.

Within months of the war's beginning, it was becoming
difficult for mothers in the workplace to secure caregivers
for their children. Former baby sitters now worked in factories, too.

A contingent from York traveled to Harrisburg to soak
up information on how to care for children whose mothers
were involved in defense work. In York alone, 2,265 children
fell into that category.

Created by William Watters, 12A.   Cut by Joyce Good, 12B.

York County residents were coping well with blackout drills, as suggested in this cartoon from an October 1942
edition of The York-High Weekly.

The U.S. Navy required contractor York Corporation to provide fingerprints of all employees to protect war industries and American fighting forces against espionage. The company assured employees that the prints would not remain in York but go to the FBI in Washington, D.C. Here, Stewart E. Lauer, Yorkco's president, is the first to get his prints done in May 1942.

The York group, led by city school Supt. Arthur W. Ferguson, learned about a statewide program to establish nursery schools.

These day-care centers would train children in hygiene, provide special diets and otherwise educate children who weren't in school and were "deprived of mothers attention."

• • •

Not all women entered industrial plants.

York Hospital publicly recruited nurses and aides to replace local nurses enlisting in the military. By late March, Marie Ketterman, hospital's school of nursing director, oversaw the training of more than 15 additional aides.

Helen Minatelli, Eva Ball and Dorcas Kehoe were among the aides receiving 80 hours of classroom and ward training for assisting graduate nurses in a disaster.

Three days a week, Barbara Witmer Young staffed a recruiting center for nurses in the Yorktowne Hotel. It was part of a nationwide effort to lure 3,000 nurses a month into the military.

The name of Hattie Brenneman of Spring Grove headed an initial list of 10 nurses posted in the recruiting center.

• • •

Ninety-six-year-old Catherine Young, confined to a chair by arthritis, kept her hands busy making scrapbooks to send to Army and Navy hospitals.

She recalled seeing Civil War soldiers in blue stacking their rifles near her farmhouse before coming into the house for milk.

"... (A)nd I didn't skim the cream from the top of the milk," she said, "before I gave it to them."

But now, she did a different kind of war work. She sat in the bay window of her York home, collecting pictures and other interesting images into scrapbooks.

• • •

The call of war was depleting the pool of male teachers in county schools. The WACs and other military opportu-

nities for women also drew away female teachers.

The waiting list for city teachers at Supt. Ferguson's office was nearly dry late in the year, particularly for music, art, home economics and other special topics.

The next step was to call married women, banned locally from teaching during the Depression to ensure enough jobs existed for male heads of families.

'Don't kill your pet'

One night in 1942, 52 county residents met at Bowman's garage, Philadelphia and Sherman streets in York, to figure out how to get to work at the Middletown Air Depot.

A growing problem had brought the group together. Transportation to and from defense plants was becoming increasingly difficult.

Rationing of gasoline and tires forced the workers — many of them skilled mechanics vital to defense production — to look for alternate means to travel to the depot, about 40 miles from York across the Susquehanna River.

The workers explored forming a cooperative to purchase a passenger bus. Another plan called for the workers to charter such a bus, if one was to be found.

• • •

One night later, about 100 air wardens, auxiliary and emergency policemen met at West York High School to enlist the county in a statewide "Pledge Campaign."

Those assembled agreed to visit every homeowner and wage earner in the county to raise awareness of bond purchases.

Philip Deane, county war bond chair, reminded emergency workers that the idea behind buying defense bonds and stamps was to aid the military, prevent inflation and ensure a post-war nest egg.

In the four months since Pearl Harbor, the purchase of bonds at county banks and post offices had topped $1 million, and payroll savings in the workplace had exceeded $4 million.

School children selling defense stamps at the Victory House had done their part. The Colonial Court House replica had been moved from Farquhar Park back to Continental Square to promote war bonds.

But the U.S. Treasury Department's $15 million goal challenged the county.

Greater York savings chairman Benjamin T. Root said the Treasury Department would not coerce residents to give, but the purchase of defense bonds and stamps must increase to preserve the life and liberty of Americans.

• • •

Later in the year, actress Hedy Lamarr sparked war bond sales during a visit to York Safe and Lock.

In a speech to defense workers, the actress stated: "I came here to sell war bonds. You came here to see what that 'dame' Hedy Lamarr looks like. Hitler and (Japanese emperor) Hirohito are not interested in that."

After the talk, workers handed Miss Lamarr their pledges and received a smile in exchange.

Worker Joseph Kindlehart reworded his pledge from

"in honor of Miss Lamarr's visit" to read: "In honor of my boy, recently killed in action."

Oscar Schmidt Jr., Medal of Honor winner in World War I, made a large pledge. The gunner's mate in the U.S. Navy earned the high honors after rescuing two men from certain death when their vessel blew up.

The previous evening, the actress attracted 200 people who pledged to purchase a $1,000 war bond in exchange for a private victory dinner at the Country Club of York.

The Spring Garden Band played Viennese music to recognize Miss Lamarr's native Austria.

"I'd be glad to dance to it," the actress told Philip Deane.

The war bond promoter chose Dr. H.P. Belknap as "the ideal partner for such an entrancing waltz."

Hedy Lamarr's appearance stimulated bond sales to almost half of the $1 million goal for the month.

• • •

The war affected pets, too, including the county's 17,737 licensed dogs.

Local Civilian Defense officials issued guidelines about caring for pets during air raids. The guidelines urged owners of dogs to leash them to their kennels. House dogs should be kept in one room. Cats should be placed in a box or basket. Residents should not turn pets loose outdoors and should not ask police officers to care for them.

Pet birds, at risk from broken natural gas lines, could be placed in a gas-proof box. The same was true with pet white mice.

Owners who could accommodate their pets in the country should do so.

But the guidelines warned against killing pets, as had happened in Britain during German air attacks. The Humane Society pointed to the impact such animals have on morale.

"Don't kill your pet," The Dispatch reported, "with the idea that you will thereby spare them the dangers of an air raid."

• • •

York County participated in numerous blackouts — both planned and surprise — for hours. Blackout drills took place to prepare for an air raid, so as not to give enemy pilots a bead on a heavily populated area.

Col. Beckner, the Civilian Defense director, told residents switching off lights was not enough. He urged them to improvise material to cover windows with blankets, dark paper and other items from the home rather than to buy scarce covering materials.

He advised families to prepare a place in their homes or property — called an air raid shelter — where games and reading matter were available.

A recreation kit for children could include favorite toys, pads and pencils for playing drawing games, Chinese checkers, Dominoes and modeling clay.

A National Recreation Association kit for blackouts suggested that harmonicas, ukuleles or kazoos could provide diversions, though "non-playing members of the family may veto this suggestion."

• • •

With more than a hint of satire, William Penn High School 12th-grader Phyllis Frey suggested that blackout drills showed how smoothly a home could run.

York Corporation promotes the value of its cooling equipment in controlling temperature within industrial plants. Stable air control meant that mass production could occur with more precision, this advertisement stated.

As the air-raid whistle blasted one night, her family rushed to blunt the glow of a roaring blaze in its fireplace.

Her mother and father fetched two large umbrellas to put in front of the fire, and her sister collected sweaters to drape over the umbrellas.

Her brother, took time to find "Bulldog Drummond" on the radio and then pulled strings to close some blinds. The blinds came down but so did some flower pots, sitting on the window sill.

"When all that noise died down, we were all set for the blackout," she wrote in The York-High Weekly, "my mother and father holding the draped umbrellas, my sister calmly sitting on the sofa, my brother listening to 'Bulldog Drummond' and I holding a curtain up at the front door. In a few seconds the all-clear sounded, and we happily flooded our home with good old electric light."

• • •

Each community developed its own system for informing residents about air raids. Spring Grove first used an old bell in its fire hall, which proved inadequate.

The responsibility next fell on Lucille White, the always-on-duty operator of the local telephone exchange.

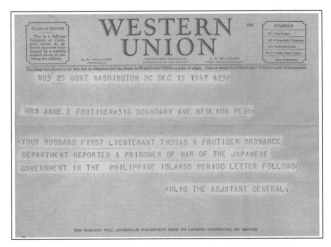

This telegram informed Anne Frutiger, wife of Lt. Thomas W. Frutiger, that her husband was alive after American forces surrendered in the Philippines. Frutiger survived what became known as the Bataan Death March.

Before the fall of the Philippines in 1942, heavy Japanese air strikes impaired the efficiency of Allied troops. The fighting men had to stay in or near foxholes because of enemy air pressure. They couldn't lay communication lines, go on patrol or inspect defenses. Here, men take cover during an air attack near Lamao. The officer, second from right, is believed to be Thomas W. Frutiger of Red Lion.

She had two phone switchboards in her home, one downstairs and one by her bed.

Equipped with a designated switch to activate the fire siren, she provided 24-hour-a-day vigilance. Her instructions: two blasts for a fire outside the borough; four blasts in Spring Grove; six times for the Glatfelter paper mill; eight blasts for an air raid. A continuous alarm meant all clear.

The warning system worked, as an unfortunate incident involving Josephine Miller of Spring Grove attested.

She arose from bed on the second floor of a residence and moved to another room. To comply with blackout rules, she did not turn on the lights.

She mistook a stairway for the room, fell down the steps and fractured her skull.

• • •

With the Spring Grove community on alert for air raids, mysterious flashing lights in the High Rock area of Pigeon Hills particularly alarmed residents.

"Some persons thought that Nazi or Jap spies were flashing messages from the Pigeon Hills," resident Barbara Kling later wrote.

Police officers could not find the source of the lights, widely presumed to be a hoax to scare the public.

• • •

In early June, men, women and children stood in line in York's recently vacated city hall on South Duke Street to receive extra sugar permits. Officials had moved to a new West King Street city hall, leaving the former city building available for Civilian Defense purposes.

Only a handful of clerks waited on the hundreds of people seeking applications for extra sugar.

It was canning season — strawberry season, in fact. Government officials in charge of rationing underestimated the demand for sugar in an agricultural area where housewives had long preserved fruit and vegetables for winter use.

The same clerks waiting on the sugar seekers also were assigned to handle automobile tires, bicycles, typewriters,

gasoline and other rationed items. This was typical of life with a war on.

• • •

Collections to send to servicemen were common, but the auxiliary of the American Legion on West Market Street sought to provide gifts as much appreciated as anything: playing cards.

The auxiliary gathered 512 decks in the first two weeks of a campaign to accumulate 1,000.

Card clubs were among the most generous donors.

The auxiliary made it known that badly worn cards could not be shipped abroad. Members were seeking new or slightly used decks.

'Every time you twist a nut'

By mid-year, Stewart Lauer's words to Yorkco workers were sinking in. Heard less often around "The Yorks" was the question, "How the heck you gonna' win a war with an ice machine?"

Writing in the company newsletter Shop News, editor Fred Gibbs acknowledged that the importance of everyone's contributions took some time to absorb:

"Although we knew that materials couldn't be acquired unless for essential priority production, although we knew that some of our refrigeration work carried higher priorities than did guns, shells, etc.; although we knew that we had close to 95% of essential war production, and although we knew of our increasing production of tank controls, tank hulls, tank parts, gun mounts, torpedo rings and that our thumbprints were on many other actual combat pieces over five oceans — still a few of us did not believe."

By July, War Bond clubs were forming, and an increasing number of Yorkco employees allotted part of their checks to buy bonds. Morale was increasing. Workers were seeing where they fit in.

The numbers alone would have convinced them. For 2,000 officers and men aboard a battleship, two-weeks' rations would have included: 1,500 pounds of smoked ham, 20,000 pounds of frozen beef, 4,000 pounds of frozen veal, 500 pounds of luncheon meat, 1,000 pounds of frozen fish, 37,000 eggs, 2,400 pounds of lettuce, plus thousands of pounds of other goods. Refrigeration was needed to preserve much of this food.

American forces caused the Japanese fleet fits in the battles of Midway and the Coral Sea. Many ships that fought in those Pacific battles were Yorkco equipped, Gibbs wrote.

"Therefore, we of York were 'in' at Midway and certainly helped cause desperation in Tokyo's Naval Office where swords are probably being sharpened and Admiral (Isoroku) Yamamoto's yen for the yanks, dulled," he wrote.

• • •

Managers at Yorkco and other area defense plants kept an eye on worker morale. Company newsletters were filled with encouraging stories and successful uses of company products in aiding the military.

Yorkco sponsored a plant-wide slogan contest that garnered 1,500 entries.

Shop News listed the winners, including George Wachter's first-prize winner: "Work for freedom. People are dying for it!"

Fred Donaldson's "Time is our ally ... don't kill it!" finished second, and James L. Mixon's "Tomorrow is another day, but don't wait!" came in third.

Shop News recorded a morale-building saying that did not appear among the winners: "Every time you twist a nut, think of Hitler."

• • •

Those on Yorkco shop floors grasped for every flake of information about co-workers in the military.

News came from letters home, stories in Shop News, and articles in York County newspapers.

Don Landis, formerly a shearing machine operator, delivered his news in person.

The fireman second class, home on furlough, told Lauer and others how he survived after the Japanese attacked his destroyer in the Pacific.

One morning, he climbed from the U.S.S. Blue's boiler room to the deck for some drinking water. On his way back down, he saw a blinding flash of amber and red, and the ship shook beneath his feet.

A torpedo blew off the destroyer's stern, but the ship somehow stayed afloat. The Japanese returned fire, and the Blue's crew safely climbed aboard another nearby destroyer.

When under fire, there is no time to think or anything else, he said.

"A battleship or any fighting craft is necessarily operated by teamwork," he said. Each man has his particular duty and knows it. This keeps you so concerned that you are aroused beyond fright."

Landis visited his former post at the Can Shop, a department at Yorkco's Grantley plant.

"... Don told the boys he felt right at home again but he

Before the war, York's Floorola Products was a maker of floor waxers and polishers. But the company effectively retooled for defense work. Here, a former weaver and repairer of looms assembles small parts for gun mounts.

thought he'd rather fire the boilers of a destroyer and give Hirohito the hotfoot," Shop News reported.

• • •

York Ice employees also followed the fortunes of their co-workers' sons and daughters in the military.

Chester Nickey, a milling machine operator in the Gun Mount Department at the Grantley plant, made gun shields for the aircraft carrier Hornet and other ships. His son, Chester Nickey Jr., served aboard the noted carrier.

From its decks, Col. Jimmy Doolittle flew Army bombers in an attack on Japan's mainland in April 1942. The assault came as retaliation for the Pearl Harbor battering five months earlier.

Later, the 21-year-old Nickey fought at Midway aboard the "Hornet." The Navy's decisive win in this battle later was viewed as the turning point of the war in the Pacific.

To give his son support, the elder Nickey manned his milling machine seven days a week to turn out shields.

This work would help his son sail into Tokyo Bay, according to Shop News, and "blast Yamamoto and Hirohito right smack dab on the seat of their most dishonorable pants."

• • •

Sometimes, Yorkco employees-turned-servicemen would write much but reveal little.

Such was the case of Johnny Arthur, located with American forces in Ireland. He was attending a school, but secrecy kept him from explaining the type of course he was taking.

Arthur liked Ireland and its beauty.

"However, not a word about the colleens (girls)," Shop News kidded. "Is that a military secret, too?"

• • •

Many at York Ice Machinery particularly strained for information about Lt. Thomas W. Frutiger, the former Yorkco engineer stationed on the island of Luzon in the Philippines.

Pledging that he would return, commanding Gen.

These young women are completing about 120 hours of engineering-drafting training, after which they would fan out into various drafting rooms at York Ice Machinery sites. During the closing weeks of the 1942 school year, Lea Becker and Charles Brillinger interviewed students at area schools for the drafting positions. Here, mechanical engineer Ed Bishop, near the window, instructs the class.

Douglas MacArthur departed shortly before Japanese forces overran the Philippines in May. Information dried up after that, and the Army simply listed Tom Frutiger as missing in action.

Fears about Frutiger's status heightened after word reached the United States that many prisoners had been subjected to a deadly forced march.

The trek, starting from the tip of Luzon's Bataan Peninsula, covered 65 miles in six days under a tropical sun. It ended with survivors trapped in appalling prison camps, subjected to subhuman conditions.

About 11,000 men died or fell victim to Japanese bayonets or clubs along the route of the march.

Anne Frutiger, residing with her two sons in the family's North Main Street home in Red Lion, received a word of encouragement from her husband's unit headquarters in August.

H. Harrison Smith, representing the 316th Infantry, speculated that Frutiger would be safe. His ordnance company, with its supplies of explosives and ammunition, would have been given as much cover as could be found.

Smith had met Tom Frutiger in 1933 when the young engineer had joined the regiment as a reserve officer.

"... I know he was a splendid, outstanding young man, and a very gallant officer," he wrote.

The 316th had 352 officers on active duty and two — Lt. Frutiger and Charles H. Langdon Jr. of York — had been in Bataan.

Langdon's father also had not heard from his son since shortly after the Japanese attack on the Philippines. Langdon was a graduate of Augusta Military Academy and a former student at Gettysburg College.

Smith wrote that the "old-timers" of the regiment thought highly of all officers but were proudest of Tom Frutiger and Charles Langdon, who were the first to go into action and were known to have fought to the last with MacArthur in Bataan.

• • •

Anne Frutiger received more encouraging news late in the year from Congressman Harry L. Haines.

Haines, a fellow Red Lion resident, had met with a

American Chain and Cable Co. of York issued envelopes for the safekeeping of war bonds purchased by its employees. Stories abounded about bonds that were lost, stolen and even accidentally incinerated.

nurse, Nancy Gillahan, at Walter Reed Hospital in Washington, D.C. She had contracted malaria and was among the last Americans to leave the Philippines before the enemy takeover.

She informed Haines she had eaten a meal with Frutiger the night before the Philippines fell and was certain he was taken prisoner and not wounded.

Schmidt & Ault Paper Co., a long-time York business, encourages paper recycling in this advertisement placed in The York-High Weekly in 1942.

"She said Tom was well and in good spirits and right on his job to the last minute," Haines stated.

Haines was proud to hear fine things about Frutiger and stories about his bravery under a trying ordeal.

"She was most interesting and told me many of her experiences," he wrote, "but what pleased me most of all was the high praises she spoke in behalf of Tom's action under fire."

Anne Frutiger would have welcomed that news — any news from her husband. It had been months since his last letter.

She had heard from him by telegram at Christmas 1941.

"Doing Fine Love Merry Christmas," one note stated.

She received correspondence from somewhere in the Philippines in February, probably the last full letter she received from him.

"Some of the old Philippine soldiers showed us how to make beds out of bamboo so except for a little noise sometimes, it is like a camping trip," he wrote, "Natives do our laundry if we furnish the soap which is becoming rather scarce."

He wrote that American forces had been taking care of themselves and as many enemy soldiers as possible.

Just before the Philippines fell, the family received a telegram stating, "Safe and well ... don't worry."

After the Japanese gained control of the Philippines, Anne Frutiger inquired about her husband through the Red Cross in York.

After checking, Martha B. Carey informed her that Thomas' name did not appear on any War Department casualty list. The Japanese government had not released prisoner lists.

Finally, just before Christmas, Anne Frutiger learned from military officials that her husband was a Japanese POW in the Philippines.

• • •

Tom's captivity did not deter his sister, Virginia, from serving.

The York Ice Machinery employee was in an early group of county women enlisting in the WACs.

She received her basic training at Daytona Beach, Fla., early in 1943 and entered Officers Training School at Des Moines, Iowa.

Her parents, William C. and Anna Frutiger of Red

Lion, were proud of both their children in the military.

"Tom always was an adventuresome and thrill-seeking boy," his father told Shop News. "But he is a thoroughly determined fellow who can 'fix' most anything he tackles. Because of this, I do believe that he will come through the 'fix' he is in now with flying colors."

Tom and Virginia's mother agreed.

"Yes, and Virginia has many of Tom's traits," Anna Frutiger said.

Meanwhile, a third sibling labored to aid military men and women. Bill Frutiger worked in Yorkco's Can Shop, producing air conditioning units for military use.

'Did I get that card?'

In December, 76 enlistees in the U.S. Navy participated in an observance marking the anniversary of the Pearl Harbor attack.

In the somber ceremony on the York County Courthouse steps, the county men repeated an oath to become Navy seamen.

At one point, the entire audience turned to the west — toward Pearl Harbor — for a minute of silence.

A trumpeter played "Taps" to end the observance.

• • •

The community also looked at the threat from the east.

Just before the Pearl Harbor anniversary, 12th-grader Natalie Butler satirized the much-despised Hitler in The York-High Weekly.

She presented notes from the Fuehrer's chefs about his menus:

"Breakfast: One slice of Czechoslovakia, nicely browned with two glasses of Poland and one boiled Norway.

"Der Fuehrer appeared to enjoy his meal.

"Lunch: Sandwiches of Denmark and Holland mixed with Belgium, also the Balkans fried in Greece; as dessert, France a la mode.

"Der Fuehrer personally congratulated me for preparing such a delicious repast.

"Dinner: Russia, baked, fried, stewed, boiled, simmered, broiled, etc.

"Tomorrow I die because Der Fuehrer had horrible indigestion from trying to consume Russia."

• • •

Meanwhile, Bob Senft continued his duties as a Yorkco clerk, doing the important home front defense work that Stewart Lauer put forth earlier in the year.

The military was not yet drafting married men, and every able-bodied worker was needed to handle mounting defense demands.

Ethel Senft remained in her Conewago Township home, doing volunteer work in her church and the Zion View community and caring for her mother and grandfather.

The couple developed a ritual.

He would come home every day and ask, "Well, did I get that card?"

He meant his greeting card from Uncle Sam, his draft card.

By year's end, his wife's answer still was no.

III

'Don't you know there's a war on?'

— 1943 —

These volunteers pose outside the Victory House, the Colonial Court House replica located in York's Continental Square, in this war stamps sales promotion photo. The stamps sold for 25 cents, and when they filled a book, they could be exchanged for a $25 war bond. Bonds sold for $18.75, bringing a $6.25 profit over 10 years. In this way, Americans helped finance the war to the tune of hundreds of millions of dollars.

Gallery

This New Freedom husband and wife served in the war. Charles Goodfellow Jr. entered the U.S. Army Air Forces in 1943 and served in the Pacific before his discharge in 1946. Margie Lynn Goodfellow joined the Women's Army Corps in 1945. She was discharged about eight months after her husband.

The Spring Grove community mounted a 77 mm field piece near Spring Grove American Legion Post 216 in 1927 as a memorial to borough residents who had served in World War I. Residents felt it appropriate to donate the cannon to be melted down for armament metal during World War II. The field piece sits, right, near a pile of scrap, to be recycled for war use.

'Use it up,' a 1943 conservation poster, gives a double example of how Americans could make do. While a man bends over to repair his lawn mower, his wife mends his trousers.

York Ice Machinery Corporation's Charlie Zeigler welds freon connections on the coils in the lock of the two-room strato-chamber while James Zinner installs the main cooling coils in the inner chamber. The insulated apartment inside the steel tube was designed to simulate stratospheric conditions for pilot training.

Bill Flinchbaugh, a William Penn High School senior, practices commando-toughening tactics in boys' gym. Senior boys received such training five days a week to prepare for military service after graduation in 1943.

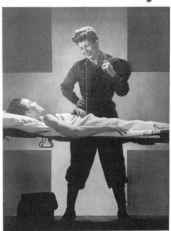

This recruitment poster addresses the critical need for nurses during the war. Medical care improved during World War II compared to the Great War. In World War I, about 4 percent of those wounded recovered. By the second war, about 50 percent lived. In 1943, the federal Victory Nurse Corps granted financial aid to women to attend nursing school. Later, the Nurse Training Act provided instruction for 124,065 medical workers as part of the Cadet Nursing Corps.

'Few tears were to be seen'

In 1940, John Lathrope Wheeler, a worker in Arthur Bury's West Market Street restaurant, was the first to register with the Selective Service in the first precinct of York's first ward.

The 23-year-old had served in the Army for two years in Panama before his discharge in 1938. Two years later, he led the enrollment line, one of 25,000 York County men to do so in the peacetime draft in the fall of 1940.

That number of registrants had swelled to 58,471 by 1943 as war overtook peace, according to numbers put forth by the county's seven Selective Service boards.

In November 1940, Robert D. Feiser, 21, became the No. 1 man from York County to complete his physical test and other examinations at the induction center in Harrisburg.

Feiser, a knitter in a hosiery mill before his enlistment, was among the volunteers who rode the rail to Pennsylvania's capital after fanfare at York's North Duke Street station.

"Few tears were to be seen, since the young men were anxious to enter the service and secure the experience," The York Dispatch reported.

By mid-January 1943, 7,368 county residents had followed Feiser into some branch of the service, many taking the same path north to the Harrisburg induction center.

By now, county fighting men and women in the Armed Forces were serving around the world.

And dying for their country.

And the county continued to produce more military men and women — 13,000 more by war's end.

• • •

America's involvement in the war reached the halfway point in late 1943, not that President Roosevelt or anyone else could know it.

The Allies had yet to establish a second front in western Europe to aid the Soviet attacks on German lines in the east. Despite taking the strategic island of Midway in the Pacific, the Allies faced a formidable foe in Japan.

Anytime York County people got together, they traded news of men and women they knew shipping out to some faraway location.

They talked about their sons, daughters or family members coming home, often for short furloughs before again departing.

They talked about some soldier or seaman they knew who would never come home again.

They talked not only about those who had left, but the many new folks now in town working in defense indus-

Rabbi Alexander D. Goode, center, behind his South Beaver Street pulpit, served as leader of York's Temple Beth Israel in 1940. Two years later, Rabbi Goode became Lt. Goode, a military chaplain.

tries. Newcomers occupied the church pews informally — or formally — reserved for the same families for years.

And many people on the home front never forgot — they were constantly reminded in the community and in the workplace — that they were doing their part in saving the lives of those in the service and protecting their own freedom.

'Just one of those things'

The same January day's newspapers that gave military induction figures to date also reported that Robert A. Elsessor, 18, was missing in action.

By now, the deaths of military men were becoming more common as fighting escalated in the Pacific and Mediterranean theaters of war.

Elsessor's parents, Mr. and Mrs. Peter Andrew Elsessor of York, learned by cablegram that the seaman was unaccounted for following action in the performance of duty.

His last letter had arrived a month before from the Pacific. From his earliest days of basic training, he wrote about his desire to get into action.

His family later learned the dreaded news — their son had died for his country.

• • •

That January, 31-year-old York Rabbi Alexander D. Goode and his wife, Theresa, met for three days in New York, near his Brooklyn birthplace.

After about six months in the service, he had learned of his pending departure for Greenland, home of two American air bases. Planes stopped there for refueling on their way between Newfoundland and Britain.

The couple said goodbye, typical of countless other hard farewells between servicemen and loved ones in those years.

"It was a difficult good-bye, and I looked at him through the window of the train," Theresa later recalled. "I was crying and he was crying. I knew I would never see him again — I just felt it in my heart."

Before he departed on the troop carrier Dorchester, Goode wrote Theresa, "Don't worry — I'll be coming back much sooner than you think."

• • •

Alexander Goode accompanied three other chaplains on the ship. George Lansing Fox, a Methodist minister; Clark Poling, a Dutch Reformed pastor; and John Washington, a Roman Catholic priest, joined Goode in working with the men aboard the Dorchester as it moved across U-boat-infested waters of the Northern Atlantic.

The threat of attack by German submarine Wolf Packs was at its height, and those aboard the ship knew of the danger.

To date, swarming subs operating in groups had sunk more than 100 Allied ships in the Northern Atlantic. Their mission was to deter troops and supplies from reinforcing Britain and thus allay or delay an attack on France, representing Germany's western front.

In the early morning hours on Feb. 3, a wolf found its prey. A torpedo struck the Dorchester, and the exploding ship immediately started to sink. The four chaplains rushed from their stateroom to the main deck, intent on creating order amid chaos.

"The encouraging thoughts and remarks of the chaplains was in no small way responsible for some of the more fearful individuals going over the side and eventually being saved," survivor William G. Bunkelman recalled.

Boats and rafts could accommodate about 1,300 in an emergency, sufficient for the 900 men aboard. But many untrained, wounded and chilled men panicked.

Some dropped into the water without life jackets. Others jumped from the ship into already-filled lifeboats.

Rabbi Alexander D. Goode is pictured at right in this mural in the York elementary school bearing his name.

A full year before Pearl Harbor, men in York County and across America from 21-36 years old received orders to register for Selective Service. This created a peacetime inventory — initially projected at 25,000 county men — of those eligible for duty and stood as the starting point for the enlistment or drafting of more than 20,000 county men into the Armed Forces during the war.

Some rafts thrown over the side hit men in the water.

The chaplains handed out life jackets, even giving up their own. Lt. John Mahoney had left his gloves in his cabin, and headed back for them. Alexander Goode headed him off, pulling off his own gloves.

Mahoney refused, but Goode said he had another pair. The lieutenant lowered himself into the water.

"I owe my life to those gloves," Mahoney said years later. "I landed in a lifeboat that was awash, and for eight hours had to hold on ... ."

• • •

Sgt. Michael Warrish saw Goode remove his life jacket and kneel beside a man with an injured shoulder. The rabbi unlaced his own shoes, placed the man's good arm through the life jacket's armhole and then tied the other side of the jacket around the injured shoulder with the laces.

On deck, the chaplains started praying, in English, Hebrew and Latin. In the darkness, Warrish could not see if they linked arms.

The chaplains were going to stay with the rapidly sinking ship.

• • •

John P. O'Brien observed the four chaplains calmly trying to maintain order. He dived into the water and climbed onto a lifeboat, which then capsized.

"So, I returned to the Dorchester and remained on it until the water on the deck ... was up to my knees," he later said. "The chaplains were still on the deck and remained there when I dove off the ship for the second time."

James Eardley has been credited as the last man to see the chaplains alive: "I was on a life raft and ... when (the ship) rolled over ... that's when I saw the four chaplains, (who) had climbed up on the keel, and they were standing arm in arm ... And then ... she nosed down (and) they slid off ... into the water."

About one-third of the passengers and crew survived.

• • •

Theresa Goode, staying with her sister in Washington, D.C., awoke with a start at 1:35 a.m., 15 minutes after the Dorchester went down.

"It was as if someone had dropped me in ice water and I was just frozen," she later said. "It seemed to me that the whole room had become illuminated, and Alex's picture on the dresser just seemed to glow. I felt as if he was trying to reach me. I was just so frightened."

Soon thereafter, the Army notified her that her husband was missing.

"I have not given up hope for his return to me," Mrs. Goode told a reporter in early March. "I can not believe that he is dead and will not return."

She pointed out that her husband was young and a good swimmer.

"There are many possibilities that he was saved," she said, "and I will not give up until it is established that he is gone forever."

Late in March, the Army sent its official word. Goode was the first Jewish chaplain to die in the war.

• • •

By year's end, pennants hanging around York Corporation listed 791 company men and women in the service and bore six gold stars for those who died.

William Ensminger Jr., George J. Ensslen Jr., Paul C. March, Charles Rotunda Jr., James L. Sawyer and John W. Walton died in uniform.

The gold star for Sgt. Ensminger, 19, was the first on the Yorkco flags.

Ensminger was part of a six-man crew in a medium-range bomber. The plane exploded or collapsed shortly after taking off on a routine training flight in Florida. Everyone aboard was killed.

The former draftsman had just returned to Florida after a 10-day furlough at home.

"It's a honey," Ensminger wrote his mother the afternoon before the flight. "I am anxious to get up again. Don't worry about me ... ."

Ensminger escaped injury or death in an earlier incident. He bailed out over a Florida swamp.

"The parachute leap did not frighten him," Yorkco's Shop News reported, "as much as the thought of landing in the snake infested swamp."

• • •

Lt. George J. Ensslen Jr. was the first former Yorkco employee to meet his death in actual combat.

Carolyn Landis, Ensslen's sister and a Yorkco worker, learned of her brother's death from his squadron's commander. It was later believed that Ensslen, a P-38 fighter pilot, died in aerial combat with the enemy over China.

Earlier, Ensslen had distinguished himself in attacks upon Sardinia, Sicily and Pantelleria in the European Theater.

"I knew his courage to be unlimited, his judgment to be always quick and accurate and his participation in our operations against the enemy always to be forceful and complete," the commander wrote.

The issue of Shop News telling of his death included a letter from the 20-year-old pilot, written from somewhere in China, to his former co-workers. At that point, he thought he had damaged two enemy aircraft in dogfights.

"It's hard to tell," he wrote, "as you don't stick around long to count the score."

In China, halfway around the world, he had enjoyed many landmarks along the way.

"I have seen the Sphinx, Pyramids, Taj Mahal, and many other much discussed places," he wrote, "but with me it is still the States.

"Why join the Navy to see the world. I say, join the Air Force."

• • •

The families of Yorkco workers also sustained losses in the war.

For about a year, since the Battle of Guadalcanal in the Pacific, Edwin Harbold, a veteran Yorkco machinist, had lived with the fear that his son, Lewis Henry Harbold, was dead. He was listed as missing in action.

In late 1943, the Navy officials notified the family of their conclusion: Lewis Harbold was dead. The 19-year-old sailor had been aboard the U.S.S. Juneau, when it went down during a battle.

Five days before that battle, young Harbold had written to his parents: "I hope you are okey as I am. If you do not receive mail from me for a long time, do not worry about me, mother, it is just one of those things. The Japs are keeping us pretty busy. No news is good news, you know."

Lewis Harbold wrote one more letter to his mother, which she did not receive until several days after the naval battle.

"I know that it will be impossible for me to come home for Christmas," he wrote, "but that doesn't keep me from wishing. I am enclosing a money order for $100. You and dad get whatever you wish as a gift from your fighting son."

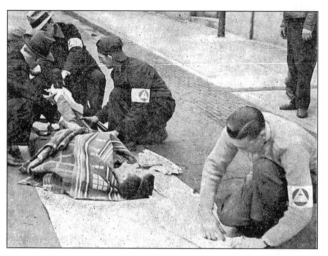

York Corporation staged a mock bombing raid in the spring of 1943, Here, Lawrence Depler, Lloyd Waller, Thomas Davies, Daniel Bumbaugh and Lewis Gibbs, members of the Plant Protection Corps, administer first aid to George Landis, who they carried out of debris during the drill. The mock raid was met with skepticism among some workers, but 'Yorkco Pete' wrote in the June 1943, Shop News that workers at the plant should be on guard. The Allied pressure on Hitler was making the dictator desperate. Air raids and sabotage were possible.

'No matter how little it is'

As the war entered its second full year in 1943, multiple members of the same family often had entered the service. And often more family members would join before the war ended.

Five sons of Mr. and Mrs. John Carter of Spring Garden Township served around the world, and a sixth son, Lloyd, 17, a William Penn High School senior, had already passed his mental and physical tests for the Air Corps Reserve.

Cpl. Emanuel Carter served with the U.S. Engineers in Africa.

Cpl. William Henry Carter attended the Coast Artillery radio school in North Carolina.

Pfc. Kenneth Carter, inducted during his senior year at Pennsylvania's Cheyney State College, was attending engineering school in Ettrick, Va.

Seaman Second Class John Carter was stationed at Camp Moffet in Illinois. He was formerly a student at Hampton Institute.

Seaman Second Class Richard Carter, inducted while a student at Tuskegee Institute in Alabama, was stationed at the San Diego Naval Base.

Lloyd, the last son to enter, did not survive the war.

He died in 1945 when the plane he was piloting crashed near South Carolina's Walterboro Army Air Field.

• • •

The John F. Bennett family of Hanover offered Uncle

Sam eight sons for service.

Frederick, the ninth son, joined the Army after the war. He was the last son who would join.

The Bennetts had 18 children, including 11 sons. Two of the sons were deceased.

• • •

Yorkco boasted about a warrior of a different type, also from a large family.

"It isn't news any more when a cute young co-ed emerges from the employment office as a truck driver or when a dainty debutante winds up as an artist in sheet metal," Shop News reported, "but when the mother of eight children ranging from 2 to 17 decides to become a maker of airplane parts, that's news."

Shop News said "Mrs. Wintermyer" was able to work in the defense plant because her 17-year-old daughter, Edna, could watch the rest of the brood. Her husband, meanwhile, worked at United Wall Paper Co. in York.

The 37-year-old Yorkco worker produced hydraulic parts for the Republic Thunderbolt, a fighter plane widely used in combat.

"Heavens knows that I want this country to be the same when my children grow up as it was before the war started," she said. "When I read in the papers about the many Thunderbolt victories in Europe, I feel that although the part I am doing — no matter how little it is — is helping make it that kind of country."

• • •

John J. Smith II and his two sons enlisted in the U.S. Navy.

Mrs. Smith and her 11-year-old daughter followed a widespread practice when the service beckoned men to duty. She moved in with her parents, Mr. and Mrs. Frank Schrom of York.

John Smith, 39, who had served in World War I, accompanied his 17-year-old son, Wesley Donald Smith, to the Navy recruiting station at York's Post Office. John Smith and his 18-year-old son, John J. Smith III, previously had enlisted in Philadelphia.

During his first hitch, the elder Smith served as an orderly — and boxing sparring partner — to then-Prince Leopold of Belgium during the royal family's visit to America.

Smith saluted the prince every time the two met, causing the future King Leopold III of Belgium to remark: "Once a day is sufficient. You need not salute so often."

• • •

John C. Sherrill battled for three years to enlist in the Army.

But the Shiloh man, found to be in perfect health, could not get a clearance to serve. The problem was his unusual height.

A regulation Army uniform could not wrap around his 6-foot, 7-1/2-inch frame, he was told. He took the advice of a friend and practiced walking under a 6-foot door in an attempt to appear shorter.

He traveled repeatedly to the induction center in Harrisburg.

'No, York is not making guns, but York men are building the intricate turntable mount that handles this 6-inch Coast Defense Rifle as if it were something you'd use for rabbits,' York Corporation's Shop News reported in January 1943. The newsletter touted the gun's prowess: 'If ever Adolph sees "eye to eye" with this Army toy, there'll be little argument concerning "the Master Race."'

Finally, in 1943, he gained his clearance.

"He has the distinction of being Uncle Sam's tallest soldier from York County and said to be among the few of that stature serving in the United States army," The Dispatch reported.

The average American soldier stood 5 feet 8 inches tall and weighed 144 pounds.

• • •

Two other physically fit York men had less success than Sherrill in joining the service.

The last two Mr. Americas did not gain entry into military service.

John Grimek's bid was rejected because of poor eyesight.

Jules Bacon's left leg had been broken, run over and shot in a series of mishaps when he was young.

• • •

Although healthy, 22-year-old Russell R. Rentzel of York was denied entry into gunnery school. He weighed 122 pounds, 3 pounds less than minimum weight.

The next day, he returned for another weigh-in with two quarts of water hidden under his belt. He passed and went on to serve as engineer-gunner on a B-24 Liberator. He flew in more than 20 combat missions over Europe and German-occupied France.

The lightweight was awarded a Distinguished Flying Cross and Air Medal with three Oak Leaf Clusters.

• • •

Leroy J. Koons of York was so eager to get into the service that he fibbed about his age.

That was in March 1941, when he was three months short of his 17th birthday. He was in Hawaii during

Japan's sneak attack and made his way to Australia in 1943 to join MacArthur's campaign to retake the Philippines.

In January 1945, he was fighting with MacArthur's Army when he was summoned home. His 46 months of service earned him a leave, and he headed stateside on the same ship as American POWs freed in the invasion.

He was still only 20 years old.

• • •

One York businessman, a World War I veteran, had no trouble entering the military. But his uniform helped him stay in the service — and out of jail.

The Internal Revenue Service hauled the 42-year-old major into federal court to collect about $25,000 in unpaid business taxes and penalties.

He stood before the judge in khakis and gold leaf insignia. His lawyer argued that he was doing important war work.

The judge suspended a prison term, and if the major met certain conditions, he would earn probation.

"If it were not for the fact that you are wearing that uniform," the judge lectured, "I'd send you to jail for a good, long term."

• • •

A special type of county fighter was shipping out in great numbers.

The Army was looking for aggressive dogs to perform special duties: patrol, attack, carry backpacks or convey messages in canisters tied to their necks.

The dogs entered the service through a Philadelphia induction center. The canines had to be 26 inches at the shoulders, weigh 50 pounds and qualify as a government-approved breed.

They also had to pass a physical.

Some of the dogs shipping out were pets of servicemen who wanted their canine friends to enlist with Uncle Sam, too.

• • •

Early in the war, the U.S. Army Signal Corps put out a call for homing pigeons.

The corps asked the six or more York County pigeon clubs to inventory how many of the county's 6,000 homing birds would be available for military service.

The military considered pigeons an important part of war communication, when other means of sending messages had broken down.

The corps also cautioned the clubs about foreign agents intercepting the birds.

John P. Bailey of York spent most of the war training homing pigeons to operate in a battle zone and teaching infantrymen how to handle them. Late in the war, the sergeant operated pigeon communications on an island in the Philippines with success, even saving a band of Filipino guerrillas trapped by the enemy.

Bailey wrote to the York Homing Pigeon Club that a Japanese sniper took a pot shot at the pigeons. The bullet severed two toes of a cadet bird.

But the birds faced a bigger foe. The Philippines were full of hawks.

SPECIAL SERVICES WE HAVE RENDERED

1. Taught 14 servicemen to dance or a reasonable facsimile.
2. Held 26 hands, 18 in sympathy, 8 in self-defense.
3. Consoled 12 servicemen wailing, "Three weeks after I left, she married someone else," with "She wasn't worthy of a nice guy like you anyway."
4. Loaned 9 handkerchiefs to as many 18 year olds who were ready to cry into their Pepsicola because we reminded them of some girl back home.
5. Swam in temperatures of 33 degrees and smiled our warmest when frozen to the teeth to be good sports.
6. Wrote letters to 405 servicemen who were about to embark on the great adventure.
7. Sent 4 watches to the watchmaker's; sewed on 18 buttons.
8. Refused 692 and ½ invitations to be taken home without harming the morale.
9. Refused 62 invitations to get married.

This list found in the York County USO's newsletter provides a tongue-in-cheek account of services provided by hostesses at the Servicemen's Club and Canteen at the old York County Academy.

'Patriotic To Look Pretty'

Men and women in the service daily disembarked at the Pennsylvania Railroad Station on York's North Duke Street.

There, they would wait for their connecting train or a ride home and enjoy the hospitality and food packages from a United Services Organization booth. Volunteers had accommodated 17,800 troops in transit by the time of the York USO's 18-month anniversary in the fall of 1943.

If men or women in uniform were looking to stay the night, they would walk the short distance to Continental Square. There, volunteers at the Colonial Court House replica, the Victory House, pointed them toward a free meal or room.

If Continental Square was the center of the bustling community, Victory House was the focal point of the square. It served as a hub for information and war bond sales in the York area.

The 1-1/2-story building, situated on the southeast corner of the square, was a miniature of the York County Court House that housed the Continental Congress during its nine-month stay in 1777-78.

In that square brick building during the Valley Forge winter, delegates adopted the Articles of Confederation, forerunner to the U.S. Constitution. The courthouse, demolished in 1841, had become a significant local symbol of patriotism.

The "Little Courthouse," newly constructed then, became a rallying point for the sale of bonds in World War I.

LODGING—Hotel prices listed in VICTORY HOUSE. Upon presentation of signed leave card overnight lodging in private homes may be secured without charge to transient uniformed men. Rooms may be secured for one dollar per night in private homes upon presentation of signed leave card. Lists are posted in VICTORY HOUSE.

MEALS—Following Service Clubs invite any man in uniform for free meal:

Lions Club of York—Tues. Noon—Yorktowne
Exchange Club—Tues. 6:00—Yorktowne
Rotary Club—Wed. Noon—Yorktowne
Kiwanis Club—Thurs. 6:00—Yorktowne
Monarch Club—Wed. Noon—Colonial
Exchange Club of West York—Alternate Thurs. 6:15 P. M.—West York Inn

If you lack change a free meal may be arranged upon inquiring from the police officer in the Square.

This page from a USO brochure provided instructions to servicemen stopping over in York. Victory House listed in this information was the Colonial Court House replica, then in use as headquarters for war bond and stamp drives in York's Continental Square. This information suggests the ongoing presence of a policeman in York's center to keep the peace, answer servicemen's questions and provide vouchers for free meals and lodging for chronically cash-poor military men.

During that war, community leaders Mahlon Haines and Edward S. Brooks feuded over who would more often ring the bell in the little building's tower. The custom was to clang the bell each time a bond or stamp was sold. Haines and Brooks would try to outbid the other until one or the other had put forth $100 to help underwrite the war.

The courthouse was retired to York's Farquhar Park after Armistice Day until called up for similar duty in World War II.

Grade school student Phyllis May bought the first war bond, a $100 note, upon its reopening in 1942. Again, the bell rang. The original bell was gone, but a fire engine bell made an adequate substitute.

In reporting on the re-emergence of the little courthouse, The York-High Weekly stated, "How about blasting that bell till Hitler and all his colleagues fall beneath the might of a steady stream of your war stamps and bonds?

"And then, little 'Victory House' will be able to again go back to its peaceful, happy resting place, having served to save its country."

• • •

Sometimes, a free meal could be found elsewhere on the square, if the Salvation Army's canteen and club car trailer were open.

The canteen offered doughnuts, coffee and sandwiches, and servicemen could lounge in the trailer to listen to the radio, chat with a hostess or enjoy records on an electric portable phonograph. The men also could pen letters in a writing room supplied with paper and envelopes.

Police officers, always assigned to the square, carried vouchers with them for servicemen in need. The USO adopted the Brooks Hotel and YMCA as their official hotels and the Ramona Restaurant for meals.

By the fall of 1943, servicemen had received 3,210 vouchers for lodging and 2,300 for meals from the USO.

• • •

Volunteers at Victory House would often point visitors to an old brick building on North Beaver Street. That was the former York County Academy, a school built in 1787, and then the headquarters for USO activities in the York area.

Using the nonprofit USO's motto of a "home away from home," the York unit had already accommodated 9,200 military guests.

The old academy served as a Servicemen's Club, and the Pennsylvania Dutch Canteen operated out of its former gym.

The club included a lounge room, equipped with easy chairs, reading and writing material and a radio/Victrola.

A "Quiet Game Room," featuring card tables and puzzles, and an "Active Game Room," for ping-pong, darts and pool, were also on the first floor.

A "Craft Room," full of tools, sewing and pressing materials, was located on the second floor.

Out back in the canteen, Pennsylvania Dutch designs covered the walls of the old brick gym, and antique lanterns and candles provided soft light.

The canteen, of course, featured Pennsylvania Dutch food, a jukebox, Victrola, dance floor and facilities for showering and shaving.

There, servicemen could eat and mingle with young women serving as volunteer hostesses. Outside, a wooden floor provided an area for dancing, basketball or shuffleboard during warm weather.

Local women acted as hostesses, chaperones and canteen workers to serve the traveling military men.

Patrons came from all over. Some sought to kill time during layovers. Others came from nearby New Cumberland Army Depot, Fort Indiantown Gap and other military bases to seek companionship. Some military men and defense officials were on assignment as inspectors with York Corporation and other government contractors.

• • •

In the USO's first 18 months, 5,840 young women from the York area volunteered to serve as dance and conversation partners.

Senior hostesses worked in shifts to oversee the activities of their generally younger, junior counterparts. The junior hostesses were forbidden to date the servicemen, a rule they sometimes broke.

USO newsletters contained regular counsel for these junior hostesses, who were at least 18 years old. They were on duty to entertain, not to be entertained. They

Some couples enjoy time out at York's USO canteen at the old York County Academy campus on North Beaver Street. This postcard touted the USO's hospitality. In 1943, Judge Walter I. Anderson served as chairman of the committee overseeing York County's USOs. Margaret Swartz handled duties as director of the North Beaver Street USO.

could be served at the canteen at all times but with smaller helpings than the servicemen. They must not wear sweaters.

In fact, a USO newsletter item, titled "Patriotic To Look Pretty," suggested that servicemen were asking for their hostesses to wear dance frocks — evening dresses. Such garb had not been worn, considered too frivolous for wartime.

"You don't know how good it is to see a pretty girl in a party frock," the servicemen told USO officials, "after you've lived with uniforms so long."

• • •

USO activities for servicemen also took place at the Crispus Attucks Community Center.

The center, a gathering spot for York's black community, sponsored dances, mushball games and dinners and also sent junior and senior hostesses to dances at Fort Indiantown Gap.

The Crispus Attucks center faced the same challenge as other USO locations: a shortage of hostesses. A number of young women were attending college or working in defense plants.

Still, more than 100 senior and junior hostesses were available when the need for them arose.

• • •

A weekend the next summer illustrates the USO's commitment to servicemen.

GIs at the Pennsylvania Railroad canteen enjoyed donated cakes, candy and cigarettes. Arlene Lehman and Mrs. Lloyd Henry were among the volunteers stocking treats at the canteen.

Sixty-five servicemen and girls attended a swimming party and picnic at the bungalow of a USO leader, Marie Strickhouser, at Long Level on the Susquehanna River.

About 225 people registered at the Pennsylvania Dutch canteen. Seventy-five of this group received breakfast served by Red Cross canteen corps.

About 100 women volunteered as hostesses or canteen workers for those weekend activities. Many of the volunteers were mothers or sisters of military men stationed overseas.

On another weekend, the USO played host to actor Edgar Buchanan and actress Leslie Brooks, in town for a pep talk to buy war bonds.

The celebrities convinced those attending to fork over $3,200 toward the war effort.

• • •

USOs often had quiet areas for servicemen to write home. Mail was the primary link between the war and home fronts.

Victory Mail Service, better known as V-Mail, was now fully in place to help residents reach their sons and daughters abroad, and vice versa.

The U.S. Post Office Department's system called for each letter, prepared with address and message on one side, to be microfilmed to lighten mailbags for air transport. When the mail reached its destination, an enlarging camera prepared the letter for delivery.

Men overseas often did not receive letters while in battle zones, but when they returned to their rest camps, a pile of old letters sometimes awaited.

Those in the military got free postage. Senders on the home front paid 3 cents for regular delivery and 6 cents for airmail.

Sometimes, V-Mail carried "Dear John" news, probably less well-received by the soldier in the field than the friend back home, surmised Conewago Township resident Norma Bear Gates years later.

"Nevertheless, in either case, 'Dear John' brought pain and tears," she wrote, "at times, even an erratic binge!"

• • •

V-Mail helped keep mail call a much-anticipated rite in camp. Servicemen would write home, too, and sometimes send along souvenirs.

Lena Bentivegna of York received a jolt in opening a package from her son, Jack, a Marine sergeant in the Pacific. She found two buck teeth from a fallen Japanese soldier on Guadalcanal strung on a piece of wire.

"The dental work appears to be of good quality," a newspaper observed, "and the gold is untarnished despite its long trip across the sea."

The sergeant previously had written his mother that he had considered sending the head of a dead enemy soldier. Postal regulations and sanitary conditions would probably prevent that.

The Marine showed his mother a sensitive side, penning a poem titled "Medals for Mother" and ending like this:

"Yes, you gave your sons to the war so they might do their part.

"While you stay at home and fight the battle raging in your heart.

"So when the war is over and we know our job is through.

"I think that all the medals won should be pinned on mothers like you."

• • •

Military men and women enjoyed packages coming their way, too. Early in the year, attorney Vincent Keesey led the county Victory Book drive, centered in York's Martin Memorial Library.

The drive called for residents to donate good books for those in the service to help combat boredom and loneliness and to prepare them for their return to civilian life.

The twin slogans for 1943: "Any book you really want to keep is a good one to give" and "Many are giving their blood; we can each give a book."

Army and Navy officials noted the most popular books were fiction and non-fiction best sellers, adventure and western stories, detective and mystery fiction and humor works.

'I've lost my victory pants'

In big and small ways, rationing affected residents in all three corners of York County — and everywhere in between.

Gasoline rationing, for example, meant many defense workers could not commute long distances. Housing for these workers became scarce in York and other populated areas where defense plants were located.

Sometimes, landlords declined to rent much-needed apartment space to men of Selective Service age. They feared the man leasing the house would be called to duty, and his family would not pay the rent. Landlords could find plenty of paying customers.

In one discrimination case early in the war, a woman refused rent to a West York couple because the husband was 24 years old.

"My decision is final," she said. "I will not rent my house to anyone within the draft age."

By mid-year 1943, efforts were under way to add more housing to the market. Representatives from the York

Scott Nicoll, chairman of York Corporation's Transportation Committee, deals with gas rationing by pedaling to and from work. 'I get plenty of miles per gallon with this jalopy, and I need not worry about A-B-C (rationing) stamps,' the native of Hawaii said. 'And I expect to ride until I am "grounded" by deep snow.' A caption in Shop News noted that Nicoll could not play a ukulele. Bicycles came under rationing rules, but another longtime form of transportation never faced restrictions. A rumor going around claimed that the horse and wagon would return. County farmers put that idea to rest: Only a few workhorses were available, and only one wagon-maker yet operated — a Lancaster maker of ice cream wagons. Rubber horseshoes would be needed on the hard roads, and rubber to make those was scarce.

Chamber of Commerce and an assortment of York defense plants toured 50 federally funded homes at Roosevelt Avenue and Fahs Street in northwest York.

The two-story homes were available for occupancy.

Architect Harry R. Lenker pointed to the conveniences in the attractive homes: hardwood floors, hot water heating, painted plaster walls, gas stoves and refrigerators.

The four-room houses rented for $33 monthly, and those with five rooms cost $35.

Another 170 homes, complete with a community building and repair shops, were on the drawing board.

• • •

About 150 trailer homes for defense workers popped up at the former York County Home tract near the county

The Gazette and Daily

The Weather
Eastern Pennsylvania—Continued warm today, somewhat colder in west portion this evening; unconfirmed showers and scattered thundershowers in west portion this afternoon.

All war news is censored at the source. We print the latest accurate news available, but not rumors or unconfirmed reports. We want you to be able to rely upon what you read in this paper.

Vol. 111—No. 18072   York, Pa., Thursday Morning, April 1, 1943—Thirty-Six Pages   Price 3c—15c a Week

ALLIES DRIVE HARD TO TRAP ROMMEL—From the Bizerte front in the north to the Axis-deserted Mareth line in the south, Allied forces pressed their advantage to deal the final blows to Axis power in Tunisia. The map shows how, in the north, the British First Army slugged forward against Gen. Jurgen von Arnim's troops to threaten Bizerte. In the central sector, American troops fought against time to reach the coast, cut off Rommel's Afrika Korps, fleeing northward to join with von Arnim's forces. In the extreme south, the British Eighth Army, having smashed through the Mareth line, swept through Gabes after the retreating Germans and Italians.

Montgomery Hot In Pursuit Of Fleeing Rommel

British Eighth Army Fans Out Over Central Tunisia Plains More Than 12 Miles Above Gabes. Captures Oudref And Metouia. First Army Recaptures Sedjeane And Is Now Only 35 Miles From Bizerte. U. S. Troops Hampered By Minefields But Bag Another 200 Prisoners

Allied Headquarters in North Africa, March 31 (AP)—The British Eighth army fanned out over the coastal plains more than 12 miles above Gabes today in a steady pursuit of Marshal Rommel's bomb-ridden troops, while the British First army in the North recaptured Sedjenane and pressed on to a point only 35 miles southwest of the big Axis-naval base of Bizerte.

Intense Russian Drive Toward Strait Of Kerch

To Our Readers

Good morning.
This is the new Gazette and Daily.
Faced with the necessity to stay within limitations in the use of newsprint set by the War Production Board, we decided that in order to print a better newspaper and stay within the limits, some new departure would have to be made.
The tabloid size seemed to us to offer the best opportunity of maintaining the complete coverage of news. With the tabloid size there is no need to "spread" to keep headlines and other material in proportion to the size of the paper. It encourages smaller advertising display without losing the effectiveness of the display.
We hope you like this new, more convenient, easier to read paper-saving size of The Gazette and Daily.

Says Russians Keep Their Word

Former Ambassador Davies Declares They Will Not Make A Separate Peace With Hitler And Not Interfere With American Form Of Government

Philadelphia, March 31 (AP)—Joseph E. Davies, former ambassador to Russia, declared tonight "the Russians' word is good" and they will keep their promise not to make a separate peace with Hitler and not interfere "with our form of government in any way."

Intended To Eject Germans From Novorossisk

Capture Important Enemy Defense Point Of Anastaevskaya In Western Caucasus. On Smolensk Front There Is Little Activity As Mud Has Hampered Military Operations There, But Red Army Knocks Out One More Nazi Defense Point, Enemy In Superior Numbers On One Area Of Western Front Red Army Newspaper Says

London, Thursday, April 1. (AP)—Russian troops captured the important German defense point of Anastaevskaya in the Western Caucasus yesterday in a renewed drive to eject the enemy from his last major foothold at Novorossisk, 33 miles to the south, Moscow announced early today.

Arnold Backs Bill To End Control Of Patents By Cartels

By VOLTA TORREY
(Special To The Gazette And Daily)

Washington, March 31—A magna charta for science, to free inventors from servitude to cartels, was urged yesterday by Judge Thurman Arnold of the U. S. Circuit Court of Appeals at Senate sub-committee hearings on a science mobilization bill sponsored by Sen. Harley M. Kilgore (D-W. Va.).

Arnold heartily recommended the bill, which would create an Office of Scientific and Technical Mobilization to:

Consumer, OPA Sides Of Labeling

(Special To The Gazette And Daily)
New York, March 41—The Eastern Co-operative Wholesale, Inc., representing consumer organizations along the Atlantic coast, and individual New York consumers were unanimous today in their opposition to proposals that grade-labeling on canned goods be dropped.

Army Lists 34 Items Small Business Can Provide For Defense

Washington, March 31 (AP)—Small manufacturing plants whose regular business has been curtailed by the war will be given an opportunity immediately to obtain army orders totalling $200,000,000, Maj. Gen. Clifford L. Corbin, director of Quartermaster Corps procurement, said today.

Victory Gardens Now Going Fast

Herbert F. Anderson, Director of Parks and Playgrounds yesterday received six plots of ground suitable for Victory Gardens, but shortly after they had been received four were assigned. One of the two remaining plots is located at the south east corner of Norway and Poplar streets and the other in the 800 block East Princess street. Mr. Anderson stated that lately he has been obtaining more applicants than plots and urges that everyone with vacant land, who is not planning to utilize it, contact him.

To conserve paper, The Gazette and Daily converted from a full-sized page to tabloid size in 1943. This is the initial tabloid edition. The morning newspaper, forerunner to the York Daily Record, was printed at that size until 1973. 'With the tabloid size, there is no need to "spread" to keep headlines and other material in proportion to the size of the paper. It encourages smaller advertising displays without losing the effectiveness of the display,' a note to readers stated. The newspaper regularly presented maps, such as the one on this page, to inform readers about troop movements. The smudge on this page probably is a printer's fingerprint. The York Dispatch remained full size. The story, bottom center, lists defense items needed, including pianos. York's Weaver Piano Co. produced sturdy, olive-green pianos for military training camps and recreation centers. 'There are many good musicians in the armed forces who enjoy leading their "buddies" in group musical activities, barber shop harmony being one of the popular pastimes of the army,' a Weaver spokesman said.

• • •

prison at the north end of Broad Street.

The National Park Service supervised the park, made up of trailers accommodating families of four and six.

Some of the trailers were equipped as shower, toilet and laundry facilities. Designers shaped the park so that none of the homes were farther than 150 feet from a trailer toilet.

As the war wore on, York County residents increasingly went without.

The government's rationing programs attempted to even distribution of scarce items at home and to preserve

Rationing robbed girls of their nylons, but Sears offered an alternative, as suggested in this advertisement appearing in The York-High Weekly in April 1943. Rayon and cotton lisle replaced the rationed silk as the hosiery of necessity as the war wore on. Rayon stockings took special handling to wash and hours to dry. At one point, the federal government accused York merchants of hoarding nylon hose for the Christmas season. Store buyers said supplies were limited, but when sparse numbers would come in, store employees often got the first pick. Women also wore a type of tan makeup on their legs in lieu of stockings, and some penned a vertical line on the back of their legs, resembling a stocking seam.

enough supplies for military operations.

The York County Salvage Committee, overseeing rationing efforts, even called for collection of used women's hosiery. Discarded silk and nylon hosiery were to be dropped off in women's wear and department stores.

The hosiery would be recycled into powder bags for guns on battleships and parachutes for paratroopers.

• • •

The war's demands for cotton goods left some women in York County wondering what to wear.

Wives of farmers and poultry men found a practical solution that became a wartime fad. For years, chicken feed had been shipped in cotton print bags — sturdy bags in bright colors.

The 100-pound bags came in about 25 different patterns — flower, fruit and striped prints. An emptied bag measured about 4 square feet, and three bags made a dress.

This poster, from York County Heritage Trust files, urges conservation and care of tires on the home front. Axis occupation of rubber-producing areas and diversion of material to the military caused domestic shortages.

Scores of county women soon wore dresses made from the fabric, giving new meaning to the expression "putting on the feedbag." The feedbag dresses came in handy around the house and even on special occasions.

County women found a use for plain bags as well as those covered with advertising. The bags made effective towels, dishcloths and sheets, as many women heeded the wartime mantra, "Use it up, wear it out, make it do, or do without."

A newspaper account told of a young girl victimized by the scarcity of elastic waistbands.

She was heard crying in downtown York, "Mama, Mama, I've lost my victory pants."

• • •

The ban on new car sales drove up the value of existing automobiles.

Some people regularly tried to improve their investment portfolios by driving off in cars not their own.

Sometimes, the rationed automobile tires and tubes were more valuable to the thieves than the car itself and gave a glimpse of how the considerable county wartime black market worked.

In one case, a York man was charged with the theft of seven automobiles and 20 tires. A farmer spotted the man acting suspiciously around a truck outside Red Lion, near Freysville. Police searched near the vehicle and found tires and tubes hidden in the bushes.

Police arrested a New Cumberland man, who had purchased 14 tires from the thief for $10 a piece. The thief then resold five of the tires for $90 and four for $70.

• • •

Police also became concerned about reports that county residents were storing large quantities of gasoline in garages and basements after rationing orders came down.

York Fire Chief L. Ellis Wagner weighed in on this practice. He released a bulletin from the National Board of Fire Underwriters reminding residents that gasoline could be purchased in safe five-gallon containers before the war.

But such containers had become scarce, and hoarders were storing gas in improvised containers. These receptacles — often glass bottles and jugs — usually lacked suitable caps.

Storage in basements was particularly problematic, the bulletin stated. Vapors might accumulate, and a furnace could ignite them.

• • •

An appreciable black market in gasoline operated in and around York County.

Police busted seven county residents for disseminating obsolete ration coupons.

The entire lot of coupons totaled 5 million gallons of gasoline and 15 million gallons of fuel oil, enough to cause serious shortages of petroleum products on the Eastern Seaboard.

The coupons originated with a Washington, D.C., salvage firm and reached the black market when the salvager shipped them to a York County plant as waste paper.

• • •

Gas station pumpers — now women attendants, too — not only dispensed less gasoline during a shortened work-day but also curtailed washing the windshields of customers' cars.

This service ended when the war started. Manpower shortages provided a justifiable excuse.

But some motorists never appreciated the retort — a common wartime reply — when they asked for help: "Don't you know there's a war on?"

• • •

Government red tape often marred efforts to acquire scarce and rationed items.

To purchase a used typewriter, for example, the government asked applicants to fill out a form in triplicate.

The rationing board must then approve the application and retain one copy of the form. The applicant would take the other two copies to the typewriter seller.

The vendor would keep one copy and return the other to the rationing board after the vendor had filled the order. To establish the need to purchase a used machine, applicants had to prove to the rationing board that all typewriters in their inventory were in use, and they did not own any that could be repaired.

Sellers were required to keep reports on sales and rentals of used typewriters for at least two years. They were mandated to supply an inventory of such typewriters to the local rationing board.

Typewriters received such special treatment because the military and a burgeoning federal government bureaucracy requisitioned them and the manufacture of new machines required scarce metal parts.

• • •

The military even demanded cooking grease.

Glycerine in the grease could be used to make gunpowder, dynamite, paint and Plexigas windows used in military planes.

Residents could earn points to purchase meat and

C.B. Yost's Meat Market in Loganville sponsored this booklet of tips to make the most of the scarcity of meat. The National Live Stock and Meat Board supplied ideas on how to extend meat's appetizing flavor. 'A little ingenuity in the kitchen, Mrs. Homemaker, will go a long way toward solving that troublesome wartime problem of stretching the limited meat supply so that that hungry family will be satisfied every day,' the booklet began.

cheese by saving grease and other fats. In conducting fat drives, the government assured the public that odors — even from fried onions or fish — did not affect the valuable fat.

Residents should keep the waste fat cool, the government advised. When residents accumulated a pound, they should take it to meat dealers.

• • •

Keys, made of scarce metals, had value, too.

Early in the war, the National Key Kollection Kampaign netted more than 50,000 keys in the county.

York City Patrolman John Judy collected 2,100 keys himself.

Somewhere, he found a large key — a cast iron "Old Home Week" celebration key from Columbia, across the river from York County.

The program particularly sought to recover flat keys for Yale locks, prized because of their high content of nickel. Judy had garnered a bunch of them, too.

888|976 EZ

UNITED STATES OF AMERICA
OFFICE OF PRICE ADMINISTRATION

WAR RATION BOOK FOUR

Issued to _____ Helen P. McLaughlin
(Print first, middle, and last names)

Complete address _____ 468 W. Princess St.

York, Pa.

READ BEFORE SIGNING

In accepting this book, I recognize that it remains the property of the United States Government. I will use it only in the manner and for the purposes authorized by the Office of Price Administration.

Void if Altered _____ Helen P. McLaughlin _____
(Signature)

It is a criminal offense to violate rationing regulations.

OPA Form R-145

16—35570-1

This image is the front of a rationing book, assigned to those on the home front to ensure sufficient food and supplies were available on the war front.

• • •

A giant bin sat in the corner of York's square, accessible to motorists to pull up and toss their payload of scrap metal.

Controversy broke out over whether the ornate iron fence around the York Fairgrounds should be scrapped for defense use.

The fence survived, but iron gates to Prospect Hill Cemetery were hauled away for military use.

• • •

Prohibition had been repealed before the war, but some residents still felt the scarcity of their favorite alcoholic beverages.

Beer supplies dwindled because of grain shortages and a government directive for breweries to set aside 20 percent of their output for military men and women to consume.

Even if beer supplies were adequate, shortages of bottles and caps became evident. Brewers called for recycling bottles, but such glassware was needed to accommodate food because of the shortage of tin.

At one point, the state Liquor Control Board limited whiskey, gin and brandy sales to one bottle per customer per visit.

The federal government placed limits on production of certain alcoholic drinks. Ingredients were needed for military purposes, as was alcohol.

Foust Distillery near Glen Rock shifted its production to medicinal alcohol and received federal funds to build a plant to dry grain used in alcohol production for cattle feed. The war ended before the plant could go into operation.

• • •

State police often oversaw the conveyance of valuable ration books to school sites where the public could pick them up.

County ration boards could request the presence of at least two uniformed American Legion members to maintain order at schools where people obtained the books containing stamps necessary to buy rationed items.

The stamps could be exchanged directly for sugar, coffee and other rationed items. Other stamps were lettered or marked "spare." Newspapers and radio reports indicated when those stamps could be used, usually when a large quantity of particular items were in stock.

Many households scrimped so much that they had lard cans full of nonperishable extra food when rationing was lifted.

"Those extras might have, at some time, been needed by a neighbor whose supply was depleted," Norma Bear Gates later observed.

Edward Spring, a William Penn High School 10th-grade student, and Gladys Wilhide, an 11th-grader, produced this York-High Weekly cartoon suggesting how the black market worked to skirt strict rationing in the spring of 1943.

• • •

The great value of war bonds attracted thieves, too. Police arrested a York man and woman for conspiring to cash in two $25 bonds.

The man stole the bonds from a Wayne Avenue home, where he was doing electrical work.

The man and the 25-year-old woman took the bonds to a bank, where they became equity for a $50 loan.

The woman forged the name of the Wayne Avenue family, for which she received $1 from her accomplice for her role in the scam.

She told police she bought cosmetics with the money.

• • •

Such incidents caused people to hide their valuable bonds in places where thieves would not look.

Some would lose the bonds or accidentally destroy them. In one case, a woman war worker entered Western National Bank with charred parts of 17 war bonds, valued at $425.

Recent robberies caused her to hide them in a kitchen stove. Then cold weather hit, the stove stoked and the bonds charred.

The bank urged residents to record serial numbers, issue dates and maturity values of their bonds. But don't store the record with the bonds, the bank officials reminded.

Holders of safety deposit boxes should store the bonds there. However, bank officials noted that so many people were holding valuable papers that banks could not meet the demand for safety deposit boxes.

• • •

Schools were heavily involved on the home front in numerous ways.

Students practiced air raid drills by ducking under their desks. Classes conducted scrap-paper drives.

Children took small change to school to buy 25-cent war stamps. The stamps were pasted into books. When a book was filled, it was redeemed for a $25 Series E war bond.

R. Elizabeth Koontz, a wartime teacher, overcame severe gasoline rationing restrictions by riding the bus to school. She walked to the bus stop.

"Each evening I returned in the same manner," she recalled, "getting well acquainted with the pupils as we traveled together."

• • •

Some county teachers asked their students to correspond with a military buddy.

Lenora Hull Bear wrote to her uncle for several months in 1943. She learned that he was killed in a plane crash in New Guinea.

The 13-year-old continued her pen pal relationship with a friend of her uncle in the military.

At Christmas, the girl received a box. It came from the sister of her uncle's friend. The friend had also died in a plane crash.

Weeks before, he had asked his sister to send Lenora a gift. The box contained a locket, which Lenora kept for years.

• • •

Many high school students who weren't yet driving age did their bit to conserve gasoline and aid defense industries.

William Penn High School students were heavy users of the buses that largely constituted mass transit within the county.

The York-High Weekly admonished students not to wander around town until 5 p.m., then board a bus for home.

That was prime time for defense workers, the newspaper noted. Those men and women, at the end of their day,

Margaret Stabler   Kathryn Stabler   Jared Stabler

Military service ran deep in many York County families. Glen Rock-area sisters Margaret E. and Kathryn I. Stabler joined the WACs in 1943, following brother Jared into the military service. Jared, a seaman, fought in the D-Day invasion in Normandy in 1944. Mr. and Mrs. C.J. Stabler were the parents of this military trio.

Marie Green, a 56-year-old grandmother, works a lathe in York Corporation's Fitting Shop in 1943.

sometimes couldn't find seats on buses because students had piled in.

"Do your duty for Uncle Sam," the newspaper urged, "and don't ride buses in rush hours."

• • •

Even milkweed pods held value, and students were called upon to collect them.

At one point, York County school children picked 2,100 bags of the pods.

The lighter-than-water pods were shipped to Michigan, where the floss was extracted and used to fill life jackets.

• • •

Gas rationing included a ban against pleasure driving. Police could tell the vehicle owner's gasoline entitlement by the sticker affixed to the vehicle windshields.

"C" stickers went to ministers, physicians and mail carriers. Black marketers preferred this sticker, allowing for the largest ration for personal use.

Mahlon Haines did not have a "C" sticker on his car, but the attraction of a toll-less bridge across the Susquehanna River may have tempted the shoe merchant and his son, Stanley, to do some ill-advised pleasure motoring.

Newspaper accounts stated that the elder Haines was the last motorist to pay a toll across the bridge between Wrightsville in York County and Columbia in Lancaster County. His son was the first to cross after the toll was lifted.

Witnesses said either the father or son's vehicle turned around after crossing the bridge in Lancaster County and returned to the York County side, without any sign of business transactions. Mahlon Haines had claimed he was on a business trip to Columbia.

The county rationing board would hear cases involving the Haineses and about 25 other reported violators of the unpopular pleasure-driving rules, considered by some to be unenforceable.

• • •

Later in the war, Stanley Haines — Pvt. Stanley Haines — was on his way to becoming a hero.

He was knocked unconscious by an enemy shell as the invading Allieds headed from Normandy, France, toward Germany. He and an officer were caught between Allied and German lines, and enemy forces eventually took them prisoners.

By war's end, Stanley Haines was wounded three times and held a Purple Heart with three Oak Leaf Clusters — and a Good Conduct ribbon.

• • •

Home appliances, already associated with America's way of life, were becoming hard — or impossible — to get.

When refrigerators, washing machines, irons, stoves, vacuum sweepers and mixers went on the blink, they often stayed that way for months. The military needed such repairmen, too, or those who remained civilians were swamped with work.

Even small, everyday items — pipe-cleaners, bobby pins, pencil erasers and rubber bands — were in short supply. The military had more pressing uses for the materials needed to make these everyday items.

• • •

Hundreds of county residents gave up the most precious of all assets to aid the military — property rights of way.

They did so to accommodate an important comrade of the military burrowing across the county's width. Workers dug a trench from East Berlin, Adams County, to a point near Accomac on the Susquehanna River to bury an oil pipeline.

The 1,400-mile "Big Inch" ran from Longview,

Bessie Elicker serves as a pilot, bombardier and navigator on the home front. Here, she operates an overhead crane high up at the Fire Weld Department at York Corporation in the summer of 1943. She was the first woman to operate overhead equipment at Yorkco.

James Zinner smoothes up a welded door frame, and Preston Smith grinds rough spots off a side seam of York Corporation's strato-chamber. 'This huge iron vacuum bottle, designed and built in the York shops, will take you 40,000 feet straight up in 12 minutes flat ... without leaving the ground!' Shop News reported. The strato-chamber enabled the testing of airplane parts, engines and pilots in 67-below-zero conditions in which 'there isn't air enough to light a match.' Flying at 40,000 feet permitted airmen to pilot planes above effective anti-aircraft fire.

Texas, to refineries at Marcus Hook, Pa., and Bayway, N.J. The pipeline was designed to ensure a constant supply of oil to the Eastern Seaboard — reserves threatened by German U-boats preying on ocean oil tankers.

Twelve million gallons of black gold — about 85 tankers or 25,000 railway tank cars — gurgled through the 24-inch pipe at a rate of 100 miles per day.

Running the pipe in a channel under the Susquehanna River was surpassed in difficulty only by running the Big Inch under the Mississippi River.

Before the line started operation, construction started on a second parallel line along the same right of way, the "Little Big Inch."

'Things are going to get cockeyed'

As the months passed in 1943, the sharp vigil against air raids, so evident earlier in the war, waned as Allied forces battled far away in Europe and the Pacific.

York began muffing blackout drills. In one drill, the York Fur Shop, North George Street, and the Father and Son shoe store, East Market Street, did not extinguish their exterior lights.

Air wardens could not operate a switch on the outside of the fur shop and finally found a breaker box in the basement. No switch could be found for the shoe store.

In Hanover, a guard light on the Hanover Trust building and lights at the R. H. Sheppard Co. plant continued to burn.

Infractions of blackout or air raid regulations could be serious. A five-person committee reviewed allegations of violations filed against residents by air raid wardens, auxiliary police and other Civilian Defense officials.

This York Corporation advertisement touts the company's strato-chamber, indicating the 12 minutes needed for the large tank to simulate stratospheric conditions for the training of airmen.

If a violation was found to be reckless, it could be prosecuted. An unintentional violation could result in a warning.

• • •

'Little Johnny' of radio fame spoke at war bond rallies in the summer of 1943 at York Corporation's Grantley and West York plants. Johnny Roventini, with his bellhop persona, was an icon of the time promoting Philip Morris cigarettes with his trademark, 'Call for Philip Morris!' Here, Johnny meets up with 250-pound Charles Chester Stine of the Fire Weld Department.

The numbers of spotters watching the skies for enemy aircraft were thinning. Not enough people were left to staff the posts.

In York County, the American Legion had organized 12 spotting stations even before Pearl Harbor. After the attack, other volunteers joined the vets in manning the stations around the clock in all kinds of weather. The county corps totaled 3,600 volunteers at one point.

By the fall of 1943, Gen. H.H. Arnold, commander of the nation's air forces, said the decision to cut back spotting hours was a matter of weighing two options.

The enemy might have some success in a limited air attack, he said. But the use of manpower to perform other tasks might contribute directly or indirectly in other ways to bring the war's end closer.

He cautioned that the redeployment of spotters did not suggest a retraction of Civilian Defense. York County went to a system of readiness training by manning the spotting stations from 1-6 p.m. Wednesdays.

• • •

Decorations in downtown York were scarce for Christmas '43. Outside lighting was prohibited because of a nationwide push to cut electric use, thus saving coal and precious metal to make light bulbs.

Federally mandated and voluntary conservation programs were designed to save 75 million light bulbs and 4 million tons of coal in the winter of 1943-44.

Herman Greiman of Mount Wolf thought it was better that Christmas decorating was low key.

In a letter to former members of his Boy Scout troop now in the military, he wrote, "What's the use of pretending any way. The real good old Christmas Spirit is lacking, and until you guys come back to this neck of the woods for keeps, things are going to get cockeyed."

• • •

Still, shoppers thronged to York. Christmas tree sellers were busy, despite a predicted shortage of evergreens.

"Prices are high and things in general are becoming scarce they say," Greiman wrote.

He told about an elderly Dover-area gentleman shopping at Wiest's department store. The man walked up to a salesgirl arranging items on a shelf. He grabbed her wrist and exclaimed, "I say lady, what you call this?"

"Why sir, that is my wrist," she replied, "what did you think it was?"

"OK Sis," he said, "no offense, things is so high in this here store I had an idea that might be your ankle."

• • •

That Christmas, boys received toy ships, tanks, guns and soldiers — often made from wood.

"The kids play commando," Greiman wrote, "and can imitate machine guns as good as you fellows used to imitate automobile and airplane engines a few years back."

Greiman spotted a woman shopper carrying packages up to her chin. He observed that she needed a periscope to navigate through the crowd.

The Mount Wolf man heard her say, "It's terrible to shop these days, you just can't get a thing."

'All of us ... have war jobs to do'

In April, President Stewart Lauer assessed how York Corporation was faring at the 16-month point of the war. The company was providing some supplies and repairs to keep civilian food plants going, but virtually all of the 73.7 million pounds of equipment shipped since Pearl Harbor had gone for defense purposes.

This was done despite about 700 Yorkco workers joining the military.

Yorkco was getting contracts by what would be called gambling in normal times, he wrote in Shop News.

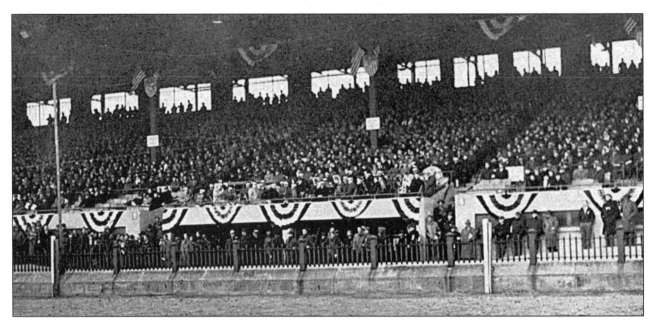

About 5,000 York Corporation employees, families and guests pack the York Fairgrounds grandstand in November 1943 to celebrate receiving the Army-Navy 'E' award for excellence in production. By war's end, 19 York-area plants had received the prestigious award.

Employees were working on gun mounts, tank hulls, marine engines, airplane pilot test chambers — jobs far removed from mechanical cooling. And they were doing the work at fixed contracts, which took four to eight months to fulfill.

Yorkco was counting on its production workers to "see us through," Lauer said.

By midyear, the name York Ice Machinery was no more. The company produced far more products than ice-making equipment.

York Corporation was the new name.

• • •

Yorkco's management labored to help employees see the meaning of their hard work. And it developed its advertising campaigns to ensure potential customers also could see the results of this labor.

Shop News spun a connection between Yorkco, a spider web and gun sights.

The publication explained the link: A spider's web is smooth and round under the high magnification of a gun sight. Web filaments worked better than split or unsplit human hairs or lines cut by sharp diamonds.

Air conditioning was needed to keep spiders productive. Web filaments were needed year-round to feed the military's needs, and spiders were known to hibernate in the winter. Yorkco equipment provided dewy, springlike mornings so spiders kept spinning their webs all four seasons.

Yorkco also developed an advertisement outlining the area its equipment was cooling for plane production — equivalent to a continuous building stretching 24 miles.

A Shop News cartoon indicated that refrigeration helped eradicate moths from wool-lined flying suits. A series of sudden temperature changes shocked them to death.

Later in the war, Yorkco put out an advertisement indi-

Robert Spangler, 83-year-old draftsman and oldest member of the company, was on the job at York Corporation in the summer of 1943. Spangler joined the company in 1895, the year the West York plant was built.

cating that a 38-million-pound cake of ice launched every hour would put forth the cooling effect of all its American installations producing for the war.

The advertisement, placed in Fortune, Newsweek and Time, showed the launch of a block of ice, sliding down a shipway.

• • •

Yorkco employees were working hard — too hard, some thought. In early 1943, frustrations boiled over, and workers at the West York plant walked off their jobs.

An estimated 65 to 100 workers, showing the strain of heavy workloads, protested hours assigned for those on the night shift. The workers wanted to put in four 12-hour days and one seven-hour night. The company sought five 11-hour shifts.

Many workers came from Waynesboro, Chambersburg and other distant points from York. They sought more time on the weekend for rest.

The company and its primary production union — the Ice Machinery Independent Employees' Association — did not count the brief walkout as a strike. The company boasted of its strong labor relations, recording only one strike since its founding in 1874.

No one could recall why the strike occurred or how long it lasted, other than it was short and took place around 1900.

• • •

Executives at York Corporation had bad moments, too.

The federal government filed charges in federal court against Yorkco for violating the Sherman Anti-Trust Act.

Yorkco and 10 other corporations named in the action allegedly transferred their patent rights to a holding company. That company could then license other companies to manufacture equipment under the pooled patents.

About 90 percent of all air conditioning installations fell subject to this licensing, and prices were fixed at artificial levels, the government claimed.

The lawsuit sought to dissolve the holding company.

• • •

Yorkco, dealing with labor shortages, sometimes scraped to find workers worthy of employment.

The company hired a 22-year-old York man as a security guard at its West York plant. One day, police showed up at work to ask the man why his fingerprints appeared on the windowsill of a South Queen Street house where a young woman was clubbed a few days back.

Armed gatekeepers at the plant, following orders to ban unauthorized visitors from the plant, kept detectives and four police squad cars at bay. Meanwhile, the security guard disappeared somewhere within the cavernous Yorkco shops and remained missing 24 hours later.

It turned out that military authorities wanted the security guard for desertion and escape, and he was awaiting sentencing on a local burglary charge.

In a strange twist a short time later, Yorkco became the sixth plant nationally to fly a "P" pennant for maintaining superior security and protection measures against enemy air raids and sabotage.

Part of the security measures called for fingerprinting employees to protect against espionage. The company assured employees that the prints would not remain in York but go to the FBI in Washington, D.C.

Stewart Lauer was the first to give up his prints.

Woodrow Oldhouser, serving in the South Pacific, wrote his former York Corporation co-workers that the war could last for some time because of the tenacity of Japanese soldiers.

William E. Loucks penned a letter from Iran to former Yorkco co-workers that Soviet fighters harbored anger toward the German troops.

While serving in the U.S. Navy, Joe Barsovitz saw production parts for York Corporation equipment that he had made as a civilian machinist at Yorkco.

Gladys L. Sheeley joined the scores of York Corporation workers who enlisted in the military instead of fighting the Axis as civilians in industry. She joined the WAVEs and reported for training to Hunter College in the spring of 1943. She had been employed in Yorkco's Material Control Department.

• • •

Despite these bumps, the year ended on a high point for York Corporation.

The makeshift work force, laboring on unfamiliar projects, did their work with sufficient quality to earn the prestigious Army-Navy "E" pennant — for excellence — late in the year.

Five thousand employees, families and guests sat in wintry November conditions in the York Fair grandstand as military officials lauded their efforts.

The award was for more than just outstanding output, Gen. H.F. Safford told those gathered. A company must be excellent in 25 different ways: low absenteeism, fine labor relations, first-rate plant protection and good housekeeping, among others.

Date ___12-18-43___

You will be interested in an excerpt from a radio message broadcast from Radio Tokyo today from ___V W Whitman___ to his relatives in ___York, Pa.___, in which he mentioned a friend's name, who is in a War Prisoner's Camp with him, who wished his relatives notified and regards sent to them. The name mentioned was -

"Lt. Thos Frutiner of Red Lion, Pa. was well when I last saw him in the Phillipines a year ago."

Very truly yours,

#844

W. E. KISSINGER
10571 Ayres Ave.
Los Angeles 34, Calif.

W.E. Kissinger monitored propaganda radio broadcasts from Tokyo. He forwarded information to relatives of servicemen heard speaking on the radio. Here, he writes that Victor W. Witman, a York serviceman in captivity in Japan, indicated that POW Thomas W. Frutiger of Red Lion was in good health the last time he saw him.

The war will be won only when we win it, Safford stated.

It will be a long war, he said. You can't win long wars by planning for short ones.

Forget rumors that the war would be over by Christmas. The rumors no doubt were fueled by reports that Axis U-boats were sinking less tonnage in the North Atlantic as destroyer escorts were taking a toll on the subs.

People were foolishly reserving rooms in New York hotels to view the "victory parade," he said.

Germany and Japan welcomed such overconfidence.

Safford applauded Yorkco workers for staying on the job to handle less exciting, less glorious tasks.

"In reality, there are not two fronts in this war — the home front and the fighting front," he said. "All of us, in uniform or out, have war jobs to do. In the total war, the men and women in overalls are just as important, just as essential, and just as honored as the men in uniform."

• • •

Foundryman Claude Baum was among the Yorkco employee representatives to publicly receive a pin awarded with the "E" designation.

"I'll go through the motions, but if they ask me to say anything right there and then you're going to see a man stricken with lockjaw," the 25-year employee said before the public presentation.

V. Marie Slenker, an employee since 1918; octogenarian Robert Spangler, 48 years with Yorkco; William C. Chambers, a 47-year worker; and Joseph F. Witman, father of two servicemen sons, including POW Victor W. Witman, joined Baum as employee representatives.

The company had a good reason for selecting Baum, father of nine. Two of his sons, George and John, former Yorkco employees, were in the service and a third was nearing the Army age of 18.

In the foundry, Baum was working on classified military equipment.

"Therefore, all we can say is that he is one of the many here in the York shops," Shop News reported, "who are backing up their boys in the service with the 'stuff that stings.'"

• • •

Frank W. Devers, a York native working as an applications engineer in Los Angeles, was among the Yorkco employees making things at home to aid a family member on the battle front.

In mid-1943, his brother, Gen. Jacob L. Devers, had been appointed commander of the European Theater of Operations. The proposed invasion of Europe was on the minds of Frank Devers and other Americans, and Jacob Devers was certain to play a role in it.

Frank Devers was familiar with the rigors of the war front. The 38-year Yorkco employee had reached the rank of captain in World War I.

• • •

The long-rumored Allied invasion of Europe was a carrot Yorkco put forth to keep worker momentum behind the military.

An Associated Press report late in the year gave Shop News an opening to suggest that the company had been making equipment for amphibious vehicles and doing other such priority military work.

The AP reported that landing boats had been moved ahead of planes, high-octane gasoline and other top-ranked programs.

This push for self-propelled landing barges, tank landing vessels and other invasion craft resembled the buildup of a year earlier, before the invasion of Italy.

"As to just how our equipment is being used on these vessels, well now don't get nosey, Bub," Shop News reported. "At least we do know that the U.S. Navy will put it to very good use."

The invasion of Northern Europe had been a talking point since Americans first stepped on English soil.

Now, it was coming in view.

"We have our part of that invasion mapped out for us," Shop News stated. "Anchors aweigh."

• • •

Yorko had some additional good news for its stockholders. The war had officially ended the Depression.

At year-end, stockholders would receive $140,000,

their first share of company profits since 1929.

The company took in $31.4 million in 1943 and turned a profit of $900,000. The remaining $760,000 was re-invested in the company "to safeguard your job after the war is won," Shop News reported to employees.

• • •

Those on the production lines also were investing part of their salaries into the military's efforts.

Late in the year, John Henry Thomas, local savings chair, presented the U.S. Treasury's "T" Award to Yorkco and its 4,255 employees.

Ninety-two percent of its workers had invested 11 percent of their total paychecks in war bonds.

'Everything isn't crashes and bashes'

For Joe Barsovitz, the war front came around and touched the home front.

He was boning up on refrigeration at the Naval Construction Training Center at Camp Peary in Williamsburg, Va.

The training included work on Yorkco compressors and FlakIce Machines, equipment that produced thin ribbons of ice.

He identified some of the parts that he had made as a machinist at Yorkco's West York plant. As he was doing the work, he wasn't aware that the equipment was going to the Navy.

"Most of the machines here are York machines," he wrote in Shop News, "of which I now am proud."

• • •

Serviceman William Varrath, a former employee in Yorkco's San Francisco office, wrote to a co-worker that he had worked on 36 York installations without a single compressor failure of any kind.

Varrath noted that the equipment under war conditions sometimes had to be lubricated with oil that resembled tar.

"Old man York himself would turn over in his grave if he could see some of the conditions under which these machines operate," he wrote from somewhere in the Pacific.

• • •

Woodrow Oldhouser, a former Yorkco employee writing from the South Pacific, saw a York-made refrigeration unit in a Victory Ship, a vessel mass-produced for war use.

He expected a prolonged war in the Pacific because enemy soldiers were dug in on every little island. It took a lot of fighting to dislodge them.

But fever was the worst foe in the tropics.

"Almost everybody has it," he wrote, "and the only cure for the darn stuff is to just outlive it, and that takes a few years ... but what a few years."

• • •

William E. Loucks wrote to Shop News from the seat

Lt. Thomas Frutiger took this photograph of his wife, Anne, before the war and carried it in captivity. The cold weather suggested by Anne Frutiger's coat must have seemed inviting to Frutiger, in captivity in the tropical heat of the Philippines. This was one of several photographs carried by Frutiger at the time of his death. Family tradition suggests that a fellow York County resident, in captivity with Frutiger, returned the photographs.

of a jeep somewhere in Iran, surrounded by five pesky Persian kids.

Earlier that morning, he had picked up several Russian soldiers in a truck. They were tough but friendly.

When the word "German" was mentioned, they got mad.

"After seeing these boys carrying their tommy-guns," he wrote, "I sure pity any Nazi they might meet."

• • •

The story of Ira Metzgar Jr., son of longtime Yorkco employee Ira Sr., made Shop News in August.

Metzgar was aboard a Coast Guard cutter in the Atlantic when it detected a U-boat underwater in the path of an Allied convoy.

Metzgar's cutter made two depth charge runs over the sub, which tried to hide under the convoy with the hope that propeller noise would throw the vessel off its scent.

Dec 15, 1943

IMPERIAL JAPANESE ARMY

1. I am interned at __Philippine Military Prison Camp #2__

2. My health is — excellent; <u>good;</u> fair; poor.

3. I am—uninjured; sick in hospital; under treatment; <u>not under treatment.</u>

4. I am — improving; not improving; better; <u>well.</u>

5. Please see that __you write to the above address direct.__
__Received your Christmas message__ _____ is taken care of.

6. (Re: Family); __Tell dad I am making cigars.__
_____

7. Please give my best regards to __Tommy, Bobby, and all__ ____

Prisoner of war Lt. Thomas Frutiger was allowed to write his wife, Anne, on several occasions during the war. 'Tell dad I am making cigars' is a message to William C. Frutiger, Thomas' father and a Red Lion cigarmaker. The prisoner used skills learned in his hometown to roll cigars in prison camp, probably for use by his captors and fellow prisoners.

The cutter remained on its trail and dropped a third "basket of eggs" on the sub, which eventually surfaced.

A gun battle between the sub and the cutter followed. The Coast Guard men won the shootout, the sub's crew abandoned ship and the U-boat sank to the bottom.

Metzgar and other crew members then fulfilled a vow. They shaved off the beards that they had pledged to grow until they got their first U-boat.

• • •

Paul Abel, a former Yorkco trucker stationed at a naval air station in Florida, was witnessing more bloodshed than some men overseas.

He wrote to his former co-workers that he was making plenty of crash calls — rushing to the scenes of downed airplanes near the base.

One large plane exploded in midair, killing all 13 men aboard. It took 36 hours to find one of the crewmen.

That day, another plane plummeted from 30,000 feet.

"All we found was a hand and part of a foot," he wrote, adding that the rest of the body was at the bottom of the hole created by the crash.

But another crash had a better outcome.

A pilot was practicing carrier landings by flying at low altitudes. His engine conked out, and he tried to slow his craft by brushing through the tops of some trees. When he hit the grove, the plane ignited but did not explode until he had crawled away from the wreckage.

"Everything isn't crashes and bashes with me," he wrote. "Many times we go into Miami and have a grand time."

• • •

Ivan H. Gates left Yorkco to serve on the other side of the world in a U.S. Army Signal Corps medical unit.

He spent two years as a medic with the corps in the

Himalayas, providing guidance for planes flying supplies from India to Allied forces in China. These "Hump" pilots had the tricky job of flying cargo planes through bad weather and high winds over the world's highest mountains.

He was part of a 12-man team that climbed through unexplored wilderness to reach remote signal corps camps. His six-month assignments were spent amid jackals and boa constrictors.

'Somehow, we survived that also'

Just before Christmas, Anne Frutiger received a card from her husband, Thomas, from Prison Camp No. 2 in the Philippines. Thomas Frutiger had survived the fall of the Philippines and the Bataan Death March and had joined thousands of other American prisoners in wretched prison camps on the islands.

Frutiger indicated that he was in good health and had received his wife's Christmas message.

He made it a point to tell his father, William C. Frutiger, that he was making cigars.

William Frutiger had been a Red Lion cigarmaker for decades, operating his own factory for most of that time.

Tom Frutiger's skill at rolling cigars might have gained him privileges in the notoriously brutal Japanese prisons. His card also said hello to his two young sons, Tommy and Bobby.

• • •

Anne Frutiger also heard indirectly about her husband that holiday season.

California residents monitoring Radio Tokyo took a shortwave message from Victor Witman, assigned to the

Robert N. Senft had just been inducted into the service in this August 1943 photo taken in Zion View, Conewago Township. He is pictured with his wife, Ethel.

103rd Engineers in the Philippines and now a prisoner in Japan.

In sending greetings to his family, the former Yorkco employee added that he had seen Tom Frutiger about a year ago, and he was "well and uninjured."

York County residents helped out, too. C.E. Mattingly of Hanover picked up the same message.

He immediately sent Anne Frutiger a cross-county note: "Trusting this may help make your Christmas happier."

• • •

The cigar business was an advantage for both the prisoner and his wife.

Cigarmaking was booming during the war. The need for nicotine remained high, and W.C. Frutiger's cigar factory, a longtime employer of women, did not have to scramble for workers.

Anne Frutiger was one of them, working the customary 6 a.m. to 3 p.m. shift. Her two boys checked in with her on their way to classes, and she was home when school let out in the afternoon.

She had to work. Allotments from her husband's military pay were sporadic, and she had payments for the house the family had purchased before the war.

She made weekly visits to the family that had loaned money for the mortgage on the Frutigers' North Main Street house in Red Lion.

Her work in the factory as a sorter was important. She was assigned the task of putting the 13 best-appearing cigars on the top row of the box, the row would-be purchasers could see.

As the months passed, she often played host at holiday meals for other women whose husbands were away at war and corresponded with other wives of POWs.

• • •

Bob Senft arrived home from work at York Corporation one summer day and asked his usual question: Did he receive his greetings from Uncle Sam?

"Look up on the refrigerator," Ethel Senft replied.

His draft card had arrived.

Senft was to report to the induction center in Harrisburg.

The summons did not surprise the Senfts. Earlier in the year, the federal government declared married men without children would be subjected to the draft.

He left for Fort Meade, Md., on Aug. 13. That was Friday the 13th, Ethel noted years later.

He underwent basic training in Fort Lee, Va., and Ethel visited Bob that Christmas.

They met at the Richmond USO, and hostesses there helped them find a private residence to spend the night.

Coal was in short supply, and the couple spent time with their hosts huddled around a blazing fireplace.

On the evening Ethel was to depart for home, a snowstorm shut down the railroad. She spent the night at the station and made it home the next day on a bus.

Soon, Bob would be stationed too far away to visit.

The Army had discovered he could type and assigned him to office work. After basic training, he was dispatched to Ft. Lewis, Wash., part of the 1778th Engineering battalion.

Now, alone with her mother — her grandfather had died — Ethel managed the household and everything else.

She adapted to the shortage of rationed goods, made easier because the family had no children.

One task weighed on her.

Her Zion View house lacked indoor plumbing, and she had to substitute for her husband in emptying the toilet.

"Somehow," she later wrote, "we survived that also."

IV

'Pray for a just if not a speedy peace'

— 1944 —

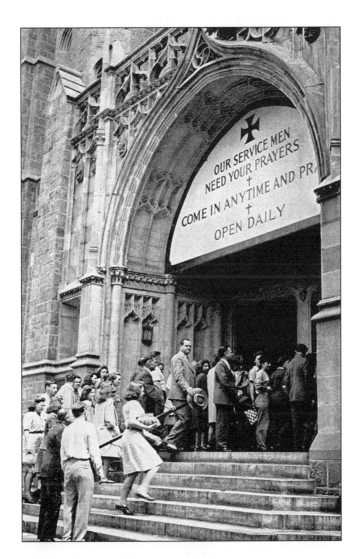

As the military hit the beaches of Normandy in northern France on June 6, 1944, many York County residents reacted to the news by going to houses of worship. The services were brief to allow workers to return to their jobs, where the demands of immense war contracts awaited them. Here, worshippers enter Union Evangelical Lutheran Church on York's West Market Street.

Gallery

As part of York County Council of Defense-sponsored emergency drills at the York Fairgrounds, workers practice catching a man jumping out of the second story of a temporary façade erected for the occasion. Ten thousand people watched as Civilian Defense officials ran through exercises on chemical warfare preparedness.

This poster encourages workers of varying occupations to support the war through payroll deductions. The federal government handed out honors to companies with high payroll savings participation.

Wilburda Murphy, a mechanical engineering graduate from Bucknell, pursued training in York Corporation's College Graduate Student Training course. 'She will be York's first female engineer,' Shop News reported in 1944, 'and she wants to be a real honest-to-goodness engineer, not just a "slip-stick" specialist.' Sometime later, Yorkco also recruited another top female engineer, Beatrice Yarov, an industrial engineer from Ohio State. She won the highly sought-after Ohio Safety Council Engineering Award.

John Hoover, formerly a machine assembler at York Corporation fighting in France, administers first aid to a French girl in the summer of 1944.

'We will not win victory in a walk'

As thousands of Allied soldiers stormed the beaches of Normandy in the D-Day assault on June 6, York County residents fell to their knees.

People prayed in churches, at special services in defense plants and in schools. For a moment in the afternoon, factories were silent. Stores and local government offices closed.

The D-Day invasion surprised the Germans in France, but not the people in York County. For weeks, they had been planning how to best observe the day Allied forces would cross the English Channel to invade northern France.

According to plan, bells pealed at 2:45 p.m. in York to mark the start of services set by the Manufacturers' Association, Chamber of Commerce and local ministers.

Thousands at the former York Safe and Lock Plant, now the Blaw-Knox Co.-operated Naval Ordnance Plant, bowed their heads to pray for their country, for those in the service, for their enemies and for peace.

Most elementary schools marked the event with homeroom prayer services. High schools held D-Day assemblies.

At William Penn High School, teacher Norman F. Trattner addressed the student body. The assembly featured the reading of a D-Day prayer written by George Seachrist, class of 1944. Principal E.A. Glatfelter read a prayer, and the educator joined class president Emanuel Cassimatis in addressing the student body.

Student Anne Ziegler provided a reading, "The Last Four Words," and a quartet played the Navy hymn. Duo Jennie Durgin and Evelyn Krone sang "Rock of Ages."

• • •

This scene played out in communities across York County.

News of Operation Overlord came via radio, including local stations, the veteran WORK and two-year-old WSBA.

First came a feeling approaching jubilation that such a campaign was under way to end the war in Europe. They knew the assault meant that Germany would face the imposing task of defending two fronts — American and British forces on the west and Soviet soldiers coming from the east. Then followed the realization that fighting men were dying on the beaches of Normandy.

"Yes, one could almost see the dead and dying strewn along the slopes leading to higher ground, the wheat fields, orchards and farm yards as wave after wave made them advance until their objective was reached," Red Lion Echoes, a community newsletter, reported.

At 3 p.m. in Red Lion, factory employees streamed toward churches. Men in overalls and women in slacks and turbans entered church doors.

"There on bended knee each person silently and later many audible prayers were raised to almighty God," the newsletter stated, "asking for guidance and safety of our armed forces as they engaged in this struggle for the liberation of enslaved people."

Afterward, many said they had never heard more fervent prayers than on this day.

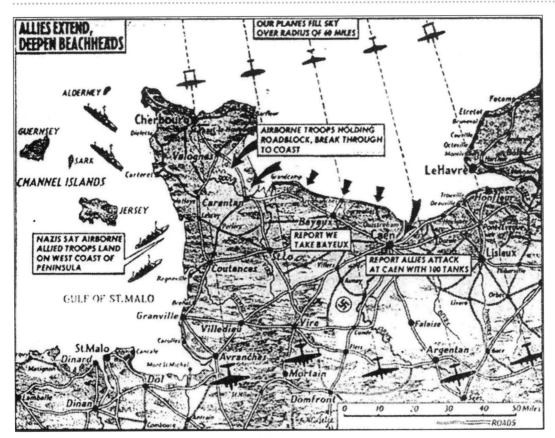

This map shows the scope of the Allied D-Day invasion — Operation Overlord — three days after troops hit the beach in Normandy. The early days of the invasion generally hit a 100-mile line between Cherbourg and LeHavre in northwest France.

"As they slowly left the worship service, many tears were streaming down the faces of participants," the newsletter stated, "each perhaps thinking of those whom they hold dear and anxious to know if at this hour God has spared their lives."

• • •

The overnight shift at York Corporation first heard the news just a few hours after workers had finished their midnight lunch.

It dominated conversations all day. At lunch, workers huddled around radios or perused late editions of newspapers.

"There was the clattering, rumbling noise of production grinding out an obligato to the howl of the planes and the roar of guns as they opened the attack," Shop News reported. "Yet there was a peculiar hush that was felt rather than heard."

Work went on that day — and subsequent days — as usual, except for the break in the afternoon when thousands of Yorkco employees went to churches.

Tools of war would be in high demand as before — perhaps even more so.

"Written on the faces of the men and women of this production army was grim determination," Shop News stated. "This was D-Day at Yorkco."

• • •

Ethel Senft, the young woman from Zion View now filing blueprints at Yorkco, was among the thousands streaming to churches near the company's plants.

She went to Trinity Lutheran Church on North West Street. A standing-room-only crowd occupied the sanctuary of the "Little Green Church," as it was called.

She stood in the narthex with co-workers during the service.

That night — Ethel's 24th birthday — she and her mother joined what seemed like the entire county in walking the streets of York, talking about the news of the day.

"It was lit up like New York on New Year's Eve," she recalled.

• • •

For many people, the invasion signaled the beginning of the end of Hitler's Third Reich.

In an editorial, The Gazette and Daily noted that Germany must defend itself against the Allies in France and Italy, the Russians on the east and Josip Broz Tito's partisans in Yugoslavia.

"We will not win victory in a walk," the newspaper stated, "But the victory will come in a relatively quick time, there can no longer be any real doubt."

The cost paid by the boys in battle will depend on the sacrifices made by those at home, the newspaper stated.

And after the Allies won, more work will be required.

"Let us resolve that we will help the boys set up a new world after victory," the newspaper stated, "in which peace shall reign forever more."

• • •

Retailers in York immediately placed advertisements in local newspapers observing the invasion.

York Corporation provided equipment for Landing Craft Infantry (LCI) and amphibious vehicles, used here in the invasion of Sicily. The company's Shop News stated in January 1944 that the Navy needs many more of these vehicles in preparation for 'the big push,' D-Day or the Normandy Invasion. 'As to just how our equipment is being used on these vessels, well, now, don't get nosey, Bub,' Shop News stated. 'At least we do know that the U.S. navy will put it to very good use.'

Bear's memorialized the Marquis de Lafayette, the French benefactor of America in the Revolutionary War and much heralded in York County during his two visits.

The D-Day invasion was a payback for France's aid in the American Revolution against Britain and would finish the job started in World War I, the advertisement stated.

"You should have known, Lafayette, we could not stand idly by," the advertisement proclaimed. "That sooner or later our wrath would rise, that one day we would come roaring to your beaches, with flaming guns and Freedom's banners flying. Come, as we have come today, determined that the oppressor shall pay dearly for every insult, every theft, every murder perpetuated against the beloved folk and upon the beloved soil of France."

• • •

Scores of York County military men participated in the invasion.

From the Delta area alone, at least seven men played a role.

Joseph Rook Creager and Bobby Harvey, 101st Airborne, parachuted into France ahead of the landing on the beach. Clarence A. Knopp and Jim Morris landed on Omaha Beach. Bud Harvey stormed Utah Beach. G. Taylor Watson, aboard a Navy ship, provided backup for the troops at Omaha Beach.

At least one military man from Delta died. Hugh Patterson was killed early in the assault.

• • •

Mr. and Mrs. Emory W. Brandt of York learned soon after the invasion that their son, Emory, died on French soil on D-Day.

The Gazette and Daily

Vol. 113—No. 18440   York, Pa., Wednesday Morning, June 7, 1944—Twenty-Eight Pages   Price 3c—16c a Week

52 SOP Employes Suspended For Stopping Work

London "Times" For Full Recognition Of DeGaulle's Gov't

Allies Land On 100-Mile Of Normandy Coast Line. Rush To Reinforce Troops

French Capture Tivoli, 15 Miles Beyond Rome

Chief Facts In Big Invasion

Beaches Swiftly Cleared, Armor Troops Move Up

The Gazette and Daily's front page tells of the long-awaited Allied invasion of France. In York County and elsewhere in America, this was correctly viewed as a major step toward ending the war in Europe. Less than a year later, the Allies declared victory in Europe.

The 23-year-old lieutenant had seen significant combat in two years of fighting. He received a Silver Star and one Oak Leaf cluster for gallantry in Tunisia.

Wounded by enemy gunfire, the William Penn High School graduate led his platoon in an attack swept by enemy fire. He insisted on evacuating casualties before seeking medical treatment for himself.

Later, he fought in the invasion of Sicily, where he was posthumously recognized for gallantry.

• • •

The second day of the Normandy invasion brought another county death.

Aileen Mundis of York learned that her 26-year-old husband, David, was killed.

Pvt. Mundis was not the only family member serving overseas in the military. A brother, Ralph, was in England. A brother-in-law, Russell Wantz, was stationed in the Pacific.

• • •

As the attack against German-occupied France moved inland, word trickled back to the county of more dead, wounded and missing servicemen. In fact, published reports of mounting casualties from escalating fighting in all theaters of war appeared almost daily from that point to the war's end.

Lawrence E. Duncan of the Hanover area, a 4th Division soldier, sustained wounds on June 9 and died three days later.

Pvt. Wilbur Hein, a 21-year-old paratrooper, died nine days after the invasion began.

Lt. John M. Lovett, 21, of York, one of four brothers in the service, died in Holland in September. About 20 days before his death, Lovett, a member of an airborne unit trained to parachute into action, used red ink to write his father. This led some family members to believe that the campaign in Holland was a bloody one.

Henry Lovett, a stepbrother, believed the red ink indicated that the lieutenant had a premonition of his death.

John Donald Gemmill, a 28-year-old private from Red Lion, died while delivering important documents to fighting units in Normandy.

He received a Bronze Star, with a citation stating, "As a messenger, he displayed outstanding courage, devotion to duty, and complete disregard for personal safety in the face of heavy enemy fire."

Two county soldiers, wounded in the Normandy invasion, were recuperating in hospitals in England. Lt. Edward A. Tuleya of York sustained a foot injury. Pvt. Nevin D. Mehring of Hanover was being treated for unspecified wounds.

Sgt. John R. Rudy of York, a gunner in a bomber squadron, was reported missing a week after the invasion. It was presumed correctly that he was a prisoner of war. In July, his parents learned by letter that he had escaped and was hiding out with the French Underground.

He had written his parents, Mr. and Mrs. John C. Rudy, that spring saying he had completed 37 missions over Germany and France and was due a furlough.

But his leave had been canceled because of the "hot stuff," the impending invasion of France.

• • •

County newspapers reported on memorial services and other such tributes to honor deceased servicemen.

The York Dispatch told of a service commemorating Sgt. Raymond G. Fishel at Fourth United Brethren Church in York.

Fishel had survived invasions of Africa, Tunisia, Sicily and the D-Day landing in France, but the William Penn High School graduate died as his invading unit moved inland in France.

The memorial service was filled to capacity, and the choir sang his favorite hymn, "The Home of the Soul."

Pastor E.W. Leech, preached on the theme, "Fighting a Good Fight." Harry P. Kissinger read the sergeant's obituary, and Freda Gaffney sang "God's Way is the Best Way."

Fishel had entered the service in December 1940, the first member of the congregation to be inducted.

• • •

Sgt. Henry I. Emig of York New Salem landed on the

'Wanted! For Murder,' a 1944 poster shows a woman — a neighbor, sister or daughter — to illustrate how loose talk can unwittingly cause the loss of American lives overseas. A National Archives exhibit stated that use of the female model drew a protest from a Hawaii resident: 'American women who are knitting, rolling bandages, working long hours at war jobs and then carrying on with "women's work" at home — in short, taking over the countless drab duties to which no salary and no glory are attached, resent these unwarranted and presumptuous accusations which have no basis in fact, but from the time-worn gags of newspaper funny men.' 'Because Somebody Talked!' and 'Careless Talk' also poignantly reminded Americans that an ill-advised word at home could lead to death in battle.

Normandy coast near Cherbourg on June 6, and his unit fought its way inland.

On the third day of the invasion, the Germans captured Emig and 18 others and marched them one-half mile behind the lines.

The Germans lined up the remnant and started executing them with machine-gun fire.

Emig had learned Pennsylvania Dutch growing up in Bair Station, West Manchester Township. Having nothing to lose, he shouted, "Halta mull die gesheeze, mir sheeze nein greekgefungne" or "Stop your shooting, we do not kill your prisoners."

A German sergeant stopped the 15- or 16-year-old executioner and approached Emig.

Where did he learn the German language?

"In die schule." ("In school.")

The captors marched Emig and his comrades to a barbed-wire enclosure.

A year later, the Russians freed him, and he returned on 60-day furlough to the home of his parents, Mr. and Mrs. Israel Emig, to regain weight and his health.

• • •

William Smallwood, a soldier of the 1310 Engineers, drove trucks through France, transporting parts to build bridges and hospitals.

When he worked in the open, he kept his gun on his shoulder. Enemy snipers were everywhere.

One night, bombs from German planes struck.

"I went to sleep one night, woke up the next morning and there were bricks and stuff all around me," Smallwood, a York resident, recalled. "Guys told me, 'Well, there was an air raid last night.' I didn't know about it."

• • •

Women from York County were part of the invasion, too.

Capt. Mildred A. Wallace of Chanceford Township served with the 59th General Hospital. The hospital moved forward with Allied troops.

She landed on Utah Beach in late July, only to be detained until the Normandy hedgerows obscuring German troops could be cleared.

• • •

Hassel Cartwright of York fought inland with Gen. George Patton's 3rd Army.

The going was tough. Cartwright went nights without sleep, spent seven days without food, enjoyed only one shower in 5 months and read month-old mail. He grew weary from the constant threat that he could be killed or wounded.

At one point, he reflected on a lesson learned early in life: Never take seriously what a politician says.

President Roosevelt had said, "No American boy will fight on foreign soil," and " We have nothing to fear ... ," he wrote years later.

Well, he was on foreign soil, he wrote, and he was fighting a fearful fight.

'You just can't stop these...dutchmen'

By this time, York Corporation's Shop News was receiving letters regularly from former workers who were

York neighbors York Corporation and S. Morgan Smith Co. combined to build this 8-inch mobile siege gun. This gun could lob 240-pound shells at targets 30 miles away. This photograph shows the gun after final assembly in the S. Morgan Smith plant in the summer of 1944.

Lt. Wilson Bernard visited his former employer, York Corporation, in the summer of 1944. At that time, the bomber pilot had flown 53 missions over Axis targets. When a Shop News photographer took his picture, he ducked with the flash, reminding him of flak aimed at his plane.

part of invasion forces.

Ross Kurtz wrote from a hospital in North Africa that he got in the way of a German mortar shell in Italy. When he awoke, he found he had been shot.

His stomach was badly mangled, causing him to spend five weeks flat on his back. His hips and arms caught some shrapnel, too, but no bones were broken.

"However, my face did not fare as well," he wrote.

Shrapnel hit above his mouth, smashing out all his teeth on the right side of the jaw. It broke several facial bones and the roof of his mouth. Later, doctors found that his lower jaw was also fractured.

"It looks as if Kurtz is going to have to keep his mouth shut for awhile," he wrote, "as they are going to wire together what teeth I have left."

• • •

Earlier in the war, Donald Landis had survived the sinking of the destroyer Blue, reappearing after making the "reported missing" list.

He now wrote to Shop News that he was part of another crew that had a destroyer blasted out from under it. He could not name the destroyer for security reasons but felt lucky to survive. Most of the crew was below deck sleeping that night, but Landis was in a forward bunk away

from the detonation.

The rocking underwater explosion threw the survivors from their bunks, and they climbed to the deck to await daylight to assess the damage.

A dawn count showed that 71 seamen died, and the tail end of the destroyer was blown away. Landis felt fortunate to live through another experience.

"But as they say back home," he wrote, " 'I hope that what is seconds isn't thirds.' "

• • •

In a visit to his former employer, Lt. Wilson Bernard told Shop News of flying 53 missions over European targets as a pilot, bombardier, navigator and tail gunner.

The hottest position is that of a pilot. It's difficult for him to bail out.

"There is also a disturbing psychological reason," the 25-year-old holder of an Air Medal with nine Oak Leaf clusters, said. A pilot is occupied with keeping the plane in the air. "He can't shoot back when attacked," he wrote.

Sometimes, German pilots, flying captured Allied planes, worked their way into a formation before opening fire.

"Nice company on a long mission," the Spring Grove resident said.

Bombing alone would not cause Germany to fold, he said. Europe was mostly steel and cement — not much is flammable — and slave labor was used to quickly reconstruct what was damaged.

• • •

David Howe Summers wrote from Italy that he had run into Don Peters, another York County soldier whom he knew from basic training.

The fathers of the two fighting men worked near each other at Yorkco.

Don Peters was wounded during a battle on Italy's "boot," receiving the Purple Heart.

"You just can't stop these York County dutchmen," Summers wrote.

Kenneth Bailey sent this photograph home to the Fire Weld Department at York Corporation. He brought down this tiger after an all-day hunt in India. He killed it with one shot from the elephant gun he is holding. 'You need a heavy gun for these playful kittens,' Bailey explained in a letter to his former co-workers.

Lt. James W. Walsh, in India, poses with a leopard cub. The leopard was not ferocious, the former York Corporation employee wrote, but he would not want to assume the same position with the animal a few months hence.

• • •

Infantryman Samuel Z. Senft wrote to his former York Corporation workers from a dugout at the Anzio Beachhead, scene of intense fighting when the Allies invaded Italy months before D-Day.

Soldiers were staying in large covered foxholes, he wrote, because of flak and shell fragments falling from the sky.

Senft fought as a rifleman soon after the landing and came under intense German artillery fire.

"It was plenty rough up front," he wrote, "and believe me I was plenty scared."

• • •

Former Yorkco employee Lt. Anthony C. Schneider,

co-pilot of a B-24 bomber, was returning from a mission over key German military oil refineries and rail yards at Blechhammer in Poland when his plane failed him.

It was flying on two engines — flak and mechanical problems had taken care of the other two.

Then, the third engine quit somewhere over the Adriatic Sea. The plane splashed down, sending Schneider through the cockpit window.

He inflated his life vest and left the relative safety of the floating plane to rescue a gunner. The York man took off the gunner's shoes and helped him get rid of the heavy outer clothing dragging him down.

The current kept them from reaching shore, but a launch rescued them 45 minutes later.

• • •

The Army decorated Lt. Robert Loucks for his deeds as a P-47 pilot in Italy's Po Valley. He first dive-bombed a bridge as part of an 11-plane flight, demolishing the structure.

The fighter pilot later machine-gunned and demolished two locomotives pulling a 30-car train. A second strafing attack caused six cars to catch fire and explode.

A subsequent attack on a smaller train put the locomotive out of commission.

• • •

By year's end, 19 Gold Stars covered York Corporation's service flag.

The D-Day invasion and its immediate aftermath added three to the group of 13 Yorkco men who died in uniform in 1944.

Capt. Albert Bodine, a reserve captain; Walter L. Boyer, mechanized cavalry; and Robert Serff, a bazooka gunner, died in France.

A few weeks after D-Day, Serff's parents learned that he was seriously wounded in fighting. He returned to action with Patton's 3rd Army within seven days and was reportedly killed in a tank battle near Nancy in France.

For the Yorkco community, the year would be the deadliest of the war.

Nearly 2,000 German prisoners, up to 500 at one time, were interned at this camp, built at the fairgrounds in Stewartstown. The seasonal workers were detained between June 30, 1944, and Oct. 31, 1945.

'They were ordinary guys'

The challenge of feeding the increasing number of men and women on the battle front fell to an ever-decreasing number of folks back home.

A fighting man in the field consumed about a ton of goods annually. Placed at Pennsylvania's wholesale farm prices, this came to $160 a year.

Leadership in 4-H clubs laid down goals for members to feed a soldier.

This could be done by producing one cow, one steer, five pigs, 60 capons, one-third acre of tomatoes or one acre of mixed vegetables.

• • •

Additional agricultural production pressure fell on York County and other southeastern counties making up the breadbasket of Pennsylvania — and America.

Before the war, the county ranked 30th nationally among agricultural counties in value of farm products sold. It ranked seventh nationally in value of products used by farm households, 23rd in expenditures on farm machinery and 11th in expenditures for feed purchased.

It was third in number of chickens on the farm and 18th in the value of vegetables grown for home use.

But labor to harvest this bounty was growing increasingly scarce.

A civil case in York County Court illustrates the importance attached to even one worker from the agricultural community.

The action was delayed after a defendant failed to show. Charles S. Snyder of the Snyder Auto Co. was needed to help harvest and transport six tons of tomatoes from his property to a cannery. The rapidly ripening tomatoes were in danger of rotting or early frost.

The judge and attorneys believed a delay was justified because the immediate processing of the freshly picked tomatoes was more important during wartime than a $30 dispute in court.

• • •

It was this seasonal need for fruit pickers and cannery workers that caused individual members of the Pennsylvania Canners Association to ask for German POW labor for the county.

William A. Free of York, executive director of the canners association, said food — tons of it — would spoil if emergency labor could not be secured.

An initial group of 80 prisoners were expected in June as a source of labor. Officials readied the Stewartstown Fairgrounds — in the heart of the fruit-growing area — for a labor camp.

Several buildings dotted the fairgrounds, including a large building for skating and Stewartstown High School basketball games. Several other outbuildings had accommodated Sunday school picnics, fairs and carnivals before the war. Residents used some of the land for Victory Gardens, a national initiative to encourage home-grown vegetables and fruit.

Workers strung barbed wire around the community park, and officials assured residents the 200 prisoners assigned there would be under armed guard.

The plan was for prisoners to be trucked to the area's six canneries and orchards during the day and stay in the camp at night.

The canneries would pay the government the same wages that a civilian would receive, and the detainees would not take work away from available local labor — a sore point in many areas where prison labor was used.

• • •

The prisoners did come, an estimated 2,000 that summer and the next. One week, 500 arrived. Lebanon County's Fort Indiantown Gap provided many of them.

The camp grew, as the POWs arrived.

Eventually, a 12- to 15-foot barbed-wire fence surrounded the 15-acre ground. Guards in towers on all four corners commanded the camp. A guardhouse stood at the entrance.

Most of the prisoners were German and Austrian privates. Many were captured during fighting in Northern Africa, still clad in their uniforms or parts of them.

Six days a week, work details left under guard by bus, truck or on foot to work in canneries or orchards. Their presence those two summers left a lifetime of stories, some contradictory.

Camp neighbor Erma Barnes later wrote that the initial concerns of residents were allayed, and they scarcely noticed the camp after that.

"It seemed like an island unto itself," she wrote.

Some townspeople believed the camp was inadequately

POW Johann Schleicher of Austria, shown in this photograph, made this wood carving during his imprisonment in York County. It was the discovery of this carving that fueled York County resident Margaret Shaub's search for the creator, culminating in the invitation to several POWs to return to Stewartstown in 1992.

guarded, and the prisoners treated too well. But Barnes wrote that some in town realized they were just boys, just like county youth who were fighting overseas.

"Pity would rise in our hearts as we thought of them so far from their homeland," she wrote. "Then we remembered the hometown boys fighting and dying on foreign soil, in a war started by their leader — and one would then feel almost like a traitor."

• • •

Eugene Blevins remembers picking apples with a dozen POWs on his family's farm near Stewartstown.

"They were ordinary guys. I liked them. But some of them cut swastikas in the apples," he said. "We just threw them away. No point in making a big deal about it."

William Blevins, Eugene's brother, recalled that the Germans, however nice, sometimes needed to be reminded that they were prisoners of war.

During a rainstorm, German pickers took shelter in a farm building. One of the prisoners began climbing a ladder, and a guard ordered him down.

The POW continued his climb anyway. The guard aimed his rifle at the prisoner and ordered him off the ladder.

"He listened then," William Blevins recalled.

• • •

Residents recalled attempted escapes and disciplinary action in which guards sprayed detainees with pressurized hoses.

Even after V-J Day marked the war's end, a prisoner decided to seek his freedom one night.

The 26-year-old inmate left the Lineboro Canning Co., where he had been working. The FBI joined state police in the search.

The prisoner was said to be wearing a blue fatigue suit with the letters "P.W." on it.

• • •

Victor Nolt guarded the prisoners.

Some were mere soldiers, he said. Others, the younger ones, were Hitler's boys, arrogant.

"They were the gods themselves, the indestructible race," Nolt said, "whereas the older ones were ordinary Germans."

• • •

About six months after the Germans surrendered — on Nov. 1, 1945 — the camp closed. All prisoners were shipped out.

Goldie Trout, who lived across from the camp, said military officials took everything back with them, except for some supplies.

Camp officials took boxes of toilet paper, sugar, rice and brooms to the Trout house.

"I called the neighbors over," she told a newspaper, "and we divvied it all up."

• • •

A similar camp sprouted up in Gettysburg along West Confederate Avenue. The prisoners worked at jobs in Adams, York, Franklin and Cumberland counties.

At first, some Adams County employers declined their labor, and employees refused to work beside the Germans.

But the need for seasonal help overcame such feelings. In July 1945, the camp had 932 prisoners. The local oversight office fielded requests for 1,100 prison laborers.

The prisoners chopped wood, filled silos, cut corn and harvested grain. They also picked fruit and worked for food processors, including the D.E. Winebrenner cannery on Hanover's Poplar Street.

U.S. Army guards, armed with submachine guns, watched the POWs at the Hanover cannery. The prisoners caused no problems, Dan Ehrhart recalled.

The 16-year-old Ehrhart worked in the food processing plant in the summer of 1945.

"I think they were happy to be there," Ehrhart told a

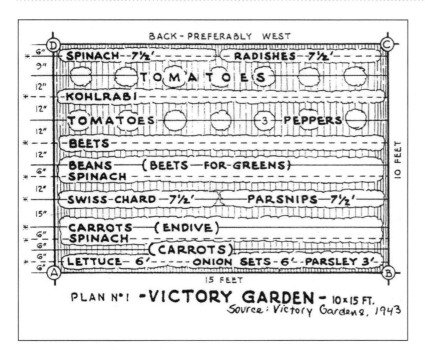

The government provided Victory Gardeners with information needed to be successful growers: Average dates for the last killing frosts. Quantities needed for each vegetable seed. Instructions on row spacing, distance between plants and preferred soil. Here, the government gives a plan for a 10- by-15-foot garden. York-area Victory Gardens had one negative result. Watering the gardens put record pressure on the York Water Co., its Lake Williams and other impounding dams. To aid meat shortages, the federal government also encouraged hunting of small game and deer. However, ammunition for hunting rifles often was in short supply. As the small game season approached in 1943, frustrated York retailers advocated pooling meager ammunition supplies and donating the cache to a worthy charity for a fund-raiser.

'Grow your own' posters promoted the home-based practice of canning fruit and vegetables, to alleviate pressure on scarce goods in markets and allow for sufficient supplies for the military. Here, a mother and daughter, with matching blonde ponytails and aprons, process food at home. Behind them, a shelf is packed with canned fruit and vegetables, grown in their Victory Garden.

newspaper. "They were still alive and being fed and everything. They were being treated as well as we were."

• • •

In York, Mayor John L. Snyder thought his city could benefit from the prison labor, too.

The war was hampering city services, he argued. Streets were filthy and in need of repair, and garbage collection was spotty.

He contacted appropriate federal authorities and found such German prisoners were available. Snyder's ill-fated proposal did not set well with a safety-conscious city council, and Highway Director Horace H. Ziegler clearly stated his opposition.

The same day council was to address the matter, York County was put on alert.

A German prisoner working at the Bayuk Cigar Co. in Lancaster had escaped. The private previously had been placed in detention at Fort Indiantown Gap, and authorities asked the public to be on the look out for him.

• • •

Jamaican workers also congregated in camps in Fawn Grove and Brodbecks along the Maryland border. When wartime labor-strapped growers needed pickers when fruit was ripening, they contracted with these British subjects.

Councils, with elected officials, governed the two camps. One leader was Elijah Lewis, a graduate of Tuskegee Institute and a teacher in Jamaican schools.

"The Jamaican accent baffles county residents, totally unprepared to hear English with a British accent complete with broad a's and extra h's," a newspaper reported. "The rising inflection of their speech, however, gives their speech a Latin emphasis so that it is difficult to understand Jamaicans speaking among themselves."

'Grow More in '44'

The Victory Garden movement became increasingly critical as the war drew more agricultural workers into the military.

The movement was based on the principle that if these home garden spots could feed families at home during war-related food shortages, it would leave more for troops to eat.

In 1943, one-third of all vegetables grown in America came from gardens. In addition, the government asked farmers to dedicate "an acre for a soldier" and donate the profits from crop sales to canteens for servicemen.

The government also dispensed gardening advice. The subtitle of one such book stated, "Vegetables, victuals, vitamins, and victory, with violets, verbenas and veronicas for variety."

Civilian Defense officials pushed for additional Victory Gardens as the 1944 growing season approached, using the slogan "Grow More in '44."

Residents with green thumbs could secure land to cultivate Victory Gardens at no cost or low cost. They could sign up for plots at York's old city hall on South Duke Street.

"Become a member of America's most formidable army at home by supporting the men on the front," Civilian Defense officials stated.

Norma Bear Gates of Conewago Township later wrote that the gardens also provided an opportunity for unity. Folks worked side by side toward a common goal.

"Neighbors shared gardening expertise as well as tools," she wrote.

The unity was not complete.

Late in the war, York Police Capt. Gorman J. Christine assigned plainclothes night patrolmen to curb looting and other malicious damage to backyard gardens.

Government directives about how to safely can vegetables also drew the ire of some county residents.

The "oven method" of preserving vegetables resulted in reports of kitchen explosions around the county.

The York Dispatch warned about the dangers of the method:

"In the interest of having some housewives save the tragedy of having her eyes put out by flying glass, or the lesser misfortune having a stove wrecked at a time when stoves are hard to get, the Dispatch today calls attention to the fact that numerous explosions are occurring as a result of a canning practice which has been recommended to York women by various 'experts' ... ."

• • •

York Corporation established two 50- by 100-foot gardens for employees on land near Richland Avenue and Grantley Road.

Tending even a small part of the three acres under cultivation brought a taste of farm life to the city or suburbs, soothed war-weary nerves and provided exercise and food, Shop News stated.

Yorkco President Stewart Lauer developed a novel approach to keep rabbits away from his East York Victory Garden. He surrounded his garden with mothballs.

• • •

With rationing firmly in place, merchants in small towns worked hard to accommodate their captive audiences — residents who couldn't venture far from home.

In Dillsburg, Ray Krall's Drug Store on South Baltimore Street sold seeds for Victory Gardens. The Sunshine Feed Store sold 1- and 2-week-old chicks to raise into egg-layers for breakfast fare or to provide meat for the dinner table.

Hatcheries outside Dillsburg sent shipments of chicks through the post office. When the chicks arrived, postal service workers would notify customers to pick up their order.

Companies sometimes celebrated their successes with banquets even with a war on. A.B. Farquhar Co., holder of four Army-Navy 'E' awards, celebrates receiving the national Security Award. This dinner took place at York's Alcazar Ballroom, seen here on the cover of the company's March 1944 newsletter. The county's defense plants stressed security. After Pearl Harbor, the Manufacturers' Association urged company officials to investigate their employees' backgrounds and to keep out unidentified visitors. Major plants hired state-commissioned uniformed guards and sent them to revolver marksmanship courses.

Jake Devers steps forward

As the months at war multiplied, Gen. Jacob L. Devers gained commands of progressively higher responsibility and the stars that accompanied them.

Just before the war, the field artillery specialist, commanded Fort Bragg, N.C.

In North Carolina, a small incident indicated his dedication to his work.

Devers was found wearing a combat helmet while sick in bed with pneumonia. He explained that he was testing the comfort and adaptability of the helmet before he, acting as base commander, gave it his OK.

He was promoted to chief of U.S. Armored Forces at Fort Knox, Ky., when the war began. He gained a reputation for administrative prowess, hard work and getting things done. At Fort Knox, he helped develop the Sherman Tank, the most successful American tank in the war.

This map, published in The Gazette and Daily on Aug. 17, 1944, shows the Gen. Jacob L. Devers-led Invasion of Southern France, lower middle. This graphic projects the probable route of Operation Dragoon toward Paris, where Allied troops would meet up with those landing earlier at Normandy in the Cherbourg area, upper left. Actually, Devers' Sixth Army Group headed toward the Rhine in the Strasbourg area, southeast of Paris. His soldiers crossed the Rhine in late March and early April 1945, and moved across southern Germany through Munich and into Austria.

In May 1943, he moved to Britain where he served as U.S. commander of the European theater.

News of his promotion evoked cheers from 70 York County residents who were members of the 94th Division.

York's Harry McLaughlin, writing for the division's newsletter "Attack," reported that the large York contingent shouted, "He did it."

McLaughlin noted that Devers was captain of the York High School basketball team in 1904. Cpl. Robert Crerand of the 94th Division headed the William Penn quintet in 1940.

For six months, Jake Devers oversaw the training of many divisions of fighting men as they prepared for an attack across the English Channel on German forces in France.

At the end of 1943, Dwight D. Eisenhower replaced Devers as the ranking officer in the European theater. This brought Ike the responsibility of final planning and execution of Operation Overlord — the D-Day assault on the beaches of Normandy.

Devers, in turn, replaced Eisenhower as Deputy

Supreme Allied Commander of the Mediterranean.

• • •

By August 1944, Devers was overseeing planning for Operation Dragoon, the long-considered Invasion of Southern France.

Devers' men had the assignment of invading the French Riviera using landing craft freed up from the offensive in Normandy 70 days before. A successful amphibious assault and subsequent operation would open the port of Marseilles. This would allow a line of communications and supplies from the south to support Allied armies as they marched on Germany along a broad front through France.

Dragoon also would prevent the reinforcement of German troops in Normandy because those reserves would be needed to stop the Allied thrust from the south. Devers' offensive would simply force the Germans to cover a broader front with thinner defensive lines.

Operations began on Aug. 15, with 350,000 Allied

IF YOU ASK ME - HOW DO YOU LIKE YOUR WORK IN AN INDUSTRIAL PLANT? - I WOULD SAY

|  |  |  |  |  |  |

FAIRIE KINNEMAN	M. HERSHBERGER	HELEN YOUNG	PEGGY KINNEMAN	MILDRED DE VONO	IRENE GREIMAN
Hench Plant	Fittings Shop	Five Story Building	Hench Plant	Fittings Shop	Five Story Building

I like it. I was formerly employed as a clerk in a department store, which certainly is much different than the work I am now doing. I like my present work much better than that of being a store clerk. The working conditions are better, the pay more encouraging, and I think the girls here are easier to work with. I like it here at Yorkco.

I enjoy working in the shop. I worked in one before I was employed here, but it was much different work. I worked at the Dental Supply Company. The work here is not as hard as I had expected it would be, but then of course my job is none of the hardest. The group of girls in my department are very agreeable to work with.

I like it very much. Before working here in the Yorkco shops I was employed in an office, and I can say that I like the shop much better. The work is different from that which women usually do, and I think my job is very interesting. Of course there is the feeling that I am doing my duty, which makes the job more appealing.

I was initiated into the machine shop sorority at the Goodling Machine Shop, and it was there that I learned to like this type of work. I still like it, always thought that working in a machine shop was rather hard and dirty. I now have found that it is not, but is very pleasant and far from being monotonous.

I think it is great. I have always liked working in a shop, and I prefer a machine shop because I think the work is more interesting than in these other shops where women usually work. I worked at the Martin-Parry Corporation before I came here to Yorkco, so I have been in the shop for some time and believe that I have about served my apprenticeship.

Swell! I was a housewife before coming into the shop, and therefore I did not know if I would like it or not. However, after working here in the Inspection Department for only a few months I would say that I like it a lot because the work is not tiresome and the girls are very nice. (Editor's Note: We noticed that, too, Irene.)

Yorkco's Shop News polled six female workers about their experiences working on the shop floor. These workers expressed job satisfaction.

troops moving ashore over a 50-mile front from Cannes to Toulon. The German defenses were softened by a heavy naval bombardment, and the Allied invaders sustained few casualties.

Within a month, the Devers-led U.S. 7th Army and the 1st French Army, freed the port of Marseilles and met up with Gen. George Patton's 3rd Army near Dijon. For many of Devers' men, it was a reunion of sorts.

Many in the 7th Army, now commanded by Alexander "Sandy" Patch, had served under Patton, as part of the first Allied forces to land in Europe. That landing on Sicily in July 1943 had added to Patton's fame, but embarrassing incidents in which Patton slapped or verbally abused soldiers undermined the volatile general.

Now, in September 1944, American and French forces, consolidated under the 6th Army Group with Devers in command, thrust toward the Rhine River for an attack on Germany.

Devers' forces were the first to reach the Rhine, but intense German offensives delayed their crossing.

• • •

Preparing a three-pronged approach across a broad front that fall, Allied forces in France looked to the Rhine as a starting line for the subsequent campaign toward Berlin and other German strongholds.

Devers' 6th Army Group was positioned on the south. Lt. Gen. Omar Bradley's 12th Army Group, including Patton's 3rd Army, would fight in the line's center. Field Marshal Sir Bernard Montgomery's 21st Army Group approached from the north.

The Germans would not make things easy for the Allies.

In fact, they counterattacked.

Their well-planned offensives — the Battle of the

Bulge in the north and Operation Northwind against Devers' forces in the south — delayed the Rhine crossings until early 1945.

Devers shifted his forces to provide defensive coverage as Patton's men moved toward Belgium to puncture the side of the Bulge. The German assault had moved deep into bending Allied lines, thus giving the battle its name.

Covering for Bradley's men fighting in the north extended Devers' lines, leaving his units vulnerable to a German offensive.

Hitler personally directed Operation Northwind, the last German offensive of the war.

Nazi forces attacked Devers' men's thin lines with initial success. But determined Allied forces finally swept remnants of the German Army from the west bank of the Rhine. The "Second Battle of the Bulge," as it's sometimes called, was over.

By March, Devers' forces were ready to move on Munich and other targeted cities in Bavaria and Austria.

The Devers-led Invasion of Southern France, called the "Forgotten D-Day," had come to an end.

• • •

Operation Northwind was the battle for which Audie Murphy, Devers' best-known soldier and the most-decorated fighter of the war, won a Medal of Honor.

Murphy's company was in a desperate position near Holtzwihr, France, lacking operational tank destroyers in the face of six heavy German tanks and 250 enemy infantry.

Murphy mounted a burning tank destroyer, grabbing its heavy machine gun. For an hour, amid the smoke, Murphy killed or wounded 50 to 100 Germans, confused about where the deadly fire was coming from.

The enemy tanks were forced to withdraw with their

Lt. Thomas Cottrell, former York Corporation employee, swears his daughter, Catherine, into the WAVEs in 1944. Thomas Cottrell was a sales engineer in York before receiving his Navy commission.

Bernice Fells Pitts of New Freedom served for 22 months after joining the WACs in September 1944. She served at several bases in the United States.

infantry support decimated. Murphy jumped off the burning tank destroyer to return to his men, and it exploded seconds later.

• • •

Other heroes emerged during this last, desperate German thrust.

A York County soldier earned a Bronze Star in nearby fighting. Pvt. William H. Hinton, assigned to a regimental headquarters in the 28th Infantry Division, moved to the rear to escort a party of soldiers toward the front. The squad would run communications wire as they walked.

When he passed headquarters along the way, the colonel to whom he was assigned as a bodyguard had already moved to the front.

Following the colonel's steps, he observed a German sniper covering the officer's path of return.

Creeping within yards of the sniper's position, he took out the enemy soldier with a spray from his submachine gun. He continued forward, found his commander and stayed with him.

To 'live a life of usefulness'

With the advancement of Allied troops through France, communities in York County planned "V-Day" celebrations.

York Mayor John L. Snyder appointed William

Beckner to coordinate the individual celebration plans already made by various organizations.

Beckner's group established the goal of inspiring people to have the proper spirit of thanksgiving when the European phase of the war ended.

The public would be urged to hold rowdyism in check and arrange a fitting celebration of church worship and community meetings. Fighting in the Pacific Theater would be far from over.

With some of the frivolity ending World War I in mind, Beckner cautioned against a premature celebration in reaction to unconfirmed rumors.

The war in Europe might end by gradual attrition, making the actual day of surrender hard to establish. In that case, Beckner's committee would decide whether the celebration would continue or be canceled.

The important thing, he said, is to be prepared for whatever might happen.

• • •

Beckner had good reason to blend caution with optimism. The casualty toll from Europe and the Pacific continued to mount.

On Nov. 4, The York Dispatch and The Associated Press released figures that placed county casualties at 659 since Pearl Harbor: 166 dead, 354 wounded, 91 missing and 48 taken prisoners.

Within 90 days, casualties hit the 1,000 mark, undoubtedly exceeding comparable county numbers for World War I in all categories.

The list of 1,000, the Dispatch-AP report acknowledged, might be incomplete.

• • •

The Red Lion Echo queried servicemen about what the community should offer when they returned.

The community newsletter contended that those in the military would not look for praise and glory.

The Echo writer speculated that those coming back would seek to return to their previous employment and need credit to purchase homes, farms or businesses. They would look for job security until they could adjust and want the opportunity to settle down to a peaceful life.

"Many of you have gone thru the dust, the wind, the cold, the heat, the insects and vermin, the stench of the battlefronts in short the 'hell of war' ... want nothing more than an opportunity to forget the past few years, and again live a life of usefulness instead of a life of destruction, to blot out the sight of the dead, the wounded, the dying and again to sit quietly in the church of your choice to worship the Almighty God," the newsletter indicated.

• • •

In Shop News, Yorkco President Stewart E. Lauer also cautioned against catching postwar fever. All Yorkco employees should try to produce more than ever.

"So, let's push a little harder each day on our war job," he wrote.

For months, groups within Yorkco had been planning for what would happen after the fighting ended. The war had taught the company much and brought more widespread use of its products than during peacetime. The company projected a postwar employee range of between 15 percent higher and 15 percent lower than its wartime total, working 40-hour work weeks.

Meanwhile, a survey showed 90 percent of former Yorkco employees in the service expected to return to the company after the war. Fifty percent of those responding to the company survey listed special skills learned in the service.

Yorkco wanted to take advantage of those new trades, not necessarily route a veteran back to his former job.

For example, Industrial Relations Manager Joseph Moody said a woman typist at Yorkco who learned to run a motor depot as a WAC officer with 300 mechanics under her supervision should not be returned to her former position.

She wouldn't accept it anyway, he said.

• • •

The York community celebrated the opening of a new building for the Crispus Attucks Community Center, a center for the city's black community and destination for returning veterans.

Community leader Dr. George W. Bowles noted that York was making history in opening its new center at the former St. Luke's Lutheran Church on East Maple Street.

"Today in Germany, because of the arrogant bigotry of the so called superior race, no such dedicatorial ceremony would be possible," he said.

The Crispus Attucks Association was a character-building organization, and character mattered.

"The loss of a firm national character and the degradation of a nation's honor is the inevitable prelude to that nation's destruction and decay," he said, in reference to Germany.

'Worst sight I ever saw'

Events late in the year reinforced the notion that fighting was far from over — that there was still a war going on.

Eleven U.S. servicemen died on York County soil when their plane crashed on Christmas Day as it attempted to land at Olmstead Field in Middletown, across the

York residents Sgt. Luther Stoppard Jr., left, and Cpl. Robert Holtzapple work at the 8th Air Force Service Command station in England. Their mission was to repair damaged B-17 Flying Fortresses. Holtzapple, a former Yorkco clerk, had the assignment of photographing the scenes of bombers that had crash-landed.

Susquehanna River.

An additional 16 were injured when the transport traveling from Jacksonville, Fla., to Minneapolis, went down on Roundtop Mountain near New Cumberland.

"It was the worst sight I ever saw," Fire Chief William Vogelsong of New Cumberland said. "The men were in the plane crying for help, and we had to cut our way to them with an ax."

Part of one wing was on a tree 200 feet from the plane.

None of the dead came from the county, but the incident gave York County residents a first-hand look at mass casualties of war.

• • •

This was not the first time that an Army plane went down in York County.

Two days after the D-Day landing, a B-24 bomber on a test flight from Olmstead Field crashed on the Walter Beshore farm, between Newberrytown and Yocumtown.

Five crew members died, but a sixth man escaped in time. He rushed to a farmhouse for help, then returned to attempt to rescue his comrades.

Mrs. W. Worrell Wagner grabbed a first-aid kit and drove to the scene. The survivor told her that he had attempted to remove bodies from the wreckage, but the

George Redman, left, and Jim Redman bale waste paper collected daily at York Corporation's West York plant. The paper would eventually become shell containers. Shop News noted in the spring of 1944 that tons of paper were salvaged at the two York plants, but many tons were also wasted. 'Save boxes, brown paper, containers, cartons, envelopes, corrugated paper, newspapers, magazines, waste basket paper and all correspondence that has passed its legal status,' Shop News urged.

heat was too intense.

The four-engine bomber's wreckage was spread over a 200-yard area.

• • •

Another plane crash in April took the life of a Women's Auxiliary Ferrying Squadron pilot.

Evelyn Sharp of Ord, Neb., was piloting a P-38 fighter plane from Long Beach, Calif., to Newark, N.J., when she stopped at New Cumberland Airport, later Capital City Airport, in northern York County.

As she was taking off the next morning, her twin-engine plane's right engine lost power, just as it was getting airborne. Sharp tried to pilot the plane back to the airfield, but it hit trees and crashed onto the Arthur Zimmerman farm, just over the Cumberland County line.

Newspaper reports stated that the 24-year-old pilot was thrown from the plane, which immediately caught fire.

• • •

Earlier in the war, a bomb-like object that dropped from a plane on a Dover Township farm proved to be a magnesium flare used by airplanes in trouble at night.

William Harbaugh, a Dover High School student, discovered the object on the Vernon Eisenhart farm near Dover. Handling it gingerly, he took it to school.

Harry M. Cooper, the principal, supervised as it was taken apart, then turned it over to county Civilian Defense officials.

The object baffled defense officials because no one in the Dover area had heard of any airplane in trouble.

• • •

In a less threatening incident in York, seven or eight planes dropped missiles from the air that were meant to recruit, not harm.

Bomb-shaped leaflets fell to the ground to recruit men between the ages of 17 and 26 for aviation cadet training.

The U.S. Army Air Forces needed pilots, and the leaflets advertised training in an enlisted reserve as aviation cadets.

All young men who made application for this training received free tickets to see the film "Bombardier," starring Pat O'Brien and Randolph Scott.

• • •

The prospects of a cold winter did not brighten moods as the long war year of 1944 was coming to an end. Coal for heating purposes was often hard to find, but rocks in coal deliveries were easy to locate.

The Solid Fuels Administration for War planned to restrict coal allocations for home use to 87.5 percent of normal that winter. The restrictions became necessary because of higher demand for coal to power defense plants and manpower shortages after the military called many coal miners to duty.

Irvin R. Shultz, York's inspector of weights and measures, noted that if coal customers were going to go with reduced allocations, the coal they did receive should not be filled with rocks.

Shultz made these statements after Edward Naylor of Grantley Street took a bag of stones to his office. He had sorted the rocks after a delivery from a Newberry Street dealer.

The inspector's calculations placed the delivery's content at, as The Dispatch reported, "21 percent unburnable, grate, wrecking rock."

To stretch coal supplies, the federal government had ruled that degradation — or substandard particles — in coal could be as high as 15 percent.

"As an inspector," Shultz said, "I know that when a maximum percentage is established, the unscrupulous producer will use it as his minimum."

• • •

York coal companies sometimes had problems finding people to make deliveries to homes, in those times that they had any to distribute.

Cpl. Robert L. Keller heard about the manpower shortage during a 13-day winter furlough.

The former York Corporation lathe operator pitched in and spent his leave delivering coal 10 hours a day. He returned to the military to add to his 34 months of service, mostly in the Pacific.

• • •

For the third wartime holiday season, the federal government banned outdoor Christmas lights.

The lights-out order came after some people questioned whether the holidays again would be dark.

The elimination of outdoor Christmas lighting nationally would save enough fuel to meet electrical requirements for a city of 50,000 — roughly the size of York — for a year, according to one estimate.

Indoor residential and store lighting were allowed. But

lighted Christmas decorations on Continental Square —
including a large star in its center — would remain dark
for yet another year.

• • •

Cpl. C.J. Williams from Camp Breckinridge in
Kentucky visited York to stump for Republican presidential candidate Thomas E. Dewey in the 1944 election.

Williams, former officer of the Republican Bureau of
Negro Affairs, spoke at a gathering of party faithful in
York. Williams said many soldiers in his camp, fighting
for their country, were unable to vote because they were
from the South, where Negroes are denied that right.

Paul Stevens, head of the local bureau, said many black
people in Pennsylvania were pro-Dewey. They had concerns about the health of Franklin D. Roosevelt, seeking
his fourth presidential term.

The racial views of Harry S. Truman, President
Roosevelt's vice presidential running mate, also concerned
the black community.

Truman had been in town earlier in the year, criticizing
defense industry "chiselers" who were using the war to
their advantage.

He commended the county for its support of the war.

"You are accepting minor privations, willingly, smil-
ingly and bravely," he said.

He sidestepped a question about his interest in the vice
presidency by stating at a York County Democratic banquet, "A statesman is only a dead politician, and I want to
live a long time yet."

In the November election, York County voters, as the
rest of the nation, solidly backed Roosevelt over Dewey.
In so doing, they showed a reluctance to change the commander in chief in the middle of the war or indicated satisfaction that the president was correctly handling his
wartime duties.

Six months later, Roosevelt died and his vice president,
Truman, became a statesman, the chief executive of the
United States.

• • •

Leon Gilbert of York was one of those soldiers fighting
for his country in a segregated unit. The lieutenant was
platoon leader for the 365th Infantry, fighting in Italy.

He was part of the bloody Allied campaign to drive the
Germans from Italy.

By early February 1945, the fighting was wearing on
him. Exhausted and shell-shocked, he was moved from the
front lines, a victim of combat fatigue.

When Germany surrendered, he returned home, combat medals pinned to his chest.

In the Pacific theater, another black soldier from York,
Henry Clayton Orr, served with the 476th Amphibious
Truck Company.

The William Penn High School graduate was wounded
in fighting on Iwo Jima.

• • •

Late in the year, York Mayor John L. Snyder irritated
many of his constituents.

He proposed a ban on playing radios, phonographs,
jukeboxes, musical instruments, singing or making any
noise between midnight and 7 a.m.

One section of the ordinance extended the ban to busi-

This York Corporation advertisement connects refrigeration with the efficient production of synthetic rubber from
petroleum products.

nesses. The prohibition was aimed at quieting the big band
sounds played at public places that interrupted the sleep of
weary war workers.

Council defeated the mayor's initiative after debate,
which included a perceptive reminder from council member Theodore F. Freed.

"If this ordinance should be passed," he said, "there
will be no Christmas caroling this year."

'Give them strength and courage, God'

Most large York County industrial plants produced
newsletters during the war.

The publications were designed to enhance communications and morale.

York Corporation's bi-monthly Shop News contained
12 pages of news about products, employees and servicemen.

Shop News emphasized content to help employees see
the relevance of their work in saving lives and ending the
war earlier. At the same time, Shop News communicated

Dora the Dope thinks she's terribly wise
With her hat tilted back and her hair in her eyes.
That peek-a-boo bang's going to give her some pain
When revolving machinery removes her blonde mane.

No sillier goop can be found anywhere
Than Gertie the Goof with her dangling hair.
For moving machinery she cares not a fig,
But some day poor Gert will be wearing a wig.

A bandana turban on Sally the Silly
Is tied so the ends flap around willy-nilly.
They'll catch in machinery some day, never fear,
And bold little Sally will look mighty queer.

Now, this Yorkette, a very smart girl,
Believes in being SAFE, so she hides every curl
'Neath a cap styled to guard her from harm.
She views Dora and Sally and Gert with alarm.

This cartoon in York Co's Shop News takes a lighthearted look at a serious plant safety issue. The cartoon was titled, 'The Three Careless Cousins and The Yorkette.' The Yorkette, 'a very smart girl,' hides all her hair under a cap.

these extensive home front efforts to former Yorkco men and women at war, who received the publication in the mail along with company-paid copies of Reader's Digest.

Editor Fred Gibbs worked to make Shop News interesting, finding anecdotes from throughout Yorkco's vast plants and emphasizing photos of attractive female employees aimed at servicemen away from home.

• • •

In one of its 1944 editions, Shop News drew a connection between Yorkco and the launching of the U.S.S. Missouri, billed as the world's greatest battleship. The 45,000-ton vessel slid into the East River at the New York Navy Yard nine months ahead of schedule.

The piping on the man-of-war would reach from New York to Philadelphia, much of which accommodated Yorkco-produced air conditioning and refrigeration.

When Gen. Douglas MacArthur accepted the Japanese surrender aboard the Missouri in September 1945, Shop News reminded workers that the ship was York-equipped.

The newsletter also told of the company's role in heavy-caliber aircraft cannon testing.

Engineers designed twin vacuum chambers where temperature and air pressure would duplicate the stratosphere nine miles above the Earth.

Shells would travel the length of the 22-foot range and smash into 20 tons of sand.

Aircraft designers needed to know more about detonation and speed of projectiles fired by high-flying bombers.

An 8-inch mobile siege gun was the most obvious Yorkco contribution to the war effort. The Army chose the neighboring Yorkco and S. Morgan Smith plants to make what Shop News billed as the "Pin-Up Gun of the Invasion."

Projectiles from those massive guns were expected to smash through the Axis' 6-foot-thick steel and concrete emplacements constructed across roads to Berlin and Tokyo.

Yorkco built parts for the gun's base. Smith workers made everything else, except for the Army-supplied gun barrel, recoil mechanism and range-finding instruments.

A piece that was started at Smith might be passed to Yorkco for the next construction step and then back to Smith workers for another piece.

The multi-ton gun could be deployed in 2 hours and then moved again in 45 minutes. Once a minute, it could throw a 240-pound shell from York to Gettysburg, 30 miles away. A 90-pound powder charge provided the power.

Materiel Command of U.S. Army Air Forces at Ohio's Wright Field ordered this refrigerator door for defense purposes. This is not the largest such door York Corporation made, but it dwarfs Roy Hamme and John Bowman. The door, which covers a 12-foot opening, reportedly moved with the same ease as a home refrigerator door. Another large Yorkco refrigeration unit — a cold storage unit meant to preserve food — saved lives on Guam shortly after the war. A typhoon packing 140-mile-per-hour winds slammed into Army installations. Robert Louey wrote back to his former co-workers at York Corporation that he and about 15 other men found refuge in the huge cast-iron Yorkco locker after the club which housed it blew away. 'I started praying and kept it up for the six hours we were in there,' he wrote. Eventually, the storm subsided and the men were safe.

The Japanese used York Corporation products, too. Left, Marines placed the sign saying 'Tojo's Ice Plant — Under New Management,' after seizing this Japanese installation on Guadalcanal. A Yorkco compressor sits in the photo's center. Right, the partially dismantled York 4 x 4 ammonia compressor sits in the plant. Makeshift, burlap-like insulation was wrapped around the pipes.

The Army touted the accuracy of this battle-ax of the invasion.

"It'll drop a projectile right on the courthouse steps," a weapons expert stated.

Later in the war, Shop News enlarged a telegram from a Navy vice admiral applauding a Yorkco air conditioning unit that withstood a direct hit from an enemy torpedo and kept operating.

The unit was aboard the U.S.S. Honolulu, badly damaged in fighting during the Battle of Leyte Gulf in the Philippines.

"The unit has been in constant service since the Honolulu was commissioned in June 1938," E.L. Cochrane wrote. "The bureau extends commendation and thanks for your high quality equipment."

• • •

Shop News published photographs of a Japanese ice plant captured in Guadalcanal in the Pacific.

The plant used Yorkco equipment to produce the ice. The publication speculated that the Japanese had captured the unit in China or the Philippines and moved it to the Pacific battle front.

Marines had placed a sign on the ice plant: "Tojo's Ice Plant — Under New Management."

Equipment in the plant was in relatively good order. The publication suggested that the Japanese left hurriedly or perhaps they found that the York equipment was difficult to destroy.

• • •

Joseph T. R. Lofland of York, stationed in a Navy supply depot in New Guinea, wrote to his former co-workers that he has handled up to 60 items made by York Corporation.

He sent along a packing slip showing that the items were checked and boxed.

Yorkco-manufactured items, he wrote, were "coming in mighty handy in these parts."

• • •

Kathryn Hamme, a former Yorkco employee, used Shop News to keep in touch.

Hamme had traded her spot at a drafting table for a

Winning the war presented a major challenge, Kathryn Hamme wrote to her former co-workers in 1944. But, she wrote, an even bigger job would follow: holding the peace.

position in the Women's Army Corps. She liked her civilian job but felt a patriotic pulling, perhaps because her father served in World War I.

After basic training, she kept charts and graphs of military activities at Ft. Meade, Md. Her Yorkco duties had prepared her well.

Hamme wrote that Army life carried with it a sense of what a big job bringing victory will be.

But, she said, a larger job awaited: holding the peace.

"Not only those in uniform are needed to win this battle," she wrote, "but all of us — everyone and every industry will have to help reestablish the men and women who return from the service."

• • •

Shop News told men and women in uniform that the

Paul T. Redman, former worker at York Corporation, mailed a prayer to his mother in 1944. Redman wrote the prayer aboard a ship somewhere in the Pacific. 'And tell them every night how much I love them, God,' he wrote about his loved ones.

In the summer of 1944, Philip Destephano, a York Corporation foundry worker, had three sons in the U.S. Armed Forces. One of them, Joseph, contacted his Sicilian relatives in the family's hometown of Caltolica. He discovered that several relatives and family friends in the town had worked at York Corporation and had returned to Sicily. Philip Destephano was proud of his fighting sons and had strong feelings against Hitler and Germany's satellites. He declared that he was a Sicilian, not an Italian.

"grand old man" of the Yorkco family had passed away.

F. Marion Dick, Yorkco finance department, collapsed as he entered the West York plant one morning.

The coroner declared that he had died of a heart attack.

Shop News stated that Dick had died as he would have wished — on the job. The 74-year-old had been with the company for almost 50 years, starting back in 1894.

Dick was among 543 Yorkco employees — 16 percent of the work force — who had been continuously employed by the company for 25 or more years.

Some of the employees were in their 70s. Bob Spangler, the oldest, was 85 when the war ended. Frank Schlosser was the longest in continuous service, starting with the company in 1888.

The sons of many Yorkco employees worked there, and during the war years, daughters or daughters-in-law. Stewart Lauer identified Twenty-five Year Club members as a stabilizing influence through the war years.

"Your record even surpasses that of many of our younger employees," he told them.

• • •

On the Yorkco assembly line one day, Adelia Smith was packing spare-part kits for cooling units when she pondered whether those grease-covered items would actually be handled by Marines, maybe even fighting men from her hometown of Red Lion.

Just before one kit was packed, she scribbled her name and address on a piece of paper and placed it among the parts.

Months later, she received a letter from a sergeant with the Sixth Marine Division in the Pacific.

He was quite familiar with York refrigeration equipment.

"York units are very dependable," he wrote, "and we like them very much."

He said the Marines even had a few bottles of good cold beer from the United States, thanks to Yorkco's refrigeration machines.

"So, you see we fellows get plenty of pleasure from these units you girls make back there at York Corporation," he wrote.

• • •

Fan mail from an island in the South Pacific reached two Yorkco employees, Peggy Kinneman and Roberta Klinedinst.

Two fighting men had run across a Shop News discarded in a jungle foxhole and were particularly impressed by photographs of the two women, who reminded them of their "best girls" back home.

The GIs wanted to hear from the women, and the letter thrilled the girls.

But they declined to release its full text to Shop News, particularly complimentary paragraphs.

• • •

Shop News regularly featured poetry from company personnel to military men and women in uniform and from those in uniform expressing their longings for home.

In one edition, former Yorkco employee Paul T. Redman wrote to his mother from the Pacific:

"Dear God, please keep them loving me,
Although I'm far, far out at sea.
Keep telling them they are the key,
The key of life which waits for me.
Please give them strength and courage, God,
To bear the aching pain
That they must feel for all the things
They love to see again.
Thank you, dear God, for love like ours
That reaches o'er the sea;
And thank you, God, for keeping us
Together, spiritually.
Please keep them trusting, loving me,
Until we meet again;
And tell them every night how much
I love them, God. Amen.

In this card from captivity in the Philippines, Thomas Frutiger urges his wife to 'Pray for a just if not a speedy peace.' The engineer also urges his wife to work on mathematics with their sons, 'Tommy' and 'Bobby.'

IMPERIAL JAPANESE ARMY

1. I am interned at—Philippine Military Prison Camp No. ____2____

2. My health is—excellent; good; fair; poor.

3. Message (50 words limit)

Love to all; stay healthy and keep the home fires burning. I have gained some weight and am feeling good both physically and mentally. Write whenevery you can, I may get one of your letters sometime. Stress Tommy's and Bobby's mathematics. Pray for a just if not a speedy peace.

Thomas W. Frutiger

Signature

'My health is good ...'

Living in Red Lion with her two sons, Anne Frutiger received several postcards from her husband, still imprisoned in the Philippines.

Sometimes, Thomas Frutiger would give practical tips: Consider selling the house if prices are up. Save current magazines and pay all insurance.

The engineer in Frutiger suggested that his wife emphasize the importance of mathematics with their sons.

He also would give an update on his health; other times, birthday greetings. He consistently listed his health as good, although in a card dated September 1943, he stated it was fair.

"Pray for a just if not a speedy peace," he wrote in one card.

• • •

Anne Frutiger was part of a network of other wives of POWs who would swap scraps of information.

She received a letter from one such correspondent in New York state who had obtained an update from a Navy commander, M.H. McCoy, who had escaped.

The letter said that Thomas Frutiger was in excellent health and had worked for the commander for about a month harvesting coffee beans.

The work was easy, and McCoy was able to provide a meal for him at noon.

A small store operated in camp where prisoners could buy tobacco, mainly in leaf form.

"Frutiger was making cigars," McCoy wrote, "hand rolled from the tobacco leaves for the store at the time I escaped."

Officers at that camp, No. 2, worked in the compound rather than outside the fence. Camp work was desirable because prisoners could steal additional food that grew within its confines. Prisoners coming in from the fields were searched.

Shelter and clothing were adequate, McCoy wrote, and the camp received an ample supply of quinine and sulpha drugs early the previous year through the Red Cross.

Ruth Blakeslee, who originally received the letter, wrote a note at its bottom to Anne Frutiger.

"Looks like your husband is a popular man in camp!" the wife of prisoner Robert Blakeslee, South Glen Falls, N.Y., wrote about Thomas Frutiger's cigarmaking skills.

She added a reference to her own husband's pre-war occupation, "Wonder if Bob is making wallpaper."

• • •

Anne Frutiger later received correspondence from a freed Robert Blakeslee painting life as a POW.

Lights went out at 8:30 each night, and POWs were supposed to be in bed by 9 p.m. Many stayed up later by keeping out of sight in the barracks and remaining quiet.

Prisoners slept in double deck bunks, but for many months Tom Frutiger lodged in the small store, the equivalent of private quarters. Frutiger had scored a position at the PX.

Most men still wore the clothes on their back during their capture, although some blue denim fatigues were issued. At one point, another American stole Frutiger's baggage.

"However, as you know, Tom is pretty resourceful and through his position at the PX and his skill at cigar rolling, he managed to acquire a pretty good wardrobe," Blakeslee wrote.

Frutiger taught the entire camp to roll cigars and even went into business for a while.

Some of the men in camp were just too lazy to roll their own, and Frutiger and another prisoner sold all the cigars they could secure tobacco for or had time to make.

• • •

Cigarmaking aside, prison was far from paradise.

Thomas Frutiger, an accomplished photographer, took this picture of his sons, Tom and Bob, with their dog, Duke. This photograph was one of several that Thomas Frutiger carried with him during captivity.

Prisoners scraped for ways to cope. Many from all ranks died of malnutrition.

On one occasion, Frutiger suffered from nutritional diarrhea, essentially starvation, Robert Blakeslee wrote.

A camp doctor later told Frutiger that he had not expected him to pull through.

"Apparently, the doctor hadn't figured on Tom's determination and will to live," Blakeslee wrote. "He literally pulled himself up from a skeleton to where he was heavier than I had remembered him in peacetime."

A prisoner in those same camps illustrated the military men's desperation by writing about an argument that awakened him one night.

Two men were arguing over how to divide a snake.

"You crippled thief," one man yelled, "the damn snake was getting away when I came along. You never would have caught him."

"It's my snake. I found it. Consider yourself lucky if you get any at all," came the reply.

"I'm having half or a chunk of your hide," the first man said.

• • •

Anne Frutiger heard from her husband on Nov. 6 through an intercepted propaganda broadcast from Japan. The War Department forwarded a telegram to Red Lion with a transcription of the broadcast.

"My health is good so do not worry," he said.

Her husband said he had received many of her letters, although only three photographs. The pictures helped him to maintain the feeling of personal interest and relationships with loved ones at home.

A recent package enhanced his memories of life at home.

"God bless you all and keep you until we meet again," he said.

That was the last she heard from her husband.

• • •

Late in the year, MacArthur's forces were fighting toward the Philippines, and Japanese authorities made plans to move prisoners to the mainland, where their labor was needed.

Moving to a new point of captivity was nothing new to Frutiger. He initially was imprisoned in Camp O'Donnell and then moved to Prison No. 2 at Davao on Mindanao Island. At the point of the Nov. 6 broadcast, Frutiger was in Camp No. 1 at Cabanatuan in Manila.

He probably knew of plans to ship him off. American planes were visible from the prison camps. This represented a danger because they were attacking Japanese war and merchant ships, prisoner transports for the 1,500-mile trip to Japan.

In mid-December, Frutiger was among more than 1,600 troops loaded onto the first Hell ship, the Oryoku Maru in Manila Bay. The group was herded into three overcrowded holds on the passenger ship where the temperature exceeded 100 degrees. Officers were stuffed in one hold, officers and enlisted men in another and enlisted men and civilians in the third.

The men had no water, no food. Some suffocated because of lack of oxygen. Five-gallon buckets served as latrines.

"Some men crazed by thirst became vampires and slashed others and attempted to drink their blood," one of the officers later wrote. "Some drank their own urine. Some murdered to satisfy their lust for liquid."

They were in the belly of the beast, someone later wrote.

The ship moved in a convoy along the coast of the island. American planes discovered their position and attacked. The friendly airmen dropped bombs and then returned with strafing fire.

The planes came and went several times that day, inflicting damage to the ship. With holes in her side and a broken rudder, the Oryoku Maru settled in Subic Bay.

The holds were filled with dead men, succumbing to overcrowded conditions, the blast of the bombs or the bullets from the strafing. Others died on the 300-yard swim from the disabled ship to shore.

Survivors were herded into a makeshift holding pen on a tennis court. There, they sprawled in their rags, with no protection from the tropical sun and little to eat or drink. Some died from exposure.

The Japanese next transferred their remaining captives to Hell ship No. 2, the Enoura Maru, which steamed toward Japan. Off Formosa, a blast from a friendly dive bomber rocked the ship.

"Hatch covers and timbers plunged into the hold along that side," one prisoner later wrote. "Hunks of metal, large and small, ripped through the air and ricocheted off the steel walls. Agonized screams of the crushed and wounded rent the air."

It was Jan. 9, 1945. More than 300 died in that attack. The survivors were crowded onto yet a third Hell ship, the

Brazil Maru, which successfully made it to Japan, where the men endured eight more months of prison.

Tom Frutiger did not survive.

Government reports placed his death on Dec. 15, the date friendly fire disabled the Oryoku Maru, killing 350.

The Frutiger family later recalled a visit by a York soldier and fellow POW, perhaps Capt. Charles Langdon, who survived the three Hell ships. Langdon was also a reserve officer from the same unit, the 454th Ordnance Company. With Frutiger, the York officer was stationed at Fort William McKinley when they first arrived in the Philippines.

The soldier returned photographs of Frutiger's family and papers taken from his body. He recounted how Thomas Frutiger survived the Oryoku Maru attack and swam to shore, where he was recaptured.

Frutiger actually died on the deadly attack on the second ship, the Enoura Maru, his family learned.

Less than 400 of the original 1,600 prisoners survived the 47-day journey from the Philippines to Japan.

• • •

Bob Senft, at Fort Lewis in Washington state, sent most of his $50 monthly salary home to Ethel. To provide spending money, he worked weekends moving groceries at a warehouse.

Without his glasses, Senft was virtually blind. He assumed he would never serve outside the United States.

But the Army readied his unit to be dispatched to Europe.

• • •

Ethel Senft had no option but to work. Whatever her husband managed to send home did not cover household costs. She arranged for her sister to look in on their mother.

She drove her mother's car the six miles to York each day.

Now at the peak of its defense work, York Corporation still was in dire need of workers.

Ethel had joined thousands of other York County women fighting the Axis from inside a defense plant.

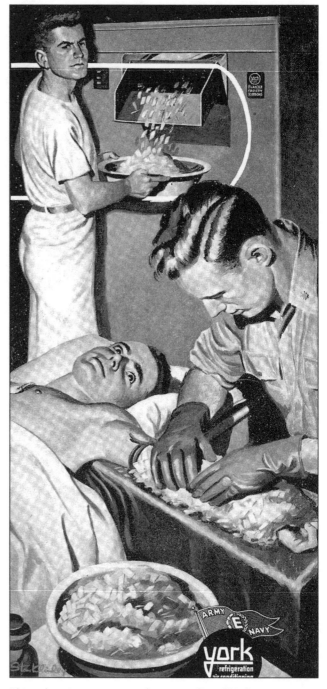

This advertisement touts the versatility of York Corporation's FlakIce Machine for military medical purposes. For servicemen, the machine did not take much selling. It was popular wherever it was found. One eyewitness tells of its arrival on Guadalcanal in 1942, scene of torrid fighting for weeks. When it was set up, a yell went out. 'Out there in the night, with its terrific heat, drama and great danger, FlakIce Frosty Ribbons flowed ... . Word passed with magical speed.' Shortly after the war, the company boasted that Eskimo fishermen in the town of Todd, Alaska, used FlakIce to preserve their daily haul of salmon. The machine cost less to operate than chipping free ice from a huge nearby glacier.

V

'The boys were kissing the girls and the girls were kissing back'

— 1945 —

On the evening of Aug. 14, 1945, York County residents joined a massive national V-J celebration, marking the war's end. The largest county assembly occurred in York's Continental
Square, where thousands of residents released pent-up emotions. Here, L. Allen Wolfgang,
Richard E. Wolfgang and Lloyd E. (Pud) Wolfgang hold a special V-J edition. Paul S. Wolfgang
is at left.

Gallery

Kenneth Smith, a former York Corporation machine tool operator, is seen in Europe with the bomber 'Hell's Belle II.' Smith, the bomber's ground chief, saved the plane from scrap. 'Smitty' and his crew put the plane back into shape, and the bomber set a record for durability in the Mediterranean Theater by completing 100 missions, marked by the bombs on the fuselage. Smith flew as a stowaway on the plane's 100th mission but did not intend to repeat the against-regulations act. 'Too monotonous,' he said. 'You fly a couple of hours. Then the Germans shoot at you for a few minutes, and you fly back for a couple of hours.'

York Corporation engineered this stainless steel-lined room, designed to simulate tropical conditions. The battery of 1,500-watt sun lamps and infrared heat lamps give these two Air Force men a strong sense of how it feels to be marooned on the sea.

York Corporation produced refrigeration and air conditioning for the U.S.S. Missouri, seen here sliding into the East River at the New York Navy Yard in the spring of 1944. Shop News provided the following statistics: A 15-story building, 150 feet square, could be erected with the area covered by the Missouri's decks and platforms. Forty-six acres of land, about one-sixth the area of Manhattan, could be flooded with the amount of water the Missouri displaced. Gen. Douglas MacArthur accepted the Japanese surrender on the ship's deck in September 1945.

'United We Win' was evidence that the U.S. government was trying to combat the demoralizing effects of racial prejudice and its impact on the war effort. The black press called for a 'Double V' — victory over fascism abroad and against racism at home.

Gen. Jacob L. Devers talks with Lt. Donald E. MacNutt, 85th Engineers, as light and heavy vehicles from the 10th Armored Division cross the Rhine River on April 1, 1945. The engineers installed this pontoon bridge across the Rhine at Worms, Germany, in nine hours, considered a major feat.

'It's all over on my front'

Once across the Rhine in early April, Gen. Jacob L. Devers' 6th Army Group formed a formidable southern thrust into Germany and Austria.

Its mission was to protect Gen. Omar Bradley's 12th Army Group's right flank and to eliminate any possibility of an embarrassing, last-ditch Nazi holdout in extensive fortifications in the rugged Alps, the rumored National Redoubt.

Devers' men accomplished their objectives.

They ground toward Munich and took that city and Salzburg. They captured Hitler's famed Alpine retreat and command post — "Eagle's Nest."

They corralled Hitler's No. 2 man, Hermann Goering, and his secret hideout. The National Redoubt turned out to be a product of Hitler lieutenant Joseph Goebbels' propaganda machine.

They freed the concentration camp at Dachau. That is, they freed the few prisoners left alive.

A moat outside the camp contained the bodies of 4,000 newly slaughtered prisoners, many of them Jews. Fifty railroad cars sat on tracks full of hundreds of bodies.

Locals had passed the camp each day, unconcerned about what lay beyond its fence. Chattering children pedaled past on bicycles.

"But even the battle-hardened veterans of the 45th (Division, 7th Army), which had fought through four countries by now, could not forget — or forgive — what they had just seen at Dachau," a historian wrote. "They had not that German gift of closing their eyes to anything that might upset them. They went on to their next objective, Munich, with murder in their hearts."

What Devers saw in Dachau and other concentration camps infuriated him. He told an International News Service reporter that the Nazi leaders should be tried and shot.

The German Army was in Allied hands, Devers said, but all the stray Gestapo leaders must be rounded up.

"We've got to destroy the Gestapo type of mentality," Devers told the reporter. "We've got to shoot them, although I guess, of course, we have got to do it legally."

• • •

Lt. M.L. Hamberger, Army Nurse Corps, was equally repulsed after visiting a concentration camp.

She saw evidences that camp officers forced prisoners to jump off a cliff. If they refused, officers pushed them. Prisoners were hung on hooks, where they slowly strangled. If they survived that, they were burned alive.

Lt. Walter P. Fridinger, son of York Corporation foreman Walt Fridinger, received a Bronze Star for heroic actions as his unit was driving deep into Germany.

This map from March 31, 1945, shows the Allied penetration into Germany after crossing the Rhine. The 21st Army Group under British Field Marshal Sir Bernard Montgomery was flooding into Germany from the north. Gen. Omar Bradley's U.S. 1st and 3rd Armies had cut the deepest into Germany. Gen. George Patton was the commander of the 3rd Army. The U.S. 7th and French 1st, under the command of Gen. Jacob L. Devers, are shown to the south. The trio of Montgomery, Bradley and Devers reported to Dwight D. Eisenhower, Allied commander in Europe.

One prisoner family member was compelled to torture and hang another one as amusement for the fanatical Nazi SS squads. The Germans made lampshades from human flesh.

"Nothing is horrible enough for the people who are responsible for such suffering," she wrote to her parents, former York residents Mr. and Mrs. Roy Hamberger.

• • •

Lt. Walter P. Fridinger, son of a York Corporation fore-

man, was one of the hundreds of thousands of soldiers serving under Devers.

During a daylight river crossing, Fridinger observed his forward units pinned to the ground by intense machine-gun fire. He executed a flanking movement with his platoon, which also drew heated fire.

But he succeeded in knocking out two enemy machine-gun emplacements and capturing seven German gunners. He spotted other enemy positions and duly reported this valuable information.

He received a Bronze Star for his actions.

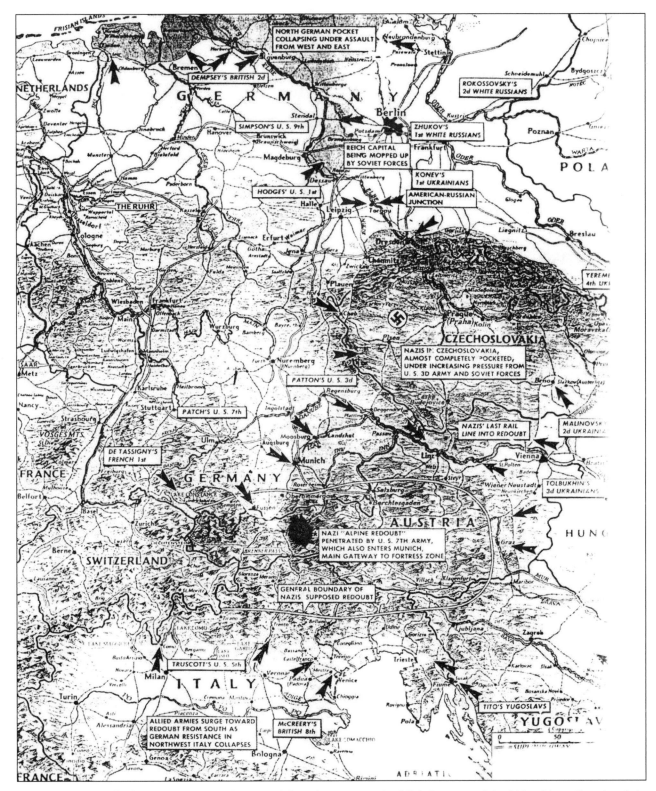

This map shows Allied penetration into Germany after about a month of fighting east of the Rhine River. Gen. Jacob L. Devers was in command of De Tassigny's French 1st and Patch's U.S. 7th Armies. Devers' forces touch the right flank of Patton's U.S. 3rd.

• • •

Devers' forces sealed passes in the Alps. There would be nowhere for the Germans to retreat, no Alpine fortresses where they could extend the war for months.

The 6th Army Group's work, which started with the textbook-perfect French landing nine months before and hundreds of miles away, was nearing its end.

The "Champaign Campaign," so-called because of the

Only 1 More To Lick!

NOW LET'S FINISH THE JOB

The War's Not Over Yet!

There's Still One More Enemy to Lick! More guns, more planes, more tanks, and more supplies of every kind will be needed to bring our boys home from all over the world. This is not the time to ease up—Now is the time to work harder for an early complete victory and peace.

Here's How YOU Can Do Your Share:

1.—Keep on Buying WAR BONDS

2.—Stay On Your Job in Industry

3.—Work "Just A Little" Harder—
          Produce "Just A Little" More

4.—Give Another Pint of Blood—Save Another Life

5.—Help Every Way YOU Can To FINISH THE JOB

York's Largest Men's & Boys' Store

Walker's
GEORGE & KING STS.

This advertisement indicates the measured celebration growing out of V-E Day. Although the victory over Hitler's regime was gratifying, Japan and its formidable forces lay ahead.

With Germany and Italy conquered, this York-Hoover Corporation newsletter shows scorekeeping Uncle Sam looking toward Japan.

relatively light resistance Devers' men faced in the landing, was hardly that. Fighting had left 15,271 Americans in the 7th Army dead and 58,342 wounded.

On May 5, Devers dictated terms of unconditional surrender to the German 1st Army commander in that sector. His Army Group took custody of a million German prisoners.

Associated Press correspondent Howard Cowan was present for the surrender. He reported Devers' conclusion: "It's all over on my front."

And the liberator of more than half of France had gained his fourth star.

'The job is only partly done'

On May 7, York braced for official word that the war in Europe was over.

It was a bit like the calm before the quiet.

Officials throughout York County were pushing for a measured celebration, a time for workers and families to go to church.

One front was closed down, but fighting in the Pacific Theater was far from decided.

The York Dispatch summarized the mood of county residents:

"Months, maybe years of blood and sweat, they knew, lay between them and another armistice such as Nov. 11, 1918, brought."

• • •

Official word from President Harry S. Truman was expected at 9 a.m. the next day — May 8.

If V-E Day came about, stores would close for the day at 3:30 p.m. to allow clerks to attend worship services.

Industrial plants would shut down for an hour at 4 p.m. for the same purpose.

In a resolution, the Manufacturers' Association recalled that industries paused on D-Day to allow workers to fill houses of worship to pray for the Allied cause. So it was appropriate to pause again when victory in Europe became official to provide an opportunity for workers to give thanks for answered prayers.

The Manufacturers' Association also recognized that the peace was only half won:

"Be it further resolved that because the cessation of hostilities in Europe will not lighten the sacrifices of the armed forces operating in other theaters of war, we continue at our tasks of supplying their needs and remain loyally in our shops until God in His time brings peace to the world."

Officials released a lengthy list of industries along with nearby churches that would be open to workers who desired to attend.

• • •

When peace in Europe was declared the next day, thousands, indeed, attended churches.

York Mayor John L. Snyder issued a reminder that boisterous merriment would be a mockery to men still in battle in the Pacific.

"Our celebration," he said, "should be simple and dignified."

The War Department was concerned that an extended celebration would cause an unnecessary interruption in war production.

• • •

The York Dispatch and Associated Press updated their ongoing list of county war casualties incurred between Pearl Harbor and V-E Day — 1,488.

That included 382 killed, 856 wounded, 155 missing and 95 prisoners of war.

"That is the price in human life and suffering that York and York County paid to bring V-E day today ... ," the newspaper stated.

• • •

A shrieking whistle at 9 a.m. brought together York Safe and Lock employees to hear President Truman's message over a public address system.

British Prime Minister Winston Churchill's announcement followed, after which those assembled recited the 23rd Psalm.

The Rev. Henry R. Gebhard, York Safe employee, offered prayer, and a company spokesman reminded workers to return to work because "the job is only partly done."

The J.S. Hershey Baking Co., Jefferson Avenue, York, gives a V-E Day thanks to the services that played a role in securing the German surrender on May 8, 1945.

...LET US CELEBRATE THIS VICTORY WITH A PRAYER!

◖ A prayer of thanksgiving that the terrible conflict in Europe has ended as soon as it has—without the additional loss of precious lives that a longer war would have inevitably brought forth . . . . and that victory in the Pacific will soon be won.

◖ A prayer of deep and lasting gratitude to the heroic men and women in the armed services who have offered their lives that the rest of us might live in peace and permanent security from dictatorships and future wars.

◖ A prayer of sympathy to the mothers, fathers, wives and sweethearts of those brave men and women who lost their lives and will not return to their homes and beloved ones.

◖ A prayer that all this suffering and sacrifice has not been in vain. . . . That it will have helped to win for this nation and the world the permanent and lasting peace and the enjoyment of the freedom for which they fought.

The Bon-Ton department store celebrates V-E Day with a prayer and a reminder to buy war bonds until Allied forces prevailed in the Pacific Theater.

• • •

In restaurants across the county, eating ceased during the president's address.

In one York restaurant, diners gathered around the radio, as tears ran down their cheeks.

• • •

In Spring Grove, the Glatfelter Paper Mill whistle blew eight long blasts. A Western Maryland yard engine worked its whistle as well, and church bells joined in.

Across from the mill, several area congregations came together for well-filled services at St. Paul's Lutheran Church at 2:15 p.m. and 4:15 p.m.

That evening, Spring Grove people joined hundreds of others driving through York with horns blaring and people cheering.

The Barker, the paper mill's publication, reported that, while people were overjoyed with the V-E Day news, the overriding feeling was that they must not stop until peace was reached in the Pacific.

• • •

After V-E Day, WAC Kathryn Hamme faced a new assignment at Camp Adair, Ore.

Before she headed out to the assignment far from home, she spent one last evening at the Non-Com Officers Club.

The band kept playing "Sentimental Journey."

This was the era of the big bands, the Dorsey Brothers, Glenn Miller and Les Brown and favorites: "I'll Never Smile Again," "Moonlight Becomes You" and "I'll Be Home for Christmas."

If music served as a universal chain to home, "Sentimental Journey" was one of its strongest links.

Years later, Kathryn Hamme Miller wrote that when she heard that song, her thoughts reached back to the night of mixed emotions between V-E and V-J Days.

'There is no glory in war'

At least two topics dominated many conversations: The human cost county families paid to win the war in Europe and the need to head steadfastly toward Tokyo.

The war was no respecter of wealth or prominence.

Maj. William L. Glatfelter II was one of six men killed in the crash of an Army transport in Mississippi.

He was the son of Philip Hollinger Glatfelter II and great-grandson of the founder of the Spring Grove paper mill and savior of York Corporation, P.H. Glatfelter.

Like the first Glatfelter, William Glatfelter was also affiliated with York Corporation, one of 24 men that Yorkco claimed among its war dead on V-E Day.

Three of P.H. Glatfelter's sons came home — P.H. III from the Navy; Ted, U.S. Army Air Forces; and George, Merchant Marine.

Sgt. Michael Glennan III was killed in Germany in April 1945, just before the fall of Berlin.

He was a descendant of longtime York resident Jeremiah Sullivan Black, secretary of state in President James Buchanan's administration.

The war took the lives of county soldiers both seasoned and young.

V-E Day Proclamation Expected

Molotov Reports Big 4 Agreed On Key Amendments

Tells press that conference is progressing so well work may be finished in few weeks. Sponsoring powers reject as untenable Vandenberg's proposal that world organization review treaties already in effect. Unanimity of Big Four also demonstrated by fact no proposals submitted seriously affecting security council, he points out.

By HARRY L. SHAPIRO

San Francisco, May 7. Soviet Foreign Commissar V. M. Molotov told the press today that if anybody was proper to do any marveling of the United Nations conference it would have to be somebody else.

After a weekend of disappointment from press and radio critics of the effect by the Soviet on the progress of the conference, Molotov called the press together this afternoon and told them he was exceedingly pleased to report that the progress of the conference was such that within a few weeks the end of the conference might well be at an end. Molotov reported that mainly among the sponsoring powers of all major amendments to the Dumbarton Oaks proposal had declared "as a result" a unanimity has been achieved which is essential to the success of the conference.

Molotov reported that the amendment particularly sought by Senator Vandenberg, that the world organization be empowered to review treaties already in effect, had been rejected which is essential to the success of the conference.

Details Agreement
Molotov also stated that the

Global War At A Glance

Report of unconditional surrender of Germany neither officially confirmed or denied. President Truman expected to announce V-E day in broadcast at 9 a. m. today.
(Page 1)

Street fighting rages in Prague, and Nazis continue resistance in Czechoslovakia and northern Yugoslavia. Breslau taken (Page 1)

Yanks score gains all along southern Okinawa front.
(Page 3)

Australian and Dutch troops capture high ground cast of Tarakan Island's Doesoraan oil field. Allied planes in operation off captured Tarakan airfield (Page 3)

International Red Cross Branded As Appeasing Nazis

Magazine praises American Red Cross but charges International headquarters with gross violation of its instructions from member organizations. Declares no considerations should have kept Geneva office from publishing facts of prison camp atrocities.

Germans Fight On In Czechoslovakia, North Yugoslavia

Street fighting rages in Prague, Breslau taken. No word from Courland peninsula or Vistula delta near Danzig. Czech pilots, airborne troops leave London to speed cleanup. U. S. Third Army battles on 150-mile front, Tito's men take capital of Slovania.

BULLETIN

London, Tuesday, May 8 (P) The Czech-controlled Prague radio announced today that the German command issued orders through all communications to German units to cease fighting.

Truman Broadcast At 9 A. M. Today Presumably To Announce V-E Day

British Ministry of Information announces Churchill will proclaim V-E Day today, declares two-day holiday in celebration of end of European war. Truman did not say broadcast would be V-E Day announcement. Story of Unconditional Surrender of Germany neither confirmed nor denied. SHEAF suspends Associated Press filing privileges from European theatre, lifts ban few hours later except for Kennedy, who sent original story.

May 7 (AP)—Britain proclaimed tomorrow as V-E Day. King George VI sent Eisenhower a message congratulating him on the "complete and crushing victory in Europe."

Prime Minister Churchill will proclaim the historic conquest at 9 a. m. (Eastern War Time) tomorrow from 10 Downing street and King George at 3 p. m. Eastern War Time.

There was nothing in the United States parallel to the British announcement that tomorrow and the next day will be holidays but President Truman made arrangements tonight to make a radio address at 9 a. m. (Eastern War Time) tomorrow.

Quiet V-E Day Observance Here

City, church and business of York outline program. Stores and plants to permit workers attend worship service. Mayor calls for no celebration.

Officials of York organizations today reiterated previously laid plans for the observance of V-E day in the main that no harassment is made at 9 a. m. today.

The Gazette and Daily projects the end of fighting in Europe in its May 8, 1945 edition. A local story, lower right, accurately forecast a relatively quiet V-E Day celebration, with the war unresolved in the Pacific. The homecoming of Gen. Jacob L. Devers in late June provided an appropriate reason for the county to celebrate. Thousands lined a 7-mile parade route, and 15,000 packed the grandstand at the York Fairgrounds to hear the native son, fresh from leading hundreds of thousands of soldiers as they fought their way across France and Germany.

Cpl. Herman Welfeld died in Europe in early 1945. The native of York County co-owned a department store in Belair, Md.

He was 39.

Pvt. Richard T. Dreisbach was killed on Christmas Eve, 1944, as his ship crossed the English Channel. Dreisbach had graduated from William Penn High School the previous January.

He was 18.

Pvt. Joseph F. Lewis, 22, of North York, was killed on a famous day in wartime: Armistice Day, 1944.

Staff Sgt. Carl S. Wills of York had the fortune of surviving confinement of more than three years in a Japanese prison camp in Manchuria following the fall of the Philippines.

He re-enlisted after the war and died in 1947 while serving in the Army during the rebuilding of Germany.

Many residents in uniform died stateside, during training or other duties. For example, Sgt. Burnell J. Willet, McSherrystown, died in an automobile accident near St. Mary's, Kan.

When twins Robert L. and James Kloker of York entered the war, Robert was assigned to the Pacific Theater and James to Europe. The twins' parents, Mr. and Mrs. Leo Kloker, learned that James had been wounded in France early in 1945.

Two months later, the parents received word that Robert, a paratrooper with the 11th Airborne Division, had been killed in the Philippines. He earned a Bronze Star for taking over a howitzer after the gunner was wounded.

At the time of Robert's death, a third brother, John, was serving in Northern France.

Pvt. Dennis J. Allen, 18, died only weeks before the German surrender. The well-known athlete at William Penn High School was a likely major league baseball prospect, and he played left end on the William Penn football team.

Edward Emanuel, who was killed in Germany nine days earlier, played right end on the same team.

• • •

Each day's newspapers brought a mixture of good and bad news.

The day before the German surrender, York County residents learned that Lt. Vernon R. Smith, a prisoner of war, had been liberated. The Air Forces officer, son of Mr. and Mrs. Ammon R. Smith, had lived in captivity for about two years.

Meanwhile, a telegram from the War Department stated that Pvt. Charles M. Frey was killed in Czechoslovakia, less than two months after his arrival in Europe.

Avis M. Hartzell, from the York Haven area, arrived home safely after undertaking highly classified Women's Army Corps work in England for eight months.

One night, she sought shelter 22 times because of V-2 attacks. The enemy launched the deadly, unmanned V-2 missiles from German and French soil.

Another time, she was among a group of WACs and soldiers standing at attention as an officer decorated them

Hannegan Heads Postoffice Dept.

Senate approves Truman's appointment of Robert E. Hannegan as Postmaster General by 60-2 vote, with Senators Donnell and Taft opposing. Motion by Donnell to send nomination back "to committee defeated 35-28.

Washington, May 7 (AP)—President Truman's appointment of Robert E. Hannegan as postmaster general was approved by a 60 to 2 Senate vote today after a debate over whether hearings should be held.

Senator Donnell (R., Mo.) sought to send the nomination back to the Postoffice committee with a view to getting hearings particularly on what he termed a "series of incidents" in Missouri during the present Democratic national chairman's political career there.

Republicans backed his motion solidly and were joined by Senator La Follette (Prog., Wis.) but it was lost 35 to 28 on a straight out party division.

Only Senator Taft (R., Ohio) went along with Donnell in voting against confirmation on the final tally.

Roll Call on Motion

Here is the vote by which the Senate refused today to send Hannegan's nomination back to committee:

For the motion—28.

Republicans for — Austin, Ball, Brewster, Buck, Burton, Butler, Capper, Gurden, Donnell, Ferguson, Gurney, Hart, Hawkes, Hickenlooper, Langer, Millikin, Moore, Morse, Reed, Revercomb, Shipstead, Smith, Taft, White, Wiles, Willis, Young—27.

Progressive for—La Follette 1.

Against the motion—35.

Democrats against — Bailey, Barkland, Bilbo, Briggs, Byrd, Chavez, Downey, Ellender, Green, Hatch, Hayden, Hill, Johnson (Colo.), Johnston (S.C.), Kilgore, Lucas, Maybank, McFarland, McKellar, McMahon, Mitchell, Murdock, Murray, O'Daniel, O'Mahoney, Overton, Radcliffe, Russell, Stewart, Taylor, Tunnell, Tydings, Wagner, Walsh, Wheeler 35.

Official Report Says Oswiecim Camp Worst Yet

One Killed, Five Wounded And Two Listed Missing In Latest Casualty Report For Area

A county youth has been killed in the fighting in Czechoslovakia, five have been wounded, all but one in Germany, and two are reported missing, according to word received by the next of kin.

They are:

KILLED IN ACTION:

Pvt. Charles M. Frey, son of Oliver D. Frey, Pleasureville.

WOUNDED IN ACTION:

S/Sgt. Clifton E. Dickmyer, son of Mr. and Mrs. Harry E. Dickmyer, tilen Rock R. D. 2.

Sgt. James Bortner, son of Mr. and Mrs. Howard Bortner, Glen Rock R. D. 1.

Cpl. Leroy Peters, son of Mr. and Mrs. Ivan Peters, 1619 Mt. Rose avenue.

Pvt. Edgar Rauhauser, son of Mr. and Mrs. C. M. Rauhauser, York R. D. 7.

Pvt. Francis T. Weaver, husband of Mrs. Betty A. Weaver, 200 East Main street, Dallastown, and son of Mrs. Cora Runkle, 237 South Pleasant avenue, Dallastown.

MISSING IN ACTION:

Second Lt. John Stewart Murphy, son of Mr. and Mrs. J. Calvin Murphy, Delta.

Cpl. James Tighe, son of Mr. and Mrs. James Tighe, 639 West Princess street.

SGT. JAMES BORTNER

Sgt. Bortner, was slightly wounded in Germany April 14, according to a War department telegram to his family recently. His parents later received a letter from Sgt. Bortner, dated April 29, which he printed with his left hand, saying he had received a scratch on the other hand. Sgt. Bortner was inducted into the army, March 28, 1942, received basic training at Ft. Meade, Md., Ft. Houston, Texas, and was stationed in Georgia before going overseas. Before induction, he was employed at the American Insulator plant, New Freedom.

PVT. CHARLES FREY

Pvt. Frey was killed in action in Czechoslovakia April 26 in Germany, his father learned recently. He had left the country for overseas duty March 19. He had been transferred into...

CPL. LEROY PETERS

Cpl. Peters was slightly wounded in combat April 18 in Germany, his parents learned recently. Cpl. Peters has been in active combat since D-Day last June and has been in service since June 23, 1942...

Ft. Meade, Md. Before his induction Aug. 2, 1944, he had been employed by the New York Wire Cloth company.

SECOND LT. JOHN S. MURPHY

Second Lt. Murphy was reported missing in action over Germany since April 10, according to word recently received from the War department by his parents. Mr. and Mrs. Murphy had received a letter from the pilot of the plane in which their son was a member of the crew, who stated that all members of his group had parachuted safely from the sinking ship. The pilot said that he had seen Lt. Murphy land safely. The pilot was taken prisoner, but later was released. Lt. Murphy received his training as a navigator at Coral Gables, Fla. Entering the service in April, 1943, he went overseas this past January. He was assigned to a B-17 Bomber crew in the Eighth Air Force. Before entering the service, he was a student at Penn State. He has a brother in the service, Seaman 1/c James William Murphy, now stationed at Shoemaker, Calif.

Cpl. Tighe has been missing in action over Hungary since February 19, according to a telegram received by his parents from the War department. Mas. 1 Cpl. Tighe, a gunner with the 15th Airforce in Italy, was inducted into the army Feb. 3, 1943, and received basic training at Camp Tyson with the balloon barrage battalion, but later transferred to the air force. He trained at Lowry Field, Colo. and Hollman Army Air Field. Because reversed for wings in Nevada. Sent over-seas last November, he was with...

Yanks Gain On Okinawa Front

Nimitz reports advances in all sectors of southern Okinawa front, lists 36,535 Japs killed thus far in land fighting on island.

Guam, Tuesday, May 8 (AP)—U. S. Tenth Army Yanks scored advances in all sectors of the southern Okinawa front yesterday, Fleet Admiral Chester W. Nimitz reported today in a communique listing 36,535 Japanese killed thus far in the Okinawa land fighting which began April 1.

American ground casualties have been given as 2,337 killed, 11,432 wounded and 514 missing.

Nimitz reported the 7th Infantry division, paced by flamethrowing tanks, scored gains in the center of the stubbornly-held Okinawa line, the First Marine division on the west flank reached Dakeshi village and the Seventh division drove ahead on the east flank to an undesignated point.

Fleet guns and aircraft gave close support, knocking out numerous blockhouses, pillboxes and other defensive structures.

Earlier, the reported silence of Japanese artillery indicated withdrawal of guns to new rear position.

A neutralizing attack on the Sakashima group of the southern Ryukyu islands, just northeast of Formosa, was carried out by U. S. carrier planes Sunday. No details were given as to damage inflicted.

Cargo Ships Sunk

Naval search bombers, again sweeping shipping lanes vital to Japan, struck in Korean waters yesterday at masthead level, sinking two good sized cargo ships and two others. In addition, two small freighters were set afire, two other freighters were damaged and a large cargo ship was seen to explode.

Three coastal cargo ships were sunk off Honshu, the main Nipponese homeland island.

The number of enemy artillery on Okinawa was reported as U. S. forces flew and elsewhere in the Pacific celebrated the surrender of Germany by fighting on against the foe in Asia.

Bomb Jap Shipping

The pressure on the Nippon mainland, whose major cities already have been heavily damaged by air raids, was increased by...

News about the missing, dead and wounded continued to filter back to York County, even as its residents observed V-E Day. Lt. John S. Murphy, one of the missing pictured here, later was listed among the dead. Earlier in the war, Yorkco's Shop News posed the question: 'How many boys from York Corporation won't come back? Nobody knows the exact number. Nobody. But — The number who do come back — on their own two feet instead of in a flag-draped box — will be in exact proportion to the job we do here at home. For every minute that we can help shorten the war will mean more lives saved.' In World War I, 213 Americans were killed on the final day and 1,114 were wounded. The answer to Shop News' question: 24 as of V-E Day and 25 on V-J Day.

---

for good conduct. A V-2 exploded 100 feet away, and no one broke rank.

Pfc. Charles E. Williams of York did not return home. He died in Italy less than two months before the end of fighting in Europe.

The infantryman entered the service in 1941 and went overseas in October 1944. He was one of six military brothers, sons of Henry H. and Geraldine Williams. Three joined Charles in the Army and two in the Navy.

An American Legion post in York is named after Charles Williams.

Lt. John S. Murphy, a B-17 navigator, from the Delta area flew bombing missions over Europe.

Less than a month before the war ended in Europe, Axis guns shot down his plane. The nine-member crew safely parachuted to the ground.

The Germans captured Murphy and three other crew members, and they were never heard from again.

Delta's VFW Post is named after Murphy.

• • •

Clergymen kept busy ministering to the many families of dead and wounded men.

The Rev. Lester Karschner stayed in contact with those in uniform. In a newsletter to servicemen, he kept track of their whereabouts.

One act of ministry brought particular gratification.

A young man in his congregation showed an interest in the Christian faith.

His father did not share his views, and the young man asked the Rev. Karschner to baptize him prior to serving in the military overseas.

The father became angry after learning about the baptism. But then the message arrived that his son was killed in action.

"It was then that the parents were most grateful," the pastor later wrote, "for their son having made his own personal decision."

• • •

Relieved York County residents learned from an article in The York Dispatch that a group of about 70 county GIs with the 94th Infantry Division in Europe were doing well.

They had survived together since basic training two years before, the article stated.

Harry McLaughlin, combat correspondent with the military newspaper Stars and Stripes, wrote that county soldiers held key jobs in the division. Many of the county men earned four battle stars.

• • •

Everyone welcomed headlines telling of Allied gains, but Ray Musser cautioned readers of York Corporation's Shop News that war has its costs.

Musser earned a Bronze Star for operating a transport boat crossing the Moselle River at Thionville, France. At one point, he was on the job moving troops and evacuating the wounded for 46 consecutive hours, consistently exposed to enemy fire.

"The Yanks are moving in; the Russians are capturing town after town; the Canadians cracked the Siegfried Line and the British are advancing. Joe, Jack, Bill, Tom and Alex are really making the Hun run. Sounds good, doesn't it?" Musser wrote.

These headlines, while attractive, were supported by suffering and heartaches.

"Joe didn't make it; Jack is on his way to a hospital and God only knows what happened to Alex," he wrote.

Even if but one Joe didn't make it, the price paid for a town or village was high.

"There is no glory in war," he wrote, "only sadness and heartache."

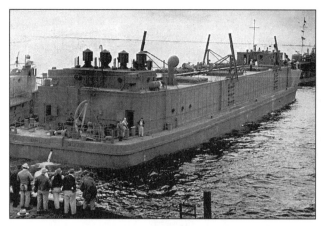

York Corporation equipped these all-concrete refrigeration or 'reefer' barges with cooling equipment late in World War II. The floating refrigerators supplied food for men and ice to treat the wounded.

Vice Admiral E.L. Cochrane congratulates York Corporation for the durability of a cooling unit aboard the 'U.S.S. Honolulu,' a cruiser damaged in fighting around the Philippines. The air-conditioning unit took a direct hit from an enemy torpedo but kept functioning.

• • •

Some soldiers returned, but with wounds that would affect them for the rest of their lives.

Cpl. Edgar Kohr was one of them.

In June, Kohr, a medical corpsman on Okinawa in the Pacific, emerged from a foxhole to aid wounded comrades. A mortar shell fell near his position, smashing his legs. A piece of shrapnel passed through his lung, barely missing his heart.

Kohr returned to the East Philadelphia Street home of his widowed mother, Elsie Kohr.

He had lost both legs, and the 30-year-old former roller skating instructor was awaiting artificial limbs to be fitted onto his two stumps.

The Rev. Homer C. Knox of Ridge Avenue Methodist Church and others were raising money to help pay off the mortgage on the Kohr house and set up the former medic in the photography business.

A benefit show featuring the color film "My Friend Flicka" was set for the York Theater to raise money for Cpl. Kohr.

• • •

Sgt. Curtis Sechrist, blinded during fighting in Patton's 3rd Army, was undergoing a series of operations to restore his facial features at Valley Forge General Hospital.

In Europe, the sergeant and another soldier were in a jeep advancing toward a German-held roadblock.

Sechrist stopped to give orders, and the Germans opened fire, catching him in the face.

The many communities back in York County were donating money to provide a home for the Railroad resident and his wife, Mary Dietz Sechrist.

A committee had raised about $7,500 early in the campaign, with the goal of purchasing and furnishing a home for the Silver Star recipient, providing a seeing-eye dog and establishing a trust fund for the upkeep of the home.

• • •

Quentin D. Grim, a former Yorkco lathe operator, was another soldier who was forced to adjust. He was part of a night raid on a German position when he stepped on a mine.

The explosion blew off his foot and knocked him unconscious. When he came to, he was disoriented but realized if he didn't start crawling, he would bleed to death.

About eight hours later, he learned he had moved in the right direction. He found friendly lines.

At war's end, he was recuperating in an Atlantic City, N.J., hospital.

"I will have to undergo another operation and then be fitted with another leg," he wrote his former co-workers. "Who knows, perhaps I can go deer hunting with you fellows next December." He hoped to attend school after getting "fixed up."

"After all," he wrote, "I don't want to be just a machine operator all my life."

• • •

Army doctors told Edward O. Kanneg to sit still if he wanted to live, after a medical discharge in 1943.

The former professional dancer had a hard time following those orders.

One day, his wife, Roseanne, observed that it was difficult to find a comfortable brassiere.

Kanneg used his experience making his own dancing costumes to fashion a brassiere his wife found acceptable.

She told her friends and co-workers about the good result. They placed orders. Then a store in North Carolina ordered a dozen. An order from Harrisburg sought two gross.

Soon, the Roseanne Manufacturing Co. was born and occupied a building to the rear of West Market Street.

Kanneg planned to give discharged servicewomen and disabled servicemen preference in hiring.

Wartime material shortages meant he had to refuse orders, but he declined to work the black market.

"I can't do it," he told The York Dispatch. He was overage when he went into the service, and he knew the risk to his health.

Instead of touting the cooling of air, this advertisement tells how York Corporation's equipment dries out the dank air of Pacific island jungles. Sensitive defense equipment operated best in dry conditions.

Charles Gangloff, formerly of York Corporation, displays a Japanese battle flag taken on Guadalcanal. After his involvement in extensive fighting on that island and Bougainville, he contracted malaria and returned stateside for treatment in New York. Charles' father, Lewis, was also a Yorkco employee.

"Now I'm out and my health is shot," he said, "but so far I've made a small success legitimately and I mean to go on that way."

• • •

The Manufacturers' Association pushed for local industries to hire disabled veterans who trickled back to York.

The Blaw-Knox-operated Naval Ordnance Plant, the former York Safe and Lock site, responded. It hired John S. Krout of York, who lost his right arm in the European Theater; James C. Lloyd of Wrightsville, who lost mobility in a leg after a wound from a Japanese sniper's bullet; and Henry S. Emig, Bair Station, recovering from detention as a German prisoner of war weighing half his normal 165 pounds.

Hiring a disabled veteran was no longer a "semi-charitable" act, Edwin A. Gentzler of the Manufacturers' Association, stated.

"It's a hard-headed business proposition," he said, "backed up by evidence that the man missing an arm or leg, provided his job is selected with careful regard for his abilities, not only equals the production of his fellow workers — in many cases he exceeds it."

'An extremely difficult problem'

In assessing the past year, York County District Attorney W. Burg Anstine expressed concern. Crime was down, but marital and non-support issues were on the rise.

"These figures, we believe, reveal the impact of the war upon the home life or our community," the district attorney wrote in his annual report, published early in 1945.

"It is our observation that this situation presents a major problem, which the churches and social agencies must cope with if we are to avoid future crime."

The war, indeed, shook up traditional family home life. Fathers were away at war. Mothers went into the work force. Children often were left alone.

Schools had to deal with increased truancy problems, and officials noted that the pupils' emotional outlook was upset.

Sometimes, speedy courtships took place so husbands could escape the draft or wives could avoid perceived spinsterhood.

Anstine's concern, in part, revolved around soldiers away at war failing to allocate part of their wages to their dependents at home.

At the same time, Anstine was busy following up on complaints from servicemen abroad about the immoral conduct of their wives back home.

"This type of complaint," he wrote, "presents an extremely difficult problem for law enforcement agencies, but we are calling such erring wives to our offices for interviews and warning."

• • •

Even before the war, York County officials had been

Anti-aircraft guns sit ready for shipment at the Naval Ordnance Plant in York. The Blaw-Knox-operated plant was credited with leadership in hiring disabled veterans. The plant participated fully in the York Plan, which drew applause from business and government leaders across America. 'In my opinion, the plan is one of the most constructive steps taken anywhere for winning the war of production,' Walter D. Fuller, chairman of the National Association of Manufacturers' said.

trying to head off public health issues spawned by vice.

Venereal disease outbreaks near military bases and defense plants presented problems on an international scale before and during the war. York County was well supplied with both.

As early as mid-1942, York County law enforcement authorities joined in a conference in Lancaster on the possibility of invoking federal control in authorizing vice patrols around local defense installations.

FBI and U.S. Public Health Department representatives attended to address the issue of commercialized vice and venereal disease.

In another conference on the topic, officials pointed out that venereal disease long had been a problem. One Pennsylvania study of 9,000 tests made on couples applying for marriage licenses in 1940 placed those with syphilis at 2.6 percent. And generally, two cases of gonorrhea could be found for every one case of syphilis.

County officials saw a crisis brewing with serious downstream effects: Among other things, venereal disease was causing absences in defense plants and military camps, thus hindering the war effort.

• • •

During these years, York had an active red light district.

One night in October 1941, more than 40 law enforcement officers raided 11 bawdy houses and nabbed three visitors. They were released on $10 bail.

Nine female and two male operators and five "inmates" — prostitutes — were held overnight in jail for physical examinations. Most houses raided were on the west side of South Howard Alley between College Avenue and Church Alley.

Police revealed the raid came after reports that two 12-year-old girls and a 15-year-old girl were schooled in sexual practices by prostitutes and left to wander the streets to solicit sex.

This led to the call for a trained city policewoman.

The ages of the girls played on Netta Ford's greatest fears. The Visiting Nurse Association official had attended a conference in Philadelphia that pointed to "glamour girls," 12 to 17 years in age, as a principal source of venereal disease infections.

The professional prostitutes were not the problem, she said. Additional women police officers and public health education could help.

• • •

Early in the war, York Mayor Harvey N. Werner called in the military police to aid in the fight against vice.

The police patrolled the West Princess Street area and several other districts known to be "hot spots."

Military police had broader authority to handle men in uniform on leave who might be lodged in places that local police power could not reach, the mayor explained.

Late in the war, military police were still in town, although their duties then included motorcycle patrols to enforce a 35-mile-per-hour speed limit for all government-owned vehicles.

• • •

In 1944, the district attorney, Army officials, York police and state health officials invited state-licensed taproom operators to meet with them at the courthouse.

Those assembled viewed a film about the spread of venereal diseases.

Anstine believed that bar owners left the meeting agreeing to conduct their businesses in accord with the wishes of law enforcement officials.

Meanwhile, the state Health Department developed new methods for handling persons suffering from social diseases.

Upon examination, those afflicted were dispatched to the Venereal Disease Hospital at Lancaster.

• • •

Reports in York's newspapers during the war did not help the confidence of military men.

In one report, two women from York — one 33 years old and the other 17 — were arrested in a raid of a Harrisburg bawdy house.

Both were wives of soldiers away on duty. The 33-

year-old was the mother of a 5-month-old baby.

Police described the house as the filthiest place they had ever seen.

The 28-year-old proprietor of the house was the mother of five children.

• • •

A Navy man came home one June evening in 1944 and found another man hiding in a closet in a bedroom of his West Philadelphia Street home.

Accompanied by city detective Ralph Keech, the seaman entered the house and heard a commotion in the bedroom. They found the man's wife and heard a noise in the closet. Upon inspection, they found an unclothed man holding his shirt and trousers in his hands.

Two children in the family were asleep in other bedrooms.

The wife was charged with adultery and the man with fornication. Both were jailed.

• • •

In a separate case, Keech accompanied a York woman back to her house after she complained that her husband had assaulted her. When the woman had entered the house, her husband had stabbed her in the back with a butcher knife and run away.

The woman later told law enforcement officials she had two husbands: the assailant and another man who was recuperating from war wounds in a California hospital.

She was forced to marry the York man, she claimed, after he threatened to kill her unless the wedding took place.

• • •

Sometimes, military men cheated with the wives of other military men.

A West Manchester man returned home from the Navy to catch his wife and a Yoe man, also home from the Navy, in a "clandestine episode," according to a newspaper.

The woman was charged with adultery, and the Yoe man was accused of fornication. The day after they waived a hearing, the husband served his wife, mother of their two children, with divorce papers.

The waiver meant that "no airing of dirty linen" occurred in court, the newspaper stated.

• • •

War conditions sometimes prompted unusual family situations. A 19-year-old defense worker met a York Springs, Adams County, man while working at the Naval Supply Depot at Mechanicsburg.

York Springs was nearer the depot than Bendersville, the young man's home, and he stayed there.

The young man met his host's attractive daughter and fell in love. A year later, the two were married.

She was 12 years old.

"I want to keep house," the new bride said, "and do everything that a wife should do."

"As long as they are in love," the girl's mother said, "it's all right with me."

• • •

The war made county police work even more difficult. The city's location on the Pennsylvania Railroad

This poster, published late in the war, urges vacationing at home to conserve. The circulating room fan, iced beverage, slippered feet and dog suggest the pleasures of such a vacation, and the picture of the family member in uniform suggests that such measures aid servicemen overseas. The York YMCA's Camp Minqua, located on the Susquehanna River in southeastern York County, offered summer family vacation camp opportunities to save on gasoline and wear and tear on tires.

ensured a constant supply of people — particularly servicemen — passing through.

And the newspapers were full of arrests for rationing and black market infractions.

Police dealt with issues that they would have considered unlikely before the war.

Military officials, for example, warned girls not to wear shoulder patches, buttons or any other distinctive parts of servicemen's uniforms. Further, storeowners who sold such items could be fined or imprisoned, the military stated.

Girls would snip off servicemen's uniform buttons — a widespread practice in York and elsewhere.

In 1944, police arrested a WAC corporal in her Rossville home on absent without leave charges. The married woman reportedly stated that her unit canceled her leave two days after she arrived home, but she stayed in Rossville anyway.

Local police turned her over to military officials in Harrisburg. This was the first time local law enforcement officers dealt with a WAC member who had gone over the hill.

County Sheriff Earl L. Wolf detained two Brooklyn salesmen for trying to persuade a York department store into carrying a line of women's rubber girdles.

At first, Office of Price Administration officials

Vol. 116 No. 18809 York, Pa., Wednesday Morning, August 15, 1945—Forty Pages Price 3c—15c a Week

JAP SURRENDER ENDS WAR

President Announces Full Jap Acceptance Of Allied Terms. V-J Day Awaits Proclamation

EDITORIAL

PEACE — MAY IT NEVER END

The war has ended. At long last the firing of arms has ceased or will soon cease everywhere throughout the world. Peace is again with us. May we all breathe a fervent prayer that it will be an everlasting, eternal one.

This war has been bad enough. What another one would be can only challenge one's wildest imagination. The airplane, the atomic bomb, the advancements that science will make in them as well as in other engines of death, make it imperative, absolutely imperative, that never again shall war show its ugly, distorted face amongst us.

The thing that really matters now is, can we win the peace? Our genius and our brains and our research and our ability to cooperate, man with man and people with people, and our spirit and our determination to protect and preserve our freedom and independence enabled us to achieve the victory over those who would have enslaved us. And achieve it in a comparatively short time considering how little prepared for it, we, a peace-loving people, were when it came to us.

That we can win the peace as well as the war there can be no doubt, provided that we put the same effort into it and display the same ability to cooperate with each other and with our good neighbors, the people of our allies, and with the other people of the world.

After the last war we were so happy to be out of it all that we forgot the future. We thought in our silly, foolish way that we could have the peace by appeasing those who were conspiring against us and against all free people everywhere.

It is inconceivable that we should not have learned our lesson and that we will not be parties to the setting up of a world-wide organizaion which eventually will be a super government in fact as well as in name, and which will keep and maintain the peace.

Peace, we should know full well this happy day, is the most precious thing on earth. To secure it we have paid a high price in human life and in limb and in wealth. Far too high a price to ever have to be paid again. The boys who will not come home are the ones who deserve our most sincere thanks and to whom we owe our greatest gratitude and our highest duty. For they gave their all, their very selves, life itself.

We dare not fail these boys murdered on the altar of man's failure to settle his quarrels without the use of force and instruments of death. We have got to tear down that altar, down to the ground and obliterate it from the face of the earth, and in its place erect a temple of peace, where love and justice, right and mercy shall reign supreme, and which shall never have its columns stained by warfare's bloody spray.

Peace is indivisible. It must be world wide. It must be continuous and unbroken. Men like those of the United Nations who can wage war so energetically and so ultra efficiently against the much militarized and best prepared for war and ruthless foes as we have overcome in Germany and Japan can do anything if they so will. They can have peace, of course they can. All they need do is want it enough.

What a wonderful word, peace. What a lovely thing after all these years. May we never forget how sweet and how good a thing it is and with what sincere and heart felt and happy enthusiasm we received it.

Britain, China, Russia O. K. Terms By Telephone

Washington, Aug. 14 (AP)—Britain, Russia and China today agreed with the United States to accept Japan's surrender note—without even seeing it.

The agreement was worked out verbally by Secretary of State Byrnes in a worldwide telephone call which he made from the Pentagon building late this afternoon. He talked with officials in London, Moscow and Chungking, told them of a report on the enemy message which he had received by telephone from American Minister, Leland Harrison in Bern, Switzerland.

He assured them that he considered the note a complete acceptance of the Potsdam ultimatum for unconditional surrender, and they agreed.

This dramatic incident in a historic day was revealed tonight by an assistant to Byrnes, Walter Brown, who told the inside story of the day-long activities by which the secretary handled details of the surrender agreement.

Proclaims Aug. 15, 16 Legal Holidays

Washington, Aug. 14 (AP)—President Truman tonight proclaimed August 15 and 16 as legal holidays with the notation that war workers who work on those days would be paid overtime.

Gen. MacArthur has been named Allied Supreme Commander to accept the Japanese surrender.

Local Comments On End Of War

Yorkers reacted in numerous ways when asked by roving reporters for comments on the "big news." Their statements follow:

"It's the greatest day to be alive!" Miss Catherine Devers, 25 North Queen street, sister of York's General Jacob L. Devers, exclaimed. She added, however, "I wish I could think of something comforting to say to those who have boys who lost their lives." The General, she believed was in Washington.

Sitting in their car parked on George street, a group of Los Angeles servicemen, when asked their opinion by a reporter, shouted, "We're very happy and we're going home right now."

Wallpaper workers, called from a union meeting by the surrender news, said, "We're very, very hap-

(Continued on Page Thirty-Eight)
See Local Interviews

President Orders Japan Stop War On All Fronts

Washington, Aug. 14 (AP)—President Truman tonight dispatched through Secretary of State Byrnes an order for the Japanese government to stop the war on all fronts.

The dispatch was sent through the Swiss government, being turned over to the Swiss legation here a few minutes after 7 o'clock.

The President ordered:

1. That the Japanese government "direct prompt cessation of hostilities by Japanese forces." General Douglas MacArthur, as supreme Allied commander must be informed by the Japanese of the effective date and hour for hostilities to cease.

2. That the Japanese government send emissaries immediately to MacArthur with information on the Japanese forces and with full power to make arrangements as MacArthur directs for the formal enemy surrender.

3. That the Japanese government stand ready to receive from MacArthur information on "the time, place and other details of the formal surrender."

Allied Offensives Ordered Stopped. MacArthur Named To Receive Jap Surrender

Washington, Aug. 14 (AP)—President Truman announced at 7:00 P. M. EWT tonight Japanese acceptance of surrender terms.

They will be accepted by General Douglas MacArthur when arrangements can be completed.

Mr. Truman read the formal message relayed from Emperor Hirohito through the Swiss Government in which the Japanese ruler pledged the surrender on the terms laid down by the Big Three conference at Potsdam.

President Truman made this statement:

"I have received this afternoon a message from the Japanese Government in reply to the message forwarded to that Government by the Secretary of State on August 11.

"I deem this reply a full acceptance of the Potsdam Declaration which specifices the unconditional surrender of Japan. In this reply there is no qualification.

"Arrangements are now being made for the formal signing of surrender terms at the earliest possible moment.

"General Douglas MacArthur has been appointed the Supreme Allied Commander to receive the Japanese surrender.

"Great Britain, Russia and China will be represented by high ranking officers.

"Meantime, the Allied armed forces have been ordered to suspend offensive action.

"The proclamation of V-J Day must wait upon the formal signing of the surrender terms by Japan."

Simultaneously Mr. Truman disclosed that Selective Service is taking immediate steps to slash inductions from 80,000 to 50,000 a month.

Henceforth, Mr. Truman said, only men under 26 will be drafted for the reduced quotas.

The White House made public the Japanese government's message of acceptance that ended the war which started December 7, 1941.

The text of their message which was delivered by the Swiss charge d' affaires follows:

"Communication of the Japanese government of August 14, 1945, addressed to the governments of the United States, Great Britain, the Soviet Union, and China:

"With reference to the Japanese Government's note of August 10 regarding their acceptance of the provisions of the Potsdam declaration and the reply of the governments of the United States, Great Britain, the Soviet Union and China sent by American Secretary of State Byrnes under the date of August 11, the Japanese Government have the honor to communicate to the Governments of the four powers as follows:

"1. His Majesty the Emperor has issued an Imperial rescript regarding Japan's acceptance of the provisions of the Potsdam Declaration.

"2. His Majesty the Emperor is prepared to authorize and insure the signature by his Government and the Imperial General headquarters of necessary terms for carrying out the provisions of the Potsdam Declaration. His Majesty is also prepared to issue his commands to all the military, naval, and air authorities of Japan and all the forces under their control wherever located to cease active operations, to surrender arms, and to issue such other orders as may be required by the Supreme Commander of the Allied Forces for the execution of the above mentioned terms."

The President made the historic announcement to a huge crowd of reporters who had been virtually living in the White House for days in anticipation of just such a development.

Smiling and surrounded by his staff, the President told the press that the Japanese had decided to accept unconditional surrender and mentioned that the reporters would not have to take any notes.

Mr. Truman said prepared statements would be available

(Continued on Page Forty)
See Jap War Ends

The Gazette and Daily's front page on Aug. 15, 1945 tells about the end of World War II — V-J Day. The only step remaining was for Gen. Douglas MacArthur to formally accept Japan's surrender. That would take place on Sept. 2. V-J Day represented a memorable moment for those who persevered on the battle and home fronts during the 44-month war. It marked the culmination of dedicated efforts to aid the military, as was the case of 11 York County men who gathered the day after Pearl Harbor and vowed in memory of those who died at the base in Hawaii: 'That we would give unceasingly of our time and our efforts to promote the speedy downfall of those who think Democracy the wrong way of life.' The men also vowed to ensure proper authorities were aware of those at home who threatened the Allied effort. 'We also promise to those in our midst who with subversive talk and smug complacency seek to unmine the morale of our glorious nation speedy retribution … .' C.C. Christensen, Norman Spangler, B.D. Baker, Percy Horn, Mervin McIntyre, Charles Miller, Clair Wentz, John Albright, Charles Bowers, Frank Mann and Harry Boltzle signed the pledge.

thought the salesmen were unloading merchandise obtained through the black market.

When the products were found to be legitimate, the O.P.A. questioned the salesmen about whether their company had ever obtained a maximum price that the girdles could be sold under wartime price controls.

Police and the public always were on the lookout for those breaking military rules.

A Spring Grove-area man was the target of one search. The FBI made the arrest of the man and charged him with violating the Selective Service Act.

The man was listed as a conscientious objector but failed to report for transportation to a camp for those declining to bear arms. Labor camps sprang up during the war for conscientious objectors in lieu of military service.

Authorities hauled the man before a York-based federal commissioner, Horace G. Ports, who demanded a $2,500 bond for his next court appearance. The man couldn't make the bond, and he ended up in jail.

In another case, state police asked local authorities to look out for four American military prisoners who stole a truck and were on the loose.

The escapees were dressed in blue denim fatigue outfits with "P" on the back of their coats.

'We must guard its secret wisely'

The U.S.S. Indianapolis dropped off components of an atomic bomb targeted for Hiroshima on July 26 at Tinian Island in the Pacific.

The heavy cruiser was heading toward Guam when a Japanese submarine targeted it. Two torpedoes struck the ship on July 30, and it went down in 12 minutes.

The ship carried a crew of about 1,200 including Yeoman 3rd Class Jack T. Yeaple of York.

The Navy did not immediately discover that the ship was missing, and survivors faced exposure and sharks for four days before their rescue. About 320 seamen survived.

The Gazette and Daily, York, Pa., Wednesday Morning, August 15, 1945

May Need Over 1,000,000 Yanks To Occupy Japan

Task of policing Japan until she can be trusted as peaceful nation expected to keep many soldiers busy for a long time. Russia may occupy Manchuria and Korea.

Washington, Aug. 10 (AP) More than a million Americans may be required for the immediate occupation of Japan once the Japanese surrender is final.

High government officials said today United States forces unquestionably will have to move in first to disarm and police the Japanese home islands. Russian troops probably will take over in Manchuria, Korea and the island of Sakhalin, which they have shared with the Japanese.

The Potsdam surrender ultimatum of July 26 said key points in Japan would be held until its warmaking power is destroyed and the terms of the U. S.-British-Chinese 1943 Cairo declaration for the dismemberment of the empire are carried out.

Because they are closest to the main islands, troops under General Douglas MacArthur, with some Marine and Naval detachments, are expected to make up the original occupation force.

If present plans are followed these troops probably will occupy seven of Japan's principal cities, maintaining only nominal control over the rural areas.

The formal arrangements for the more permanent control of Japan still are a Big Three secret, but the speculation here is that individual Japanese islands may be assigned later for occupation by the United States, Great Britain, China and Russia.

If Emperor Hirohito is allowed to stay, the expectation is the Allies would merely step into the place which has been occupied by Japanese army leaders in recent years, laying their orders before the Emperor for his automatic signature.

In such event the form of sovereignty exercised by the Emperor would be followed with the Allies actually ruling Japan just as they rule Germany. This same could be used to carry out the objectives laid down in the Potsdam surrender ultimatum which the Japanese say they are willing to accept.

Ultimatum Program

These terms were in an 8-point program, summarized as follows:

1. Elimination for all time of the authority and influence "of those who have deceived and misled the people of Japan into embarking on world conquests."

2. Occupation of key points in Japanese territory until a new order of peace, security and justice is established.

3. Limitation under the Cairo declaration of Japanese sovereignty to the island of Honshu, Hokkaido, Kyushu, Shikoku and such minor islands as the victors later designate.

4. Complete disarmament of Japanese military forces and their return to their homes.

5. Removal by the Japanese government of all obstacles to the strengthening of democratic tendencies among its people, including freedom of speech, religion, thought and respect for human rights. War criminals are to be dealt stern justice but the Jap-

York Gives News Of End Of War A Riotous Welcome

Surging, swirling crowd in autos and on foot throngs downtown streets. Impromptu parades staged.

"Banzere!?"

With a great sigh of relief tension broke across the city of York seconds after official word of Jap surrender was broadcast at 7 p.m. this afternoon.

There was a moment when people looked stunned, incredulous, then jubilant at the person across the dinner table, at the man beside them on the bus. Then the noise began.

It started with a single auto horn screaming madly across Con-

girl who jumped first on one running board, then on another. A little boy grabbed the bellcord hanging from the Victory House in Continental Square and rang the miniature Liberty bell until the rope broke. Then he climbed on the roof and rang it some more.

Overhead planes from local airports did happy flipflops against the sunset sky. A baby rode downtown in her bunting-draped walker, with a tiny flag clutched tightly in a fat fist. Flags of the United Nations were marched across the packed square, preceded by drums and carried by veterans of two World Wars.

The service of thanksgiving for the end of the war at St. John's Evangelical Lutheran church, 140 West King street, Rev Edward Kraus, pastor, will begin at 4:15 this afternoon.

Stores, taprooms, offices closed instantly. Immediate closing of state liquor stores was ordered, but by 8 p.m. the one on South George street, near King, was still jammed, and there was some drinking on the street.

Dr. David Dunn, professor of

ginning. Today and tomorrow are legal holidays, and there's still plenty of celebrating to do.

But they will be sad and solemn days for the hundreds of York county families whose young men are in spirit by more than three and a half years' of terrible warfare.

Those men will be remembered in the solemn services of penitence and gratitude today in churches of all faiths in the city and county. Bells will ring at 3:45 o'clock this afternoon, and rival leaders expect thousands to gather to thank the Divine Providence when the services begin at 4:15 p. m.

The York County Ministerial association announced its plans for the half hour services several days ago through its president, Rev. D. Perry Burke, who asks that wherever possible the services be held in the county many individual churches and communities had already publicized their plans for afternoon services.

It will be the first holiday in

Russians Drove 93 Miles Before End Yesterday

Armored troops swept unchecked across western Manchuria. Moscow announced capture of Korean port of Seishin, invasion of South Sakhalin.

London, Aug. 14 (AP)—Russian armored forces burst 93 miles unchecked across western Manchuria today, the Soviet high command announced tonight, wrecking key Japanese communications and threatening to split 1,500,000 Japanese troops on the Asiatic mainland.

There was no let-up in the fury of the Russian punch in Manchuria. The Red Army, with lightning-like blows, was tearing up Japanese lines at points along a vast 2,300-mile front heedless of peace talk. The Kharbarovsk radio exhorted Red Army men to increase their attacks and mercilessly "break the enemy's resistance."

Moscow announced a seaborne invasion of Korea. Russian naval forces and Marines captured the Japanese port of Seishin, the Soviet communique said.

Moscow also said 8,000 Japanese prisoners had been captured in the five first days of the Russo-Japanese war which began Aug. 9.

The Russians also announced they had invaded Karafuto, Japanese-owned southern half of Sakhalin island which lies only 26 miles north of the Japanese homeland. Besides landings on the west coast, they signaled aims to 12's miles away frontier defenses, Moscow declared.

The Soviets rushed toward Harbin from the west and the east. On the east, they captured the key rail junction of Mutanking, after forcing the Mutankiang river and capturing four other towns. Thus Mutanking, which carried the Soviets to a point 165 miles east of Harbin, was made by Marshal Kerill A. Meretskov's First Far Eastern Army.

On the west, the mighty Trans-Baikal Army severed the vital 500-mile-long railroad linking Harbin with extreme northern Manchuria by capturing the key rail town of Taonan, 185 miles west of the war production city of Harbin. Taonan was taken in a 60-mile advance.

Gaining speed as they hit flat country after breaking across the great Khingan mountain range, the Russians advanced up to 93 miles on a 160-mile front in southwestern Manchuria and, among other towns, captured Linsi in the former Chinese province of Jehol.

Linsi, 265 miles northwest of the ancient Chinese capital of Peiping, is 240 miles from the Yellow Sea and the Russian advance was part of a general offensive toward the coast that would isolate enemy forces in China.

---

plant; Samuel Sweeney, Roosevelt plant; Edison Ludwig, Poplar street plant; Miriam Grove, Roosevelt Oil Service; Bruce Rost, Pennsylvania avenue plant; Ray Gerberick, Valencia office, and Jacob March, Jr., Grantley Bulk plant.

SCENE AS YORKERS CELEBRATE VICTORY—Beaming spectators surround a bewhiskered veteran of the German campaign as he kisses his wife in Continental Square a short while after peace became official. The soldier is Cpl. Sam Epler, who has just one more day of his redeployment leave; his wife is Mrs. Betty Epler, of 115 Prospect street. They didn't seem to mind in the least that five hundred people were watching.

— Photo by The Gazette and Daily

Sam and Betty Epler embrace in York's Continental Square on V-J Day. 'They didn't seem to mind in the least that five hundred people were watching,' the caption states. The celebration marked the beginning of a return to a way of life for some that Flo Snyder, a York Corporation employee, wished for in a 1943 poem published in Shop News:

'When this is over
I want to see
Dresses on women
At the knee.
Instead of slacks
And grimy hands
High-heeled shoes
And wedding bands.
Feminine hair do's
And feminine talk
Feminine ideas
And feminine walk.
Housewives and mothers
At home again,
With the "bread and butter"
Up to the men.
Sugar and gas,
And ration cards gone.
Plenty of canned goods
For brides to start on.
Peace world-wide,
And on the Capitol dome.
Won't it be grand
When our boys come home.'

Yeaple, 22-year-old son of Mr. and Mrs. George T. Yeaple, was not among that group, one of the last York County casualties of the war.

• • •

Lt. John W. Emig, formerly of Shiloh, came back after 33 days of bobbing in the Pacific Ocean or drifting in a lifeboat.

Emig and three others survived after their Liberator bomber went down near the Philippines.

They drifted 400 miles, living on fish and birds captured with their bare hands. Their only water came from rainstorms.

During their ordeal, they spotted at least four enemy submarines and countless Japanese planes.

Finally, they struck a reef and waded ashore, sustaining cuts on the sharp coral.

The airman was reported missing on Nov. 1, 1944, and his wife, Margaret Zimmerman Emig, and family learned that he was alive two months later.

The Army had told the family he was probably a prisoner of war.

• • •

Soon after the atomic bombs devastated Hiroshima and Nagasaki, York County residents learned about the involvement of five local companies in the Manhattan Project.

Companies involved represented a who's who of county industry: York Corporation, Read Machinery Co., York Safe and Lock Co., New York Wire Cloth Co. and S. Morgan Smith Co.

Yorkco workers later learned that they had fulfilled a $1.5 million refrigeration contract. The contract was listed under "Manhattan Engineering District," a deceptive name that shrouded the eventual use of the refrigeration equipment.

One of Yorkco's pre-war engineers served as a member of a special engineering detachment in Oak Ridge, Tenn. William H. Shank assisted in research work on Uranium 235's separating processes.

• • •

In one of the local plants working on the Manhattan Project, FBI agents were regularly on duty.

Each evening, they locked blueprints in a vault.

Employees were sworn to secrecy, although they did not know exactly what they were working on. Even manufacturers, often subcontractors for Delaware's DuPont Co., lacked a clear understanding.

York Celebrates Victory

Yorkers literally went mad with joy following the announcement of the acceptance of surrender terms by Japan last night, signifying the end of the war.

Swirling mobs in automobiles and on foot ran rampant around the city, with an ear-deafening accompaniment of horns and yells of "The War's Over," "The War's Over."

The din made by crowds all but stifled the sounding of the church and fire bells and factory whistles.

Strangers were seen to turn from one person to another, kissing at random in the final joy that the war was at end at long last.

Long lines of snake dances formed and pranced over the downtown streets.

This short story from a special four-page V-J edition published by The Gazette and Daily summarizes the Aug. 14 celebration.

WE SALUTE

THE WOMEN
WHO MADE THIS DAY POSSIBLE

V-J DAY
August 14, 1945

In this York newspaper advertisement published on Aug. 15, The Chic, 33 W. Market St., observes women's contributions in winning World War II.

Japan had not yet surrendered, and the War Department clamped down on the specific part county industries played in the project.

Stories from defense plants elsewhere had already revealed too much about work that went on there.

• • •

Lt. Paul Hyde reviewed the receiving end of the Nagasaki bomb.

Hyde, navigator on a Coast Guard-manned landing craft, was greeted with a stench as his craft moored in Nagasaki's harbor. The smell, the type that would make people lose their appetite, came from the scene of the bombing, four miles away.

He observed the point of impact, a field of devastation. A series of brick smokestacks stood among the ruins.

It was not difficult to understand, he wrote, why no humans came out of those ruins alive.

The bomb's impact opened his eyes about its power.

"We must guard its secret wisely," he wrote his parents, Mr. and Mrs. Paul Hyde of York, "and make a real effort toward world peace everlasting."

• • •

Yorkco's Shop News published a list of fighting vessels in the Pacific Theater with the suggestion that some would be headed toward Tokyo Bay.

The publication pointed out that all of the ships were equipped with Yorkco refrigeration and cooling equipment.

Aircraft carriers Enterprise, Essex, and Independence and battleships Iowa, Alabama, and Massachusetts were among the York-equipped marquee ships that were ready for action.

"You can clip the list and paste it inside your old straw hat or the lid of your toolbox," Shop News stated, "and use it to follow these York equipped fighting vessels as they move in against the Island of Japan."

'It is a wonderful thing'

Someone observed that the quietest place in town was the city police station.

News of Japan's informal surrender reached York County at 7 p.m., Tuesday, Aug. 14, touching off celebrations unlike any since the end of World War I.

As soon as the radio news signed off, York-area residents rushed toward Continental Square.

Whistles blew. Auto horns blared. Church and fire bells

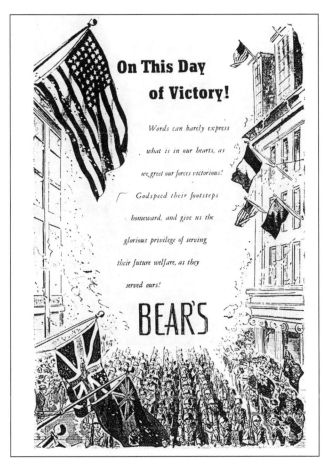

On This Day of Victory!

Words can barely express

what is in our hearts, as

we greet our forces victorious!

Godspeed their footsteps

homeward, and give us the

glorious privilege of serving

their future welfare, as they

served ours!

BEAR'S

V-J Day meant that Americans could celebrate without reservation. Bear's department store's advertisement forecast the many celebrations that would come as American troops came home.

rang out. A boy grabbed the Victory House bell cord and pulled it until it broke. He climbed on the roof of the miniature courthouse and rang it some more.

Celebrators even took to the air.

"Overhead planes from local airports did happy flipflops against the sunset sky," The Gazette and Daily reported.

Police rushed to block off traffic from entering the square. Too late.

Confetti, paper streamers and torn paper clouded the air.

Blaring bands waded through the crowds, past the Ritz Theater movie marquee touting the current feature, "Conflict."

A York-Shipley Inc. truck carried a military-type generator designed to lay down a smoke screen. Occasionally, the truck stopped and belched smoke. At the end of the evening, a haze covered the downtown.

Children and youth grabbed their mothers' pots and pans and utensils to add to the noise. They particularly surrounded servicemen, serenading them with their noise-makers.

The merrymakers came in all ages.

"A baby rode downtown in her bunting-draped walker with a tiny flag clutched tightly in a fat fist," The Gazette and Daily stated.

On the York County Courthouse lawn, youngsters tore apart a big poster stating, "The Jap's in the Fight — are You?"

"Scrap Paper Drive"
BY
York Post No. 5, Society of 28th Division, A.E.F.
Regular Scrap Drive—Zone 2.
WEDNESDAY NIGHT
☞ STARTING AT 6 P. M.
In case of Rain, Collection will be made Friday Night.
"Save Your Scrap and Lick the Jap"

This undated advertisement alerted York County residents of an upcoming scrap paper collection effort. Scrap paper could be recycled into a variety of paper products. Volunteers were conducting such a drive in York when victory was declared on Aug. 14, 1945. The collectors had a field day — or field night — cleaning up confetti.

Across the bottom of the billboard, someone had written, "We Did It Again."

The official ceremony came at 10 p.m. when an American Legion color guard, bugler and firing squad stood before the tablets bearing the names of the World War I dead on the courthouse facade.

The bugler sounded "Taps," and the flag bearers dipped their banners.

The only disappointment that night came when the city's park director locked the comfort stations, located beneath the square, so attendants could celebrate. Most restaurants and taprooms were closed as well, leaving thousands discommoded.

Mayor Snyder's criticism of that decision sparked verbal brickbats at the next city council meeting.

• • •

The mayor instructed police to let the celebration take its course.

Excitement overtook decorum.

An exuberant girl was seen kissing two soldiers riding in a classic car around the square.

She jumped first on one running board and then the other.

"The kids had a swell time," The York Dispatch reported. "The boys were kissing the girls and the girls were kissing back and no one, even the adults ruled out of the game by age or matrimony or both, seemed to object."

• • •

The Gazette and Daily garnered a variety of reactions from those strolling the downtown that night.

Ida M. Malone, a teacher at William Penn High School, pondered what would happen after the reality of peace settled in.

"I wonder what forty million people are going to do when we go out of the murder business?" she asked. "The temperature of the crowd amazes me — I never thought York would go up this way."

Servicemen, spouses and volunteers pose at York's USO in June 1945. Clara E. Wright, standing, fourth from left, and her husband, Porter Wright, sitting, fourth from left, are identified in this scene, at the Pennsylvania Dutch Canteen on the York County Academy's North Beaver Street campus. On the wall, right, a drawing is posted of the placement of the flag on Mount Suribachi on Iwo Jima in February 1945. George Bixler, a Marine sergeant, observed the flag after it was raised. '(I)t was like a ballgame, everyone hollering all over the place. I could just see that baby waving,' Bixler, a Hanover resident, said years later. In 36 days of fighting on the Pacific Island, 6,800 Allied fighting men died, and 19,000 were wounded.

She worried about all the automobiles moving around town.

"Gas rationing isn't over yet," she noted.

Martin Rhinehart, a World War I veteran and York Corporation worker, was happy about the war's end. He said he would not comment but then remarked, "I said too much in the other war."

He added, "It is a wonderful thing."

A wounded veteran, foot in a cast, believed a sober celebration made more sense.

"I am glad the war is over," he said, "but after serving three and one-half years overseas and seeing my buddies die one by one, I am sorry to see the home folks celebrating the way they are. I can't help but think of those who have lost loved ones in the conflict."

But another veteran, wearing a Purple Heart, had a different reaction: "I am so tickled I could squeeze everybody."

The wife of a drugstore owner, waiting for her spouse to return to the store, stated: "I wish my husband would come back. It doesn't look right, having the store open now."

Ruth Miller, whose husband was home on furlough, couldn't understand the raucous celebration.

"I don't see why people have to carry on like this," she said. "It's over and we're really glad — why make a fuss?"

Mrs. William Schreiver, discharged from the WAVEs, summed up the feelings of many.

"I'm just glad no one else will get killed," she said, "and that all the boys can come home."

• • •

At first, celebrators weren't sure whether to throw confetti to the wind.

Scrap paper was still valuable, but an hour after news broke about the surrender, paper trickled down from York's tallest buildings.

Soon, it littered the streets.

Mayor Snyder said that night's scheduled scrap paper drive would go on as planned in southeast York, but it would possibly be extended to capture debris then being tossed in the streets.

• • •

Communities throughout York County staged similar celebrations.

In Spring Grove, everything stopped. The paper mill shut down. Wednesday afternoon, stores closed. No sandwiches could be purchased. No cigars. Liquor sales were banned throughout the state. Bus service halted.

But church services at St. Paul's Lutheran went on.

And each community added its own twist to the celebration.

Some in Spring Grove took out their guns and aimed at the sky.

"There was more shooting on Tuesday night than on any Fourth of July since the government had banned the sale of fireworks," one observer wrote years later.

A group broke into the Spring Grove High School building after midnight and pulled the bell rope so hard

Pfc. Charles E. Williams died in Italy less than two months before the German surrender. He was one of six military brothers to serve.

and often that the bell turned over and the rope snapped away from the bell.

• • •

The York community observed the Allied victory with an interfaith religious service at the York Fairgrounds the Sunday after V-J Day.

The Rev. D. Perry Bucke presented the keynote address to 7,000 people.

He read an address originally presented by Marine Chaplain Roland B. Gittelsohn at the dedication of the American cemetery at Iwo Jima. In that cemetery, two county residents were known to be interred.

The address consecrated the "officers and men, Negroes and whites, rich men and poor" who lie together in "the highest and purest democracy," and dedicated the living "to the right of Protestants, Catholics and Jews, of white men and Negroes alike, to enjoy the democracy for which all of them have here paid the price."

William H. Eckenrode read a poem, written by Joseph Auslander, as a tribute to the four chaplains who gave their lives on the Dorchester in 1943. It was dedicated to "all in our armed services in York and York County who have made the supreme sacrifice."

Many in the audience that day had known Lt. Alexander D. Goode, one who made the sacrifice.

• • •

York County residents absorbed other news coming out after the celebration.

The federal government estimated that 7 million men would be discharged from the military in the months ahead. In fact, local newspapers regularly ran passenger lists of servicemen returning from overseas.

At the same time, the loved ones of hundreds of York County families were buried beneath white crosses in military cemeteries in faraway lands.

The York Dispatch/Associated Press count established the county death toll at war's end at 433.

A few days after V-J Day, that number became outdated.

The Navy notified Mr. and Mrs. Admiral Irwin, parents of Vernon Leroy Irwin, that their son was killed in action in June.

He was the victim of a kamikaze attack on the carrier U.S.S. Curtis, off Okinawa, in June.

'When Your Man Comes Home'

That fall, York's USO welcomed the 100,000th man or woman in uniform to use its services. Cletus Ruby of East Prospect received a special certificate to recognize this milestone.

This was part of the USO's new role to aid the military in the demobilization, redeployment and training of returning veterans.

The organization distributed pamphlets to hostesses, wives, husbands, sweethearts, sisters, friends and mothers to help them prepare for the return of military men and women.

The titles of the pamphlets provided a glimpse of the post-war issues people were being prepared for: "Welcoming the Wounded?" "Nervousness in the Returned Serviceman?" "Understanding People in Wartime," "Make the War Strengthen Your Marriage" and "When Your Man Comes Home."

• • •

The war's end meant temporary closure for many county plants that had primarily handled defense work for the past four or more years.

They loaded in new materials, retooled and prepared for production during peacetime.

"This is the first enforced idle period for many persons in many years," Red Lion Echoes stated.

County plants closed down for Labor Day, the first time in four years.

On V-J Day, the Navy canceled nearly $6 billion in defense contracts. The Navy's post-war projections called for the production stepdown.

This also meant a respite for the New Cumberland Army Services Depot in northern York County.

In some cases, York industries shipped the fruits of their war work only a short distance to this distributor of food, ammunition for rifles, Tommy guns and large caliber machine guns.

Employment at New Cumberland topped 1,400 late in the war as men and women worked to make sure fighting men had all the equipment they needed.

• • •

Not everyone sought time off, however.

Many women preferred to stay on the job. A Department of Labor survey in 1944 found that 80 percent of the women in the work force wanted to stay there. When the war ended, many returned to domestic life.

A Manufacturers' Association survey of company post-war projections as of June 1 showed that York Safe and Lock expected to reduce its force from 1,700 to 400.

Practically all those laid off would be women.

The York-Hoover Body Co. plant employed 306 people and expected to lay off its entire female force of about 75.

"These employees will be replaced by men and the force should be increased to around 350 as soon as they can get the materials to make their peace time products," the report stated.

The report placed York Corporation's employment at 3,492, including 693 women. Projections called for an

IF YOU ASK ME - WILL WOMEN STAY IN THE SHOPS WHEN THE WAR IS OVER? - I WOULD SAY

GLORIA SHARP	HILDA BAHN	ARLENE KRAMER	MARY LAUER	DORCAS NEFF	VIVIAN YOUNG
Drill Press Operator	*Stock Clerk*	*Stock Clerk*	*Lathe Operator*	*Inspector and Assembler*	*Milling Machine Operator*
Age 19—Single	Age 26—Married	Age 21—Married	Age 27—Married	Age 19—Single	Age 24—Married

Sure, women will stay in the shops. More women are in the shops today than ever before, and they have found it a good place to work. I like my work, and I would like to stay. I intend to get married, but that won't make any difference; I will still continue to work. Shop work isn't any harder than housework. But, I don't believe that women will be permitted to remain in shops throughout the country when this war ends and men return to the job.

Yes, some of them will stay in the shops. I would like to remain on the job myself. I have always worked, and I guess I always will, so I might as well work in the shop as any place else. Although I would not want to keep a returning veteran out of his job, I believe that there are plenty of jobs around the shops that do not require a man, and which women can do equally as well. Therefore, why shouldn't women remain on these jobs after the war?

Yes, most women will remain in the shops if they are not forced out at the termination of the war. Women have become independent and many are earning good money for the first time. They had to work for a few dollars a week before. They will be reluctant to give up these jobs, married and single alike. With modern appliances simplifying housework, a married woman can easily work eight hours a day and keep a home. That is, of course, unless her family is exceptionally large.

I don't want to, and most of my associates don't, either. When my man comes back I want to stay home and stay put. He worked here before the war, as did many other husbands, and I feel that I am taking somebody's place here in the shop, and when they return I am ready and willing to step aside so that they can have their job back. Of course I am satisfied now, but I am only here to do a job as long as I am not keeping a man out of that job.

Most of the girls with whom I work and with whom I talk are waiting for V-Day to quit. They do not want to stay in the shops. However, some of them do. I believe that the more efficient workers will want to stay. They have an interest in their jobs and like the work. Therefore, they are more efficient and also desire to remain on that job regardless of the war. Yes, I would like to stay if the company will retain women workers after the Armistice.

No. I don't think women will remain in the shops after the war. Many of the girls I know expect to quit when the men return. My husband is in the Navy, and when he returns I am going back into the home. From what I hear, I believe that most of the married women now working in the shops do not intend to work in a machine shop after the war, but most of the single girls desire to stay if allowed. I like my work here, but I feel that my place is at home when the war ends.

This sampling of women workers at York Corporation respond to the question of whether women would work in industrial shops when the war ends.

---

addition of about 500 people, and no layoffs.

Six months later, Yorkco's employment stayed at V-J Day levels, with work weeks adjusted to 40 hours. The high demand for refrigeration and cooling equipment offset cutbacks in defense work.

Also losing their jobs at America's factories were 16- and 17-year-old girls, permitted to work during the war by special exemption. Production could go on without the aid of the girls under 18 years old, the government concluded.

• • •

This refitting to produce non-military items meant that residents would have to make do with worn-out appliances and furniture for several more months.

In August, furniture-makers predicted that replacement items would not be available in time for Christmas. Mattresses, as one example, would be slow in coming because of scarcity of wire for springs and fabric for cushioning.

Table and floor lamps should be available by Christmas, although shades would be made from paper parchment. Fabric shades would come later when the materials became available.

Waffle irons, toasters and percolators would also be available by year's end. But larger appliances — refrigerators, washing machines and stoves — would come off production lines after the smaller appliances.

• • •

At this retooling point, 19 York-area plants had won the prized Army-Navy "E" award for their war production performance.

A.B. Farquhar Co. and York-Hoover Corporation plants won the award four times. General Electric was a three-time winner.

'Same old shop, but some big new jobs,' stated a caption under this photograph in a York Corporation booklet designed to prepare returning veterans for the workplace. 'It will be a big day in your life when once again you change into civilian clothes,' the booklet began. 'We here at York anxiously await that day because York Corporation needs you when the war is won.'

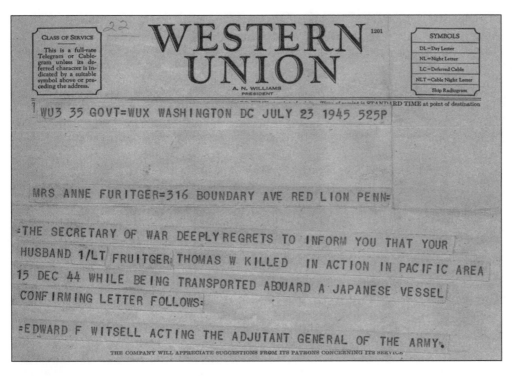

Anne Frutiger learned of her husband's death about seven months after Lt. Thomas W. Frutiger's prison ship was attacked by friendly fire.

Local production achievements were impressive.

Only 5 percent of the country's war plants — 4,283 out of 85,000 — won the Army-Navy "E." Eighteen percent of York-area plants engaged in war work garnered the award.

Sixty-five percent of all employees in York industries wore the "E" pins.

The comparable number elsewhere in America was 20 percent.

• • •

Late in the war, York Corporation had sent a special publication, "Back to York," to hundreds of former employees still in the service.

The booklet made it clear that the company wanted those workers — now military-trained — to return.

"You are still a member of the York family as far as we are concerned and we are planning a job here for you," the booklet stated. "We will be happy to help you fill that job successfully."

The company, thus, was keeping its word given in 1940 that employees entering the service would be granted a leave of absence and gain reinstatement upon discharge at the rate of pay applicable to their positions.

"Back to York" also stated that when the military men and women returned, their reception would be simple and informal. The company conjectured that returnees did not want to come back to flags waving and drums beating.

The booklet suggested that military veterans go to their former department, meet the boss and talk with fellow workers.

"This informal introduction will give you the feeling of again belonging at the "York's," the booklet stated.

An employment interview would follow, part of the process to determine the best spot.

The company had changed — expanded into new branches of research and new products, "Back to York" stated.

Indeed, York Corporation was stronger than before the war. Defense contracts had brought in $132 million. Before 1943, the company had not paid stockholder dividends since 1929. From 1943 to 1945, Yorkco earned $2.58 million in profits.

Still, the same familiar buildings and shops were there, the booklet stated. Many employees would be the same. Generally, the West York and Grantley plants would look as they always did.

" 'The Yorks' still means York Corporation to York, Pa., in everything that the word meant to you when you left," "Back to York" stated.

'A loss shared by all of us'

In July, Anne Frutiger was vacationing in Maryland with her two sons when her brother-in-law, William, brought her the news.

Her husband, Thomas, was dead. He had died about seven months before when fire from friendly forces struck his prison ship.

The war widow calmly drove home to Red Lion that summer night. But when she entered the garage, she broke down and rammed the car into the back of the structure, pushing the wall out a foot.

Tom and Bob, her sons, would later repair the damaged wall.

• • •

The Western Union telegram that gave the official news of Thomas Frutiger's death began with the standard format for such announcements: "The Secretary of War deeply regrets to inform you ... ."

Other official notifications followed.

A printed card from Chief of Staff George C. Marshall stated, "Your husband fought valiantly in a supreme hour

THOMAS WILLIAM FRUTIGER
First Lieutenant—Army

Parents: Mr. and Mrs. W. C. Frutiger, 316 Boundary Ave. *Wife:* Anne E. Frutiger, 221 N. Main St. *Children:* Thomas W. Jr., and Robert Allen. *Born* Nov. 24, 1911. *Service:* May 1, 1941 to Jan. 9, 1945. *Basic Training:* MacDill Field, Tampa, Fla. *Service Schools Attended:* Ordnance School, Aberdeen Proving Ground, Aberdeen, Md. Assigned to 454th Ordnance Company, Aviation (B). *Type of Work:* Executive officer. Sailed Nov. 1, 1941, from San Francisco, Calif. Arrived Philippine Islands Nov. 23, 1941. Engaged in combat in Philippine Islands and Bataan Peninsula. Was in "Death March" imprisoned at Camp O'Donnel and Military Prison No. 2 at Davao on Mindonoa Island until June, 1944. He was then transferred to Camp No. 1 at Cabantuan in Manila and on Dec. 15, 1944, he was placed on board a prison ship to be transferred to Japan. He was killed when that prison ship was sunk off Formosa on Jan. 9, 1945. *Awarded:* The Purple Heart (posthumously), American Defense Ribbon with one star, South Pacific Ribbon with two stars, Philippine Defense Ribbon with one star, Philippine Liberation Ribbon and World War II Victory Medal.

'Those Who Served,' a 1946 book memorializing Red Lion-area military men and women, tells the story of Thomas W. Frutiger's heroism. The book remembered the more than 30 community men who died: 'These dead have joined the ranks of those whose deeds are recorded in history ... the heroes of Bunker Hill, Valley Forge, Gettysburg, Argonne Forest and the Marne.'

of his country's need."

Secretary of War Henry L. Stimson signed a letter awarding Thomas Frutiger a Purple Heart.

"We profoundly appreciate the greatness of your loss," he wrote, "for in a very real sense the loss suffered by any of us in this battle for our country, is a loss shared by all of us."

Gen. H.B. Sayler, deputy chief of Ordnance, writing after the Japanese surrender, stated: "The great cause for which he fought, for Victory and Peace, has been achieved. He has not died in vain! A grateful nation will forever cherish the memory of his supreme sacrifice."

In a letter of condolence, Stewart Lauer of York Corporation noted that the loss of Thomas Frutiger was deeply moving, particularly because of his sister's and brother's service with the company.

"I hope that you may take some consolation in knowing that if he had to die," Lauer wrote, "he did so in the service of his country and for your protection."

• • •

Anne Frutiger's concerns must have grown as the months passed since her husband's last communication in November 1944.

She had remained part of the network of wives and relatives of prisoners of war. This group had heard from many of those who had survived, freed by American forces reclaiming the Philippines.

Robert B. Blakeslee was one of the survivors, a friend of Thomas Frutiger before and during captivity. Anne Frutiger notified him of her husband's death, and he replied that he counted it as a personal loss.

"He was the anchor man of our organization and the one we all depended on if the going got tough," he wrote Anne. "I always admired Tom's ability to accept any kind of situation with complete calm and equanimity."

He wrote of one instance in which three Japanese dive bombers plastered an ammunition dump on Bataan. Frutiger climbed from his foxhole, observing three fires blazing around the ammunition. He called the dump's

commander to advise him that it was going to blow and notified the base ordnance depot to send additional ammunition.

Then he checked all the foxholes in that area to make sure that no injured men were left behind.

He left the area, just before the ammunition started exploding.

"It was hours before I could establish contact with Tom because he evacuated in the opposite direction," Blakeslee wrote, "but when I did find him he was as cool as a cucumber."

Thomas Frutiger and Robert Blakeslee never exchanged messages to carry back, but if he had, he would have wanted Anne and her sons to live as happy and normal lives as possible.

"Tom didn't feel any bitterness toward anyone as a result of his position, and I know he doesn't want you to feel that way," Blakeslee wrote. "We all sort of figured that as soldiers, we had been unlucky enough to be in the wrong spot at the wrong time, but it was just our lot and didn't complain about it."

• • •

Thomas Frutiger's obituary noted that he was assistant superintendent of St. Paul's Evangelical Sunday School in Red Lion. He had been re-elected repeatedly to that position, even when in captivity.

Church officials applauded both Thomas and Anne Frutiger.

"We have admired your Christian courage and fortitude throughout these recent years," the Rev. Joseph Willard Krecker wrote to Anne. "We now pray for you the peace and hope which is surely ours in Jesus Christ, and which alone can satisfy."

Thomas Frutiger was the 11th member of that church to die in the service. He was the 25th and last Yorkco worker to die in the conflict. About 1,200 company men and women had served.

Frutiger had survived the grueling Bataan Death March

Myra Gerbrick Clark of Glen Rock was discharged from the Women's Army Corps on Dec. 31, 1945, after 33 months of service.

Raymond R. Clark, husband of Myra Gerbrick Clark, entered the service in 1941 and served for six years in the Army, including duty in the European Theater.

with its clubbings, bayonetings and cold-blooded killings. He had survived horrendous conditions for more than two years as a POW.

But he fell to an attack by friendly forces shortly before Gen. Douglas MacArthur fulfilled his pledge to return to the islands he had left in 1942.

In leaving, the commanding general invested the lives of the men in the hands of his officers. Thomas Frutiger was one of those officers.

• • •

The Red Lion community lost at least one other son in the Philippines.

Pvt. Paul A. Steinfelt's assignment was to help rebuild airfields and rice mills on Luzon. After the Philippines fell, he participated in the forced march, survived Camp O'Donnell but died of malaria and dysentery at Camp Cabanatuan in November 1942. He was 27 years old.

His parents, Mr. and Mrs. Jacob L. Steinfelt, received a wire late in 1943 that he died in a Japanese prison camp.

• • •

In an intriguing turn of fortunes late in the war, an American Red Cross executive from Red Lion saved the life of a Japanese soldier in the Philippines.

Warren R. Lock, assistant Red Cross field director, was driving a jeep loaded with medical supplies to soldiers near the front lines. He rolled into a village, and residents flagged him toward a Japanese soldier, hands tied behind his back, surrounded by angry Filipinos. The soldier had been trying to escape the island by boat.

Lock loaded the soldier into the jeep, drove to a nearby village and turned him over to military authorities.

• • •

Cpl. Boyd E. Sower of York also died as a POW in the Philippines. He died in Camp O'Donnell shortly after the forced march.

His parents, Mr. and Mrs. John F. Sower, learned a year after his death that he was missing in action, and the military sent word a year after that he was presumed to be dead.

Still later, in September 1945, his parents learned of his death in the camp, one of several prisons where survivors of the Bataan trek were detained.

The same day county residents learned that Sower had not survived captivity, the community received word that Capt. Charles H. Langdon Jr. of York would be coming home.

The son of Gladys Langdon of York survived the attacks on the same ships, the Oryoku Maru and Enoura

Maru, that killed Thomas Frutiger. Langdon and Frutiger were in the same unit.

Langdon ended the war in a prison camp in Japan and gained his liberty after its surrender.

• • •

Lt. Victor Witman also came home from the war, released from captivity after the Japanese surrender.

Joseph F. Witman, the Yorkco executive, had learned earlier in the war that his son was in a camp on Skikoku Island, one of Japan's home islands.

The father was relieved upon receiving word of his son's release.

"We have been anxiously awaiting word of Victor ever since we heard of the release of American prisoners in the camps of Japan," he told Shop News.

"His mother is much relieved since we have received definite word that he is safe."

Victor Witman was a former Yorkco employee, as was his twin brother, Warrant Officer Vincent Witman, stationed at Lewes, Del.

• • •

Families of those who did not come back from the Philippines learned about conditions in the prison camps from those who survived or escaped.

The Rev. Harold Sechrist and his family were among those rescued by American paratroopers.

Sechrist, his wife and three children, formerly of York and missionaries in the Far East, were captured in Manila in early 1942. They remained in captivity in Las Banos camp in the Philippines for about three years. Their captors provided little food, even though wild fruit was available in the jungle, and cattle grazed in the hills.

"It was deliberate starvation," the missionary said.

Malnutrition led to an assortment of diseases. Sechrist lost 50 pounds, and other prisoners twice that.

The Sechrist family faced harsher treatment than another missionary family with York ties. Earlier in the war, Japanese forces in China apprehended the Rev. Calvin Reber, his wife, the former Audrie Fox of York, and their daughter. After a period of detention, the Japanese put the Rebers on a freighter to a neutral port.

Some of the Japanese officers later were convicted of war crimes for their treatment of prisoners.

• • •

Bob Senft celebrated V-E Day on a train stopped on a rail siding somewhere east of Fort Lewis, Wash. His unit had been heading east for deployment in Europe. But during a wait on that siding, Senft and his comrades found

Bob Senft of Conewago Township is shown somewhere in Montana during his duty out West. He was on his way to Europe when Germany surrendered. The troop train he was riding returned him to Fort Lewis, Wash., and he later shipped out to Okinawa and then Korea.

This group of American prisoners of war gained their freedom as Allied forces headed toward Berlin. Fred Auchey, fourth from left, a former York Corporation employee, was among those freed. Yorkco's Shop News, where this photo originally ran, pointed out the Hershey chocolate bar sticking out of the pocket of the soldier on the left.

out that fighting was over in Europe.

Their unit immediately did an about-face, heading back to Fort Lewis. He would do service in the Pacific Theater.

So Senft celebrated V-J Day on Okinawa. His engineering unit was assigned to build roads on that island, scene of intense fighting.

The first job was to dig burial ditches. The island had not been cleaned up since fighting ended in June.

"The stench of decaying bodies was near unbearable," Senft wrote years later.

Unaware of the war's end, Japanese soldiers occupied caves throughout the island.

"... (W)e found it necessary to block cave entrances and eliminate the contents," he wrote.

One night, Senft was on guard duty near a critical watering hole. Contamination of this scarce water source would have been disastrous.

Senft saw a set of eyes moving across the marsh, and he tensed.

"All of a sudden ... a cat popped up," he said.

• • •

He and Ethel kept in touch by letter.

"I wrote every day the whole time he was gone," she said.

The two developed a code to keep her abreast of his whereabouts. They correlated an island where he was stationed to towns near Zion View. Bob would ask in a letter about how some person was doing in Manchester or Mount Wolf, and that would give Ethel the clue.

After helping clean up Okinawa, Senft's unit shipped

out to Korea. In February, six months after V-J Day, he was back in the states.

He had met former Yorkco co-worker Bob Boring in a chow line in Korea, and the two traveled back to Fort Indiantown Gap together. Ethel met the pair at the station in Harrisburg.

Before long, Bob was back in Zion View, back to his duties at York Corporation.

Her husband had left on Friday the 13th, 1943, Ethel noted.

He was discharged on Washington's birthday, 1946.

• • •

Ethel Senft left her clerical position at York Corporation.

The Zion View woman did so willingly. Her aged mother needed to be watched.

With the end of the war, Ethel Senft also gave up an important patriotic duty. For months, she had ironed service stars on Quickel Church's American flag. A blue star on the flag represented congregation members in the military.

A gold star signified, "Killed in action." At war's end, she had sewn only one gold star, among many blue ones.

"Naturally, everyone was happy as the men slowly returned to their homes," she wrote, "and that flag could be stored away."

• • •

The past war remained much on the minds of York County residents on the fourth anniversary of Pearl Harbor, according to county newspapers.

On Dec. 6 — the day before the anniversary — Gen. Jacob L. Devers told 400 people attending William Penn High School's football banquet that competitive athletics helped the United States win the war.

The former William Penn quarterback said teamwork,

Through war's end, government posters urged the need for Americans to work together. From left, 'I'll carry mine too!', a conservation poster, compares the efforts by those working at home to servicemen fighting overseas. 'Private Joe Louis says' highlights the achievements of blacks in military and civilian life. 'Together we win' shows Uncle Sam joining the handshake between a factory worker and a businessman, designed to promote a healthy relationship between workers and management.

endurance and leadership qualities developed on America's playing fields contributed to victories in Europe and the Pacific.

Sgt. Philip S. Weinbrom had returned home from overseas. Meanwhile, his brother, Lewis, and Lewis' friend, Edward H. Faber, had just enlisted in the Army. Both graduated in William Penn's class of 1945.

WAC Cpl. Mildred P. Schumaker, who grew up near York, had married Everett L. Householder in Compton, Calif. The couple had met in Texas, where Householder, a staff sergeant, had been stationed at Camp Walters and the bride as an occupational therapist at Long View hospital.

In a similar manner, the war would disperse hundreds of county residents, who never permanently returned home.

A Victory Loan Drive was under way to help Uncle Sam with his war debt.

Sugar remained scarce. Caribbean crops were not yet at their pre-war vigor.

York's American Legion post was seeking at least 1,000 holiday gift packages for vets in government hospitals suffering from wounds or illness from military duty.

An estimated 25,000 men and women in Pennsylvania hospitals would qualify for "Gifts for Yanks Who Give" packages.

Local Catholic churches were campaigning for food donations for those living in war-torn areas of the Pacific and Europe.

In an editorial, The York Dispatch pointed to a current congressional investigation into how the Japanese surprised the United States at Pearl Harbor.

"There was a general failure, in the White House and on down, to take the true measure of the Japanese," the newspaper stated.

Students at a William Penn High School assembly had witnessed a re-enactment of the flag-raising on Iwo Jima. The assembly honored high school graduates who died in

the war.

The flag-raisers included former servicemen who were taking post-graduate courses at the high school in preparation for college enrollment under the G.I. Bill.

Veterans Milford Robertson, Howard Schucker, Wade Lehr and George Schenck joined students Richard McIlvaine and James Benton in the re-enactment.

The war had changed the reading habits of Martin Library's patrons.

Some library patrons were switching to non-war books, a survey suggested.

Readers were demanding lighter reading or anything that did not mention the war. Fiction readers were looking for books with non-military settings.

It had been a long four years since word of Pearl Harbor had reached York County. Some in York County were seeking a diversion.

But the Martin Library survey showed returning servicemen were interested in war books, particularly publications about their former units.

These former servicemen also were asking for vocational reading, including books on salesmanship. Those who were good readers before entering the military came out better readers.

Ex-military men and women were asking about information on schools and courses. They were calling for college catalogues.

There was no longer a war on.

• • •

York County, indeed, had changed in those years since the Japanese attacked Pearl Harbor.

Following Stewart Lauer's words on Yorkco's shop floor that cold day four years before, the county — at home and overseas — had entered the fight for freedom with both feet.

And it would never back out.

Epilogue

Gen. Jacob L. Devers, at microphone, earned a reputation for achieving what he set out to do. Here, Devers addresses the 4th Armored Division in Europe after conferring the Presidential Unit Citation on the unit in June 1945. Later that month, Devers received rousing accolades from his hometown of York.

Gallery

Gen. Jacob L. Devers, third from left, surveys Hitler's home in Berchtesgaden, Germany. From left, Sgt. John Turnipseed, from Devers' staff; Gen. Wade H. Haislip, commanding general of the 6th Corps, and Gen. Maxwell D. Taylor, 101st Airborne Division, join Devers.

Gen. Devers confers with George C. Marshall, Army chief of staff and fellow Pennsylvanian, in October 1944 in France.

Much of the Army's leadership in the assault on Germany gather in France in this March 1945 photograph. Those with the stars of general officers are, from left, Jacob L. Devers, Alexander (Sandy) Patch, George S. Patton and Omar Bradley.

'We had plenty of it'

One day in late June 1945, a group of York's war-weary citizenry looked northward along the Susquehanna Trail.

Native son and war hero Jacob L. Devers was due from Harrisburg, and he was certain to travel that primary north-south route through the county. The general was expected to enter the city's Continental Square on his way to the Yorktowne Hotel, his headquarters for the night.

Once again, history had granted York County strong ties to a major war. The York Plan, the heroics of Jake Devers and Alexander D. Goode and the 571 or more men who would never come home provided proof of that.

In typical expansive fashion, the people of York planned a massive celebration for their most prominent soldier. But Devers, home from Europe awaiting a command in the Pacific, directed a flanking maneuver before entering the square. His car moved west toward his boy-hood home on West York Avenue, now Roosevelt Avenue, named after President Theodore Roosevelt.

He had planned a rolling inspection of house number 254 but ran into an ambush. A crowd of about 1,000 people milled around the block, all awaiting Jake. York Corporation, just south on Roosevelt, had added to the crowd, closing up early to give employees a glimpse of one of the U.S. Army's ranking generals.

Devers asked his driver to stop, and the general immediately started shaking hands with old neighbors. He remembered many by name.

He made his way to the house where he was born. George A. Swartz, the current resident, offered him a mahogany cane. The wood came from York County's second courthouse, demolished in 1898 when Jake was just 11. Its metal tip came from a courthouse clock.

The cane bore the name James Devers, the general's paternal grandfather. A band below the handle carried the inscription of Devers' father, P.K. Devers, with the date, 1900.

At one point, the general looked around his former neighborhood.

"That's where I was blamed for breaking some windows," someone heard him say.

• • •

Devers' homecoming pulled together several strands of York County's long, deep history. The date Devers would depart York for the next stop on his American tour — June 27 — had gained significance in two previous wars cross-ing the county's soil.

That day in 1778, the Continental Congress returned to Philadelphia after a nine-month exile. The citizenry had ever since grandly celebrated the nation's founders' depar-ture and the role York had played as America's capital dur-ing the Revolutionary War.

On June 27, 1863, Jubal Early's division of Richard E. Ewell's II Corps, Robert E . Lee's Confederate Army, stepped across York County's western border. That inva-sion prompted a controversial surrender of York and dead-ly fighting in Wrightsville and Hanover. It would cover most of the county, to the banks of the Susquehanna River,

Gen. Jacob L. Devers received his fourth star on March 30, 1945, as his Sixth Army Group crossed the Rhine in its campaign through the south of Germany.

the easternmost point the rebels would reach.

Three days later, Lee recalled the rebels, and the long gray columns countermarched. A battle was brewing in Gettysburg, about 30 miles away.

When Jacob Loucks Devers shook hands with the scores of York Corporation employees cheering him on Roosevelt Avenue, it marked the reunion of the general with a company his maternal grandfather and namesake, Jacob Loucks, helped form.

The business prowess of P.H. Glatfelter, who purchased his Spring Grove paper mill from his kinsman Loucks in 1863, gives a glimpse of how the Industrial Revolution took the fruit of the earth and turned it into goods used and enjoyed by late 19th- and 20th-century Americans.

Glatfelter later bailed out the struggling York Manufacturing Company at the time of Devers' birth. Philip Henry Glatfelter made his fortune converting trees into a useful consumer product. His acquisition of York Manufacturing and its developing refrigeration and air conditioning lines was another step toward modernity, bringing the cool of winter into the warmest days of sum-mer.

The company's advances in cooling technology increased the productivity of future generations of produc-tion, office and defense workers.

Glatfelter recruited Thomas Shipley in 1897, and the Shipley influence transformed the company, later York Corporation, into an international cooling giant with the know-how to help equip multiple armies and fleets. The connection of Jake Devers and York Corporation in this late-June 1945 celebration linked a four-star giant on the war front with a major home front contributor of services and equipment to fighting men and women overseas.

Gen. Devers, 57, holds his family's cane, given to him by the resident of his boyhood home, 254 Roosevelt Ave. in York. A large crowd greeted Devers outside his home during the late June 1945 visit.

William S. Shipley, Thomas Shipley's brother and York Corporation board chairman, joined the general at a Yorktowne Hotel banquet later that day.

When the two shook hands, it marked more than a salute between two distinguished achievers. York County's greatest soldier greeted the York Plan's foremost promoter and corporate heir to the county's greatest industrialist, P.H. Glatfelter.

The handshake celebrated the synergy of the vital American industries that supported the soldier in the field and the soldier who fought so that the industries could continue to freely prosper.

• • •

Eventually, Devers made his way from the Roosevelt Avenue gathering to his East Market Street hotel. Later that day, he would again pass near the Roosevelt sign, this time as the featured rider in a parade that extended to the York Fairgrounds.

Thousands of residents lined the seven-mile route, cheering as the noted general passed by.

The turnout would be larger than past and subsequent official V-Day celebrations, including the middle-of-the-night romp along city streets marking the end of World War I.

According to one estimate, it was almost as large as the 150th anniversary of York County in 1899 — a celebration marked by three parades. If propriety would not permit the county to celebrate V-E Day with the appropriate frivolity, the great general's visit provided a prime opportunity.

A fairgrounds crowd of 15,000 residents crowded into the grandstand or wherever they could find a perch, as the general mounted a platform constructed on the racetrack.

In an extemporaneous address, he maintained he did not deserve the honors.

York County comes out to honor its most famous soldier, Gen. Devers. He was on his way to the York Fairgrounds, where 15,000 turned out to hear his speech.

"I know it was meant with the greatest sincerity, and I accept it as a very precious tribute to me, but it was earned with the help of those great soldiers, sailors, marines and airmen, WACs — those who have won this war."

Then he extended the line to connect the two fronts — at war and at home.

"Our workers have produced more," he said, "than anyone in the world."

York County workers know how to do it, he said, and do it right now. They do not wait.

"With this great effort put out in York, you have given us the equipment and the food and the incentive to go ahead, without which we could not have done what has been done," he said. "We have received this equipment, and we have received it at the right time, and the right place, and we had plenty of it."

Afterword

Lt. Thomas W. Frutiger in full uniform outside the home where he grew up, 312 Boundary Ave. in Red Lion. Before the war, the Lehigh College graduate worked in his father's cigar factory and later served as an engineer for York Ice Machinery Corporation. The reserve officer was called up when war seemed inevitable in 1941. He died in late 1944 or early 1945 from friendly fire, when he was on his way from the Philippines to Japan aboard a prison ship.

Gallery

As owner of a large cigar factory, William C. Frutiger, shown here with his wife, Anna, also contributed to the war effort. Cigarmakers in Red Lion and elsewhere in York County were busy during the war because cigars remained much in demand. Frutiger started in the cigarmaking business years before by turning out his first 10,000 cigars for free. Those just starting out often worked for no pay because they would ruin a lot of cigars in the training process. Thomas Frutiger took this photograph of his parents before the war in their Red Lion home.

Virginia Frutiger wears the bars of her brother, Lt. Thomas Frutiger, prisoner of the Japanese since the fall of the Philippines, when this photo ran in York Corporation's Shop News in August 1943. Both Frutigers were employed at Yorkco before they enlisted.

Anne Karone Frutiger is seen in this wartime photo with her sons, Tom, left, and Bob. He remembered 'Tommy' and 'Bobby' in his letters and cards to his wife before and during captivity.

'One of the Nation's finest'

In the months that followed V-J Day, thousands of soldiers returned to their York County homes.

The war had changed them, and they would help transform York County.

Many carried the war with them for years.

Some marched in parades and supported American Legion and Veterans of Foreign Wars posts. Others simply never talked about their experiences. No one could understand what they had been through. Why try to explain?

War hero Audie Murphy, walking among celebrators in Cannes, France, after the German surrender, summarized the feelings of many:

"I feel only a vague irritation. I want company and I want to be alone. I want to talk and I want to be silent. I want to sit and I want to walk. There is V-E day without, but no peace within."

• • •

When GIs came home, a pattern emerged.

The former soldiers and their brides, many now back home from the factories, often moved in with their parents.

It was a matter of practicality. Housing, scarce during the war, remained so. Many transplanted defense workers had stayed, making York their new home.

Some vets went back to school, without leaving town. The county now boasted York Junior College, and Penn State offered classes to train veterans in engineering and management under the GI Bill. York Corporation and others set up training institutes within their companies.

The newlyweds started families of their own, placing further demand for housing in York and small towns throughout the county.

By July 1946, York Hospital was reporting a record number of reservations set for deliveries in August. Between 200 and 300 deliveries were expected and possibly more for "duplications" — twins and triplets. Births in June had come in at 156.

The city hit its highest population of 59,704 in 1950, and the county's population increased by more than 13 percent in the war decade to surpass 200,000.

Building demand brought a scarcity of lumber.

In some parts of the county, wood was more readily available to build garages than houses. People built those structures and lived in them until lumber became available for a house. Some people built basements where they resided until supplies for a house became available.

Few building sites were available in the City of York, so developers created suburbs, showing a voracious appetite for the farmland that had nourished York County since its beginning.

Many veterans gained employment at Caterpillar's new plant in Springettsbury Township. Haines Acres and other suburbs went up a tract at a time to accommodate these workers.

By the mid-1950s, young families shopped at Sears in the York County Shopping Center and other strip plazas spinning off of downtowns elsewhere in the county. Malls followed the strip centers.

VETS HOME-COMING and HALLOWE'EN PARADE Thurs. Eve., Oct. 31

Sponsored By **DOVER POST No. 7374 V.F.W.**

Prizes Will Be Donated By Merchants of Dover and Vicinty

Parade will form at Schoolgrounds at 8 P.M.

Kilroy will be there

Military men and women gradually returned home after V-E and V-J Days, as their obligations ended. Dover and other communities waited to celebrate their return, as seen in this 1946 poster. The notation 'Kilroy will be there' plays on the widespread wartime saying, 'Kilroy was here.' Legends abound about the source of the saying and the familiar cartoon character accompanying it. It suggested that an American had been there before. At least seven men from Dover died in the war.

Caterpillar brought another element to York County — outside ownership.

One by one, companies with out-of-town headquarters acquired York's venerable, locally owned industries. Cat's wage scale changed the industrial environment, pulling skilled labor from other manufacturers and introducing a higher wage scale to the county marketplace.

• • •

York Corporation was among those homegrown companies that attracted outside investors.

William S. Shipley's death in 1951 ended the family's relationship with Yorkco that began with Thomas Shipley's arrival in York in 1897.

Stewart Lauer headed the still-private enterprise until 1956 when Borg-Warner, an international conglomerate, purchased it. Lauer retired as president in 1957, ending 46 years with Yorkco. The company again became independent in 1986, changing its name to York International.

Today, the Fortune 500 company's equipment operates in the Kremlin, Empire State Building, British House of Parliament and English Channel Tunnel. The company

Veterans of the WAVEs, Women Accepted for Volunteer Emergency Service, and WACs, Women's Army Corps, parade through the streets of Hanover in 1946.

Hanover-area residents line Broadway as U.S. Navy veterans parade toward the town's Center Square.

Lawrence Baker Sheppard, president and general manager of Hanover Shoe Inc., speaks at the celebration for troops returning to the Hanover area from World War II. Sheppard served as a consultant with the War Production Board on shoes, shoe leather and shoe material. He was in the Army in World War I. About 40 Hanover-area men died in the service in World War II.

consolidated its operations at the Grantley plant, and the West York plant fell into decay for a number of years.

But in the 1990s, part of West York was rehabbed and carved into suites for startup businesses. BASCO Associates, an engineering firm, occupies another part of the renovated structures.

This plant, home of so many technological innovations in the refrigeration arena at the turn of the 20th century, continues to house high-tech companies in the 21st century.

• • •

While heading the predecessors of York Corporation, Thomas Shipley launched other businesses.

In 1926, Shipley and brothers Samuel and William formed Thomas Shipley Inc., to market York Ice Machinery products overseas. In 1929, Thomas Shipley opened Roosevelt Garage and Supply Co, in a block full of blighted houses and bordellos across the street from Yorkco's Roosevelt Avenue plant.

That business serviced, fueled and parked the automobiles of Yorkco's employees. Shipley also made and serviced home and industrial oil furnaces.

This business was a forerunner of the service industries that are replacing York County smokestack factories today.

The Shipley Group, headed by William S. Shipley III, continues in the service field, distributing oil, natural gas and propane.

The mascot for 30 Tom's convenience stores ties back to the company's beginning. The 6-foot talking blue cat is named Tom, after the company's founder.

• • •

Two P.H. Glatfelters headed the Spring Grove's paper company after the founder's death.

The first P.H. Glatfelter's role in saving the struggling York Manufacturing Company in 1888 is often forgotten because of the long-term success of the paper mill that bears his name.

Today, descendant G.H. Glatfelter II heads a company that produces paper for books, tea bags, postage stamps and disposable medical garments.

President Harry S. Truman, right, spoke at the retirement ceremony for Gen. Jacob L. Devers in 1949. Devers retired at the age of 62 with 40 years service.

• • •

Stephen Morgan Smith, whose Moravian ministry was curtailed because of a throat ailment, left a considerable York County industrial legacy.

He was the catalyst behind the foundation of York Manufacturing Company and founded his own company, S. Morgan Smith Co., in 1890. S. Morgan Smith's products included the manufacture of water wheels and turbines. In 1959, the company was sold to out-of-town owner Allis Chalmers.

Today, three York County companies trace their origins to S. Morgan Smith. Voith Hydro and American Hydro, makers of hydraulic turbines, and Precision Components, whose enterprises include the manufacture of vessels to contain and ship radioactive materials.

Another major York Plan player — A.B. Farquhar Co. — passed into the hands of an outside company in 1952. Oliver Corp. purchased the high-profile York company, and the last owner, Hess Oil Co. of New York, gave the deteriorating North George Street shops to the City of York for redevelopment in the 1960s.

The heroes

Jacob Loucks Devers never gained an assignment in the Pacific Theater.

The same week as his triumphant return to York in late June 1945, Devers was reassigned to the largely administrative position of commanding general, Army Ground Forces, at the Army War College in Washington, D.C.

When Devers retired in 1949, President Truman commended the York native: "As one of the Nation's finest, you undertook the most severe task one can be called upon to perform."

U.S. Sen. Henry Cabot Lodge also wrote into the Congressional Record: "Here is a soldier who commanded about 700,000 men in battle, who has been honored by every foreign government ... . He is indeed the very archetype of the man on whom the Nation completely and utterly depends when its life hangs in the balance."

Today, he is most remembered for his leadership in the Invasion of Southern France, Operation Dragoon, an offensive overshadowed by the D-Day Invasion, Operation Overlord.

Devers' clashes with European Theater commander Dwight D. Eisenhower did not help his legacy.

Eisenhower listed Devers 24th on a list of 38 most-able field commanders in Europe. Eisenhower wrote his superior, George Marshall, that Devers was "most inaccurate in statements and evaluations... . He has not, so far, produced among the seniors of the American organization here a feeling of confidence and trust."

Devers and his chief lieutenant, Alexander "Sandy" Patch, lacked the fire of Patton and others of high rank. Devers never published an autobiography. No one wrote his biography until the late 1990s. Indeed, the Patch-led 7th Army has been called "America's Forgotten Army."

"Devers' problem was that he wasn't flamboyant like Patton, nor did he have General Bradley's publicity machine," historian Charles Whiting wrote. "He lacked the flair that made him good 'copy' for correspondents. They wanted stories for the 'folks back home.' Devers could not provide them."

Jake Devers often returned to York County to give speeches and make appearances in his hometown after the war. He died in 1979 at the age of 92 and was buried in Arlington National Cemetery.

• • •

The 7th Army first helped oversee the million German prisoners accumulated in the sector of southern Germany that it conquered.

But it has never been mustered out.

It stayed in a rebuilding Germany through the Cold War, providing a buffer against the Red Army. It played host to Elvis Presley during his military stint, provided extensive manpower for Vietnam and served as a major part of NATO, even observing the fall of the Berlin Wall in 1989.

It served as the Army of generations of young officers, including Colin Powell and Norman Schwarzkopf.

• • •

After the war, many York County residents of German background heard from struggling relatives in Germany.

Henry and Margaretha Cordes of York, for example, received a letter from German kinsmen Mr. and Mrs. Emil Meyer. The Meyer letter indicated that Germans daily froze in their beds, and mass suicide among families was common.

"If people are given no help or opportunity for a better life in the future, then the end is a redemption," they wrote. "People should not forget when they are punishing us, that they are doing the same thing as Hitler did to us."

The writer was working by candlelight. Electric power was turned on only a short time each day. The Marshall Plan offered billions in relief starting in 1947, but it took months for the aid to reach freezing and starving people in Germany and elsewhere in Europe.

• • •

York County military men and women continued serving in occupation forces long after V-E and V-J Days.

Carlton Schroeder was one such soldier. The 11th Airborne private was assigned to a military police unit to stand guard at the war crimes trial of Japanese Prime Minister Tojo.

On the trial's last day, Schroeder and others, armed with weapons and gas bombs, stood guard as the 200 defendants boarded buses to return to their quarters.

But all went quietly.

Life did not end quietly for Tojo, who ordered the Pearl Harbor attack. He was hanged in 1948 for ordering and permitting atrocities and committing other war crimes.

• • •

Darrell Allen, who survived the Pearl Harbor attack, moved to York after the war.

His grandson, Petty Officer Evan Allen Jr., fulfilled his grandfather's wish to be buried at sea.

In 2003, he brought his forebear's ashes aboard the amphibious assault vessel "Peleliu."

When the ship reached Pearl Harbor, his captain ordered a full service, complete with rifle salute and the playing of "Taps" at the U.S.S. Utah Memorial, not far from where Darrell Allen helped defend his submarine from attack.

• • •

Fewer than 10 Pearl Harbor survivors live in York County today, less than half the number alive at the turn of the 21st century.

The York County Veterans Affairs Office sponsors a Pearl Harbor Remembrance Breakfast each year.

The office recognizes the deceased vets by placing a single place setting on a small table, decorated with a red rose and a plate sprinkled with salt and a lemon slice — symbolizing tears and bitterness.

• • •

York County vets continue to come together on Memorial Day, Veterans Day and other occasions.

Each Memorial Day, members of the Alexander D. Goode Post No 205, Jewish War Veterans, meet at the South Hill Hebrew Cemetery in York Township for a service. Members put flags atop the graves of their fellow

Maj. James F. Lind, formerly of York Corporation's Cost Department, wrote to Shop News that he saw plenty of Yorkco equipment in Florida. 'Makes me feel good,' he wrote. As happened so often, Lind's career blossomed with post-war prosperity. Lind represented York County in the post-war U.S. Congress.

veterans' graves.

"Every year, there are more and more flags," Jerry Cohen, commander of the post, said in 2003. "I think if anybody pinned me down and asked me why I do it, I would say it's because I was one of the lucky ones that came back."

Each year, Temple Beth Israel holds an observance of Yom HaShoah, Holocaust Remembrance Day.

• • •

The courageous actions of Alexander Goode and his three comrades — the Four Chaplains — have been detailed in several books and a made-for-TV movie.

The school in the York City School District that bears Goode's name honored the foursome with a mural, and an annual ecumenical breakfast in York County commemorates their names. The Four Chaplains are memorialized in numerous stained-glass windows and murals.

Theresa Goode remarried, and her second husband, Harry Kaplan, died in 1968. Alexander's and Theresa's daughter, Rosalie, died in an automobile accident in 1999. Theresa, a Washington, D.C., resident died at the age of 93 in 2004.

• • •

The Charles E. Williams Post No. 794 of the American Legion opened on York's East Princess Street in 1947.

Williams, one of six military brothers, died on March 31, 1945, in Italy. William Green served as commander at the time the post opened.

Other veterans organizations in towns through York County bear the names of those who served in World War II.

• • •

Bronze tablets affixed to the front of the York County Courthouse, listing a final roll call of the names of those who died in 20th-century wars, were dedicated in November 1991.

The name of Eugene Burnell Bubb, believed to be the first county serviceman to die in World War II, was initially absent. His name was later added to the memorial.

Lt. Col. George
Cechmanek, Anne
Frutiger's brother-in-law,
wrote words of condoles-
cence upon hearing of
Thomas W. Frutiger's
death.

Virginia Frutiger
Cechmanek, sister of
Thomas W. Frutiger, mar-
ried Lt. Col. George
Cechmanek in the service.
The WAC second lieu-
tenant specialized in
motor transportation.

The roll of the county war dead stood at 451 by July 4, 1946, according to The York Dispatch-Associated Press count. Over the years, as omissions such as Bubb's were uncovered, that number grew to 571 or more, according to York County Veterans Affairs Office numbers.

A Selective Service count on July 1, 1946, placed the number of York County residents who enlisted or were inducted at the nine county draft boards at 20,604. About 8,000 entered through City of York boards and 3,000 through Hanover's board. About 5,000 of those enlisted or inducted remained in the service in mid-1946.

For several years after the war, the remains of the dead were exhumed from temporary burial grounds in all theaters of war and brought back to York County for re-interment.

As late as 1948, the bodies of seven war dead were returned upon request of next of kin. Six served in the U.S. Army and one in the Marines.

Even after that, news about military men who died came back to York County.

In 1951, the military informed the family of 2nd Lt. Chester A. Griffith Jr. that the B-17 pilot's body had been found.

Griffith's plane went down in an air attack in Germany in July 1944. His body, along with the remains of two of his comrades who died in the same crash, were shipped for burial in a national cemetery near Louisville, Ky.

The community

The USO Club in York closed in July 1946 with an accounting of funds. Contributions came in at $29,853 over four years, and gifts of food amounted to $25,000.

The York County Academy was later demolished, but the old gym once housing the Pennsylvania Dutch Canteen stands, as does the North Duke Street railroad station where volunteers at the USO booth treated thou-sands of servicemen with packages of food.

• • •

By July 1946, the Victory House again was standing in Farquhar Park.

As decades passed, it fell into disrepair and later was sold to a Conewago Township pet resort, where the reno-vated structure stands today.

• • •

The Manufacturers' Association of South Central Pennsylvania, successor of the group that molded The York Plan, operates today.

It sold its longtime North Duke Street building — the site where the York Plan was organized — in 2004 and moved to new quarters at 160 Roosevelt Ave. in York. The organization's offices are located in York Corporation's former West York plant.

• • •

The White Rose Post of the Veterans of Foreign Wars constructed a monument honoring war mothers at Penn Park in 1946.

The $1,500 monument paid tribute to the sacrifices of mothers, who watched their sons and daughters serve in the military.

• • •

Two years after V-J Day, veterans and city dignitaries broke ground for Memorial Stadium, a complex to honor World War II veterans.

Construction took place on the Stauffer tract, near South Pine Street and Rockdale Avenue.

The White Roses baseball club and the York Roses professional football team played at the stadium, still used for athletic competition today.

• • •

Red Lion was among many York County communities that erected memorials after the war.

The 12-foot granite shaft at Fairmount Park, the high-est populated area of York County, honored the estimated 808 Red Lion-area men and women who served their country. Throughout the war, the borough added stars to the service flag in the town's square as news came back that one of the town's sons had been killed. The Fairmount monument made the names of those who died permanent.

Thomas W. Frutiger's name and those of 31 other area men who died in uniform were inscribed. The monument stands less than a block from the 312 Boundary Ave. home where he grew up.

Frutiger's actual burial site is half a world away. He was interred in a mass grave in Japan, a nameless white cross joining scores of others on the spot. A directory lists his name among the dead.

He had written to students at his alma mater, Red Lion High School, before he shipped out of the states in 1941.

The Red Lion Hilltop, the school newspaper, reported Frutiger's sentiments: "And he wishes that we would real-ize that our nation's future depends upon us, and that we should be willing to cooperate with our government to preserve this great American democracy."

• • •

After her husband's death, Anne Frutiger continued to

Robert N. Senft, now back home, celebrates July 4, 1946, with his wife, Ethel, at Caledonia State Park in Franklin County.

Bob and Ethel Senft pose for their 50th anniversary photograph, 1990.

work in the W.C. Frutiger & Co. cigar factory. Several years later, she married Gerald Zarfos, a World War II veteran and member of another prominent Red Lion family.

At about that time, she placed numerous wartime letters from Tom Frutiger, his medals and other documents surrounding his imprisonment into a cardboard box. She had a new family to care for.

She was active in St. Paul's Church in Red Lion and the church's United Methodist Women's group.

She died at the age of 87 in 1999.

Thomas and Anne Frutiger's sons, Thomas and Robert, live in Pittsford, N.Y., and Red Lion, respectively.

• • •

Lt. Col. George Cechmanek sent a letter of consolation to Anne Frutiger shortly after she received news of Thomas' death.

The officer was Anne's new brother-in-law. He had met and married Lt. Virginia Frutiger, who had received a Women's Army Corps commission, during the war.

"Ann, I know that it is much easier to say than to do," he wrote, "but you must be brave, and live in the future, live for your family. Time heals all wounds. These are cruel and trying times, but wars are that way."

Virginia Frutiger Cechmanek, living in California, never returned to her position at York Corporation.

• • •

Robert N. Senft retired from Borg-Warner Corp., successor to York Corporation, in 1982. He had risen through the ranks from a clerk's position to become a parts and materials manager.

After the war, Bob and Ethel Senft moved from Ethel's mother's house to a next-door ranch home in Zion View, where they lived for more than 25 years. They later moved to a retirement cottage in York.

He was active in the community both before and after retirement, serving on various church boards and as district governor of Lions Clubs in York, Adams and Cumberland counties.

Ethel also was committed to community and church matters. She never returned to the full-time work force but occasionally helped with heavy seasonal loads at Wolfgang Candy in North York.

The story of Bob and Ethel Senft mirrors that of thousands of other York County families who sacrificed much on the home and war fronts.

Often, the jobs they did in civilian life and on military assignment were everyday in nature, but when thousands did routine work well, they collectively created an Arsenal of Democracy such as the world had never seen.

• • •

Bob Senft celebrated his 85th birthday at his home in York on Nov. 20, 2004. He excused himself from an interview that day to take a phone call.

Upon returning, he said, "It's an emergency. A resident has a bloody nose, and she can't stop it. I have to run her to Memorial Hospital."

Ethel explained that such emergency runs were common. "He's never here," she said.

Sixty years later, Bob Senft continued his work on the war front. Ethel Senft looked after the home front.

Still in the thick of the fight.

Appendix

This outdoor mural observing the Four Chaplains' sacrifice was dedicated on York's West Market Street in late 1998. About 670 people died when a German U-boat torpedoed the Dorchester on Feb. 3, 1943, in the North Atlantic. The chaplains, including York's Rabbi Alexander D. Goode, second from left, were among the dead. These religious leaders relinquished seats in lifeboats and removed their own life jackets to give to fellow servicemen.

Gallery

This South George Street mural, one of more than 20 'Murals of York,' highlights themes undergirding the York Plan. This includes the overarching theme: 'Do What You Can With What You Have.' Men and women in the community produced a variety of defense products. The Army and Navy recognized excellent local efforts with the 'E' flag, left.

This two-panel mural celebrates four-star Gen. Jacob L. Devers, York County's most prominent World War II soldier. The panels are painted on the YMCA, only a few blocks from Devers' Roosevelt Avenue childhood home. His grandfather, Jacob Loucks, help found York Manufacturing Company, also located a few blocks west of this mural on Roosevelt Avenue.

A giant flywheel for a 600-ton refrigeration unit dominates this mural at York Manufacturing Company's, later York Corporation's, former West York plant. This was the first panel in the Murals of York initiative, started in 1995.

7
years of
wartime
events

1939

Sept. 1 — World War II begins: Germany invades Poland.

Sept. 3 — Great Britain and France declare war on Germany.

1940

April 9 — Germany invades Norway and Denmark.

May 10 — Germany invades Belgium, Holland, Luxembourg and France.

June 10 — Italy declares war on France and Britain.

June 22 — France signs a cease-fire with Germany.

July 10 — Battle of Britain begins.

Sept. 27 — Germany, Japan and Italy sign Axis agreement.

1941

March 11 — President Franklin Roosevelt signs Lend-Lease Act.

April 6 — Germany invades Greece and Yugoslavia.

June 22 — Germany invades the Soviet Union, Operation Barbarossa.

Sept. 8 — German troops initiate 900-day siege of Leningrad.

Dec. 7 — Japanese attack Pearl Harbor.

Dec. 8 — The United States enters World War II, joining Britain and the Soviet Union as primary Allied nations against the major Axis countries: Germany, Italy and Japan.

1942

Jan. 20 — Hitler regime initiates plans for the Final Solution.

April 18 — U.S. bombers strike Tokyo in the Doolittle raid.

May 4-8 — United States checks Japanese assault in the Battle of the Coral Sea.

May 6 — American forces surrender in the Philippines.

June 4-6 — U.S. Navy triumphs over Japanese naval forces in Battle of Midway.

Aug. 7 — U.S. Marines land on Guadalcanal.

Aug. 25 — Hitler orders the capture of Stalingrad.

Oct. 23 — Britain attacks Axis forces in Egypt.

Nov. 8 — Allied troops land in Northern Africa, Operation Torch.

No Time for Stewing

York refrigeration is speeding up the manufacture of explosives. York men are fighting the war in York plants today and every day.

KEEP ON FIGHTING

The advertisement touts York Corporation equipment's role in the production of explosives and ammunition deployed in all theaters of World War II. The company's cooling machines aided in the production of synthetic chemicals used to make the ordnance.

1943

Jan. 14-24 — Allies call for unconditional surrender of Axis at Casablanca Conference.

Feb. 2 — Germans issue final surrender demand at Stalingrad.

May 13 — Axis forces in Northern Africa surrender.

July 10 — Allied forces invade Sicily.

Sept. 3 — Italy surrenders to the Allies.

Sept. 9 — Allied troops land at Salerno, Italy.

Nov. 20 — U.S. forces invade Tarawa.

1944

June 4 — Allies enter Rome.

June 6 — D-Day forces land at Normandy.

June 19 — U.S. Naval Force defeats the Japanese in the Battle of the Philippine Sea.

June 22 — Soviets attack German forces in USSR.

July 18 — Japan's Prime Minister Tojo resigns.

How to Visualize America's Rising Air Power!

Project New York's famous Fifth Avenue on up through the state across the Harlem River, through the Bronx, Mt. Vernon, Bronxville, Scarsdale to the outskirts of the city of White Plains. Next, erect a continuous building over it from curb to curb for more than 24 miles!

Then you would be able to see the amount of war plane producing area in which York is playing a vital role as this is written.

How many bombers, fighters, trainers, and transports can be built in this space is obviously a military secret. But you may be sure that no other plants in the world will be able to build them better ... or faster!

Control of temperature, of humidity, of dust, grit and fumes gives control over lost time and wasted material

by keeping gages faithful, by keeping dimensions constant in raw stock, work-in-process and finished parts, by preventing the scratching of mirror-finished parts and preventing rust and corrosion. Industrial air conditioning today is an essential instrument of war.

York services to the aircraft industry are but one phase of York war services which include all types of mechanical cooling for warships and cargo carriers, cantonments and bases, great chemical and ordnance research laboratories and housing, besides direct action on York on tanks, coast guard ships and other instruments of ordnance of war.

York Machinery Corporation, York, Pennsylvania.

YORK *Climate for Production*
REFRIGERATION AND AIR CONDITIONING FOR **WAR**
HEADQUARTERS FOR MECHANICAL COOLING SINCE 1885

York Corporation outlines the amount of war plane production area its equipment was cooling — equivalent to a continuous building stretching 24 miles. 'How many bombers, fighters, trainers, and transports can be built in this space is obviously a military secret,' the advertisement stated. 'But you may be sure that no other plants in the world will be able to build them better ... or faster!'

Eagle Eyes for the Groundlings of War

Within the smoky, reeking gloom of a hurtling tank, the commander must see through the eyes of flyers far above him. And at modern flying speeds, pilots, observers, bombardiers must be protected from the air stream. Plexiglas, said to be "the most useful plastic in aviation," provides tough, shatter-proof colorless transparency for cockpit enclosures, observation hatches, gun turrets and bomber noses. And in its manufacture, Plexiglas is protected by York air conditioning, a specially engineered installation that frees the air of dust that might otherwise settle on the warm plastic, that maintains the exacting temperature and humidity levels necessary to perfect hardening. Here, as in a hundred other industries, air conditioning is stepping up the production of what-it-takes to stop the enemies of freedom. York Ice Machinery Corporation, York, Pennsylvania.

"KEEP 'EM FLYING"

YORK *Plastics*
REFRIGERATION AND AIR CONDITIONING
HEADQUARTERS FOR MECHANICAL COOLING SINCE 1885

This advertisement suggests that York Corporation's air conditioning helps shield plastic-making industrial plants from dust. Further, the cooling ensured constant temperature and humidity levels required for hardening.

July 20 — Plot to assassinate Hitler fails.

Aug. 15 — Allies invade Southern France, Operation Dragoon. York native Gen. Jacob L. Devers commands the assault.

Oct. 20 — The Allies begin landing in Philippines.

Oct. 23 — Allied Naval Forces win the Battle of Leyte Gulf in the Philippines.

Dec. 16 — Germans go on offensive in the Battle of the Bulge.

1945

March 16 — U.S. Marines capture Iwo Jima.

March 31 — The Devers-led 6th Army Group crosses Rhine River into Germany.

April 12 — President Roosevelt dies.

April 25 — U.S. and Soviet troops meet on the Elbe River.

April 28 — Italian leader Benito Mussolini killed.

April 30 — Hitler takes his own life in Berlin.

May 2 — Soviet forces capture Berlin.

May 5 — Devers' 6th Army accepts the surrender of a million prisoners in southern Germany.

May 8 — Germany surrenders unconditionally to the Allies, ending war in Europe, V-E Day.

June 1 — Allied forces secure Okinawa.

Aug. 6 — Atomic bomb blasts Hiroshima.

Aug. 8 — Soviet Union declares war on Japan.

Aug. 9 — Atomic bomb strikes Nagasaki.

Aug. 14-15 — America celebrates Japan's informal surrender, known as V-J Day.

Sept. 2 — Japan signs surrender agreement aboard battleship U.S.S. Missouri in Tokyo Bay, ending World War II.

571

or more

made

supreme

sacrifice in

World War II

———

Hundreds of servicemen from York County died in World War II, according to a Supreme Sacrifice Memorial Committee booklet published in 1993.

Representing Gold, Silver and Blue Star mothers, these women unveil a memorial at York's Penn Park on Veterans Day, 1946. From left, Lizzie Doll, Gold Star mother; Mrs. McKinley Harley, Blue Star mother; and Bessie E. Lloyd, Silver Star mother, are part of the ceremony. In World War II, the Gold Star hung in windows of families who had a member killed in action. Blue Stars were awarded to families with a member in the service. Silver Stars were awarded to families with a member who showed gallantry in action.

Pvt. Eugene B. Bubb, on board ship en route to Hawaii, was the first York County soldier to die in battle. He was a victim of the attack on Pearl Harbor.

World War II roll of honor

A

Vincent G. Aldinger and Dennis J. Allen, both of York; Edgar W. Allison Jr., York County; Reed D. Allison, Glen Rock; Earl L. Alloways, York; Clair E. Altland, Dover; Paul W. Altland and Eugene L. Alwood, both of York County; Morgan E. Amsbaugh, York; Edward C. Amspacker, Hanover; Gene L. Anderson, Winterstown; Howard M. Anderson Jr., Stewartstown; Budd H. Andrews and George L. Angel, both of York; Robert A. Angelo Jr. and Milton F. Appler, both of York County; Robert L. Arthur, York; John W. Askrew, York County.

B

Daniel C. Babcock Jr., Dallastown; Frederick Babcock, York; George A. Bagley, York County;

George F. Bailey, York; Walter A. Bailey, York County; Clarence U. Bair and Ellis L. Baird, both of York; John W. Baish Jr., Franklin Township; Richard A. Baker, Dillsburg; James E. Bankes, Wrightsville; Glenn L. Baublitz, Glen Rock; Lawrence S. Baublitz, York; Woodrow W. Baugher, Codorus Township; Leo H. Baughman, York County; Reginald T. Beattie, York; Julian L. Beavers, York County; Allen J. Beck Jr., Spring Grove; Monroe L. Becker, Hanover; Paul L. Becker, Hanover; John A. Bennett and Spurgeon E. Bentzel, both of York County; Guy U. Berkstresser, York; Franklin E. Biller, York Haven; Warren H. Billet, Wrightsville; Richard L. Black, Glen Rock; Richard K. Bluste and Karl B. Boll, both of York; Harry J. Bollinger, Thomasville; Cletus H. Bortner, Hanover; Harold T. Bose, Glen Rock;

Clarence M. Bowen, New Cumberland; Philip R. Bowman, Seven Valleys; Herbert H. Boyer and Roy D. Boyer, both of York; Walter L. Boyer, York County; George Brabham Jr., York; Francis H. Brady and George J. Bragam, both of York County; Frederick L. Brandt and Kenneth E. Brenneman, both of York; Kenneth N. Brown, Dover; Norman C. Browne, York County; Glenn R. Bruaw, York Haven; Durwood F. Brunk, York; Elwood B. Bubb, York County; Eugene B. Bubb and Kenneth C. Bubb, both of York; Richard E. Bull, York Haven; Ervin F. Bupp, Jacobus; Ross A. Burkins, Red Lion.

C

John F. Cacciola, York County; Harold R. Cain, Washington Township; Cecil B. Caldwell and Lloyd A. Carter, both of York; Thomas B. Chapman, York County; Paul W. Cheever, Bernard H. Cohen and Joseph A. Concino Jr., all of York; Arthur H. Cooper, Red Lion; Horace J. Cooper, York County; Thomas Cosaftes, York; Carroll W. Cramer, Glen Rock; Ralph W. Craul, York County; Kenneth W. Craumer, York; John H. Craver and Walter L. Crowl, both of York County; Harold E. Crumling, Wrightsville.

D

Gail F. Daily, York; Bruce W. Danner, New Cumberland; Donald J. Davis, York; Philip D. Davis, Dover; Robert E. Day, York County; Robert O. DeCheubell, Hanover; Gail R. DeWitt, York County; Charles C. Deller and Thomas A. Deller, both of Dallastown; Henrie Descheemaeker, Hanover; George J. Devono, Dallastown; Louis J. Didio, Leon A. Diehl and Harry E. Dietz, all of York; Raymond G. Dietz, Wrightsville; Joseph J. Dilullo, Red Lion; August A. Dinkle, Washington Township; Stanley M. Disney, York; Joseph D. Donnelly, York County; Richard E. Dougherty and Richard T. Dreisbach, both of York; Stanley M. Drezeroski, Washington Township; Lawrence E. Duncan, York County; Vernon E. Dundore, York.

E

Thomas J. Eckenrode, York; Calvin M. Edelblute, Dover; Edward C. Ehrhart and Joseph G. Eline, both of Hanover; Clarence E. Ellwein, Wrightsville; Eugene E. Elmore and Robert A. Elsesser, York; Harry W. Eltz, York County; Edward C. Emanuel, York; Albert B. Emig, Hellam; J.D. Ensminger Jr., Windsor; William D. Ensminger Jr., Leroy C. Erwin and Allen J. Estep, all of York; Charles R. Ettinger, York County.

F

Charles H. Fahringer, Hellam; Glendon L. Fahringer, York; Elmer L. Faircloth, York County; Nevin W. Fake, York; Luther F. Farner Jr., Hanover; John E. Fauth, Red Lion; George W. Ferree, Hellam; Lloyd J. Fishel, Glenville; Raymond G. Fishel, York County; Milton L. Fletcher, York County; Richard L. Flickinger Jr., Hanover; James T. Flinchbaugh, Felton; Preston S. Flinchbaugh, Red Lion; Francis W. Fogle, York; John B. Forry, Hellam; Raymond S. Fox, Franklin Township; John J. Frank, Red Lion; Warren L. Frank, York; Hugh French, York; Charles M. Frey, York; Gordon B. Frey, Manchester; William E. Frey, Red Lion; Thomas W. Frutiger, Red Lion; Maynard P. Fuhrman, Glen Rock.

G

Donald J. Gallagher, York County; Donald R. Galloway, York; Leroy A. Gantz, York County; Harold H. Garbrick, York County; Ralph Gardner, Dillsburg; Ray F. Garman, Glen Rock; Everett D. Gehb, Stewartstown; Eugene H. Gehly, Windsor; Bill A. Gembar, York County; John D. Gemmill, Red Lion; Leo P. Getz, New Freedom; Charles A. Gillespie, Washington Township; E.W. Gladfelter Jr., York County; C.F. Glatfelter,

SERVICE OF THANKSGIVING
at the
CLOSE OF THE WORLD WAR
held in
St. Matthew's Lutheran Church, York, Pa.

MAY LIBERTY WITH LAW AND PEACE WITH RIGHTEOUSNESS COME TO ALL THE WORLD

More than 250 men and women (Dorothy Chronister, Ruth F. Corbin, Helen C. Rodewig and Emma Rudy) from St. Matthew's Lutheran Church served in World War II. Lewis H. Harbold, George L. Spangler, Charles E. Hoffman, Philip D. Davis, George F. Bailey, Morgan E. Amsbaugh, Roy F. Shultz, Charles E. Myers and Roy Reichard gave their lives for their country. The church was located in the vicinity of York Corporation's Roosevelt Avenue plant, and many of its workers worshipped there. This is the cover of a bulletin for a service celebrating the war's end.

Yoe; William L. Glatfelter, York County; Day C. Gohn, Dallastown; Dale E. Good, York; Morris L. Good Jr., York; Alexander D. Goode, York County; Harold W. Gordon, Airville; James L. Gouker, Hanover; Gerald F. Griffen, Washington Township; C.A. Griffith Jr., York County; Harold E. Griffith, York County; Jesse M. Grogg, Hanover; Franklin L. Gromling, Hellam; James S. Grossman Jr., Newberry Township; Robert E. Grossman, York County; George H. Grove, Jefferson; Llewellyn A. Grove, York County; Robert M. Grove, York; William F. Gunnett, York; G. William Gunter, Delta.

This World War II memorial, designed by York County sculptor Lorann Jacobs, was unveiled on York's Continental Square in August 2002. Organizers started planning for a memorial two years before, raising $250,000 from companies and individual donors to create this bronze statue resting on a granite stand.

H

William B. Hafner, York; Charles Hake Jr., Newberry Township; Peter M. Halesey Jr., York County; William E. Hall, York County; Vincent D. Halloran, York County; Charles R. Hamsher, Newberry Township; Dale V. Hannigan, Red Lion; Lewis H. Harbold, York; Fred J. Haring, York County; Joseph J. Harkins, York County; Clark M. Harmon, Laurel; Lester L. Harrold, Spring Grove; Clinton C. Harry, Dillsburg; Russell W. Hartman, Hanover; Jack T. Harvey, Red Lion; Harvey E. Haugh, Delta; Nelson L. Haugh, Wrightsville; Alexander Heckel, Wrightsville; Eugene C. Heffner, Felton; Harold R. Heilman, York County; Morgan E. Hein, York; Wilbur W. Hein, York County; William E. Heist, York; Roman E. Helfrich, Dallastown; Carl W. Helm, Dallastown; Nevin H. Herman Jr., York County; Laverhn E. Hershey, York; Clarence V. Hess, York; Howard A. Hess, York; Albert L. Hetrick, York; Robert C.E. Hetrick, Hanover; Harry H. Hildebrand, York; Homer H. Hildebrand, York; Preston Hildebrand, York County; Arlin E. Hilt, Hanover; Richard E. Himes, Yorkana; Hobart B. Hivner, Red Lion; Charles E. Hoffman, York County; Lewis H. Hoffman Jr., York; Millard E. Hoffman, York; Richard C. Hoffman, Red Lion; Richard M. Holland, Red Lion; Carroll L. Holloway, New Freedom; Kenneth C. Holtzapple, York; George A. Hoover, York; John W. Hopkins, York; Joseph E. Horn, New Freedom; John R. Hubley Jr., Dover; Donald E. Humbert, York County; John H. Hummel, York; Benjamin S. Hunt Jr., New Freedom.

I

James E. Ingoe, Stewartstown; Arthur H. Irons, York; Vernon L. Irwin, York.

J

Robert L. Jacobs, York; William F. Jacobs, Dover; Russell M. James, York County; Clarence L. Jamison, York County; Willard G. Jamison, York; Jack A. Jasper, York; Leonard R. Johns, Washington Township; James I. Johnson, York County; William K. Jordan Jr., York County; Carl Justh, Lewisberry.

K

Peter F. Kadusky, Washington Township; Edward Kajarick, Washington Township; Donald P. Kane, York County; Harold R. Keener, Washington Township; Clifford E. Keeney, York County; Donald B. Keeney, York; Paul D. Kehr, York County; Charles L. Keister, York; Elmer M. Kelbaugh, York County; James S. Kellenberger, York County; Richard G. Kerchner, Thomasville; Dale S. Kerlin, York County; Carl S. Kilmore, York; Vance M. Kimmel, Dillsburg; Charles R. King, York County; Irvin S. Kline Jr., York; Robert Kline, York; Julian S. Kling, York; Paul A. Kling, York County; Richard J. Klunk, York County; Walter M. Klunk, York; William J. Knaub, York County; Samuel N. Knisely, Red Lion; William F. Koch Jr., York County; James W. Kohr, Mount Wolf; Robert W. Kohler, Dallastown; Eugene J. Kraus, York County; William V. Kraus, York; Emory L. Kreeger, York County; Robert C. Kressler, York; Lester Kuntz, York County.

L

Joseph Latrovich, York New Salem; Earl R. Lau, York; Charles A. Laucks, Red Lion; Paul J. Laughman, Hanover; Arthur H. Lease and Burnell K. Leash, York; Kenneth E. Lecrone, York; Lige Lee and Joseph E. Lefever Jr., York County; Roy E. Leinert, Spring Grove; Gilbert E. Lentz, Joseph F. Lewis and Donald K. Lightner, all of York County; Leon J. Livelsberger and Cyril L. Livelsberger, Hanover; Cyrus B. Lloyd, York County; Phil Lofink, York; Francis A. Lombard, Washington Township; John M. Lovett, York; Henry L. Lynn Jr., York County.

M

Walter H. Malles, Stewartstown; Edward W.L. Manifold, Donald F. March and Paul C. March, all of York; Kenneth D. Marsh and Chester F. Marshall, York County; James H. Marshall Jr., York; Calvin E. Martin, York Haven;

The New Freedom community observes Memorial Day 1946, its first since the end of World War II.

Joseph Edward Horn was among the most decorated servicemen in the New Freedom-Glen Rock areas. He died in the Battle of the Bulge, one of about 20 military men in the community to lose their lives.

Edward L. Matyas, York New Salem; Lewis Mayer, York County; Preston L. McCleary, Red Lion; Edward M. McDonald, York; John E. McDonald, York County; Robert F. McElroy, Wrightsville; Garvin C. McKonly, York County; Bernard L. McSherry, York; Clair A. Meckley, Hanover; Donald W. Miesky, York County; Arthur J. Miller Jr., Mount Wolf; Charles S. Miller, York County; Charles R. Miller of Hanover; Edward Miller, Washington Township; Elson E. Miller, York County; Garland S. Miller, Mount Wolf; Harold E. Miller, York; John D. Miller, Airville; Joseph H. Miller, Red Lion; Lavere L. Miller, Yoe; Ralph R. Miller, Hanover; William J. Miller, York; Kenneth L. Minnich, Red Lion; Stanley M. Mitzel, York; William G. Mohr, Mount Wolf; Everette N. Morris, Fawn Grove; William L. Morrison and Raymond M. Moul, Hanover; Paul S. Mowery Jr., Dillsburg; David M. Mumper and David E. Mundis, York; Robert W. Muntz, Hanover; John S. Murphy, Delta; Wilbur H. Musselman, Hanover; Charles E. Myers, York County; Earl E. Myers, York; Ellis C. Myers, Hanover; Eugene E. Myers, Red Lion; George W.

Myers, Menges Mill; Gideon K. Myers, Red Lion; Marlin R. Myers, York; Paul W. Myers, Red Lion; Raymond H. Myers, Hanover.

N

Edward P. Neiderer and Robert J. Nunemaker, York County; Eugene M. Nesbit, William F. Noel Jr. and Mertis A. Noble, Hanover; Warren R. Ness and Vernon B. Noble, York.

O

Paul J. Oaster and John E. Orendorff, York County; William L. Oldfield Jr., Spring Grove; Grier P. Osborne, Peach Bottom.

P

Edward B. Palmer, Grover C. Parr, Lewis W. Phillips and William D. Poole, all of York; Bernard Paniczko, Charles W. Pennel and Paul W. Potorff, York County; Norman H. Parrish, Glen Rock; Earl M. Paules, Mount Wolf; Harold E. Peterman, Mechanicsburg; John R. Price, York County.

R

Luther G. Raby, Charles H. Rahe, Robert E. Ramsay,

John F. Reever Jr., Roy R. Reichard, Robert C. Reichelt, Earl H. Roach, Charles E. Roberts, Robert J. Robertson, William F. Robinson, Ralph K. Roderick and Charles F. Raifsnider, all of York; James A. Raine, York Haven; Francis B. Rang, Hanover; Charles A. Raver and Jacob T. Raver, Glen Rock; Charles R. Rawheiser, New Bridgeville; Levere J. Reider, Windsor; Albert W. Reinecker, York Haven; James M. Reisinger, John C. Reiter and James E. Rhine, York County; Ernest R. Rhoades, Delta; John P. Ring, Stewartstown; Russell H. Ritz, Freysville; Frank W. Rodgers Jr., York County; Arthur E. Rogers, York County; William J. Rohrbaugh, York New Salem; Charles E. Rohrbaugh, York County; Paul O. Romich, York; Elmer G. Ropp Jr., York; Emory E. Rosh, Hellam; Donald L. Rossier, New Freedom; Cloyde M. Ross Jr., New Cumberland; Charles L. Rowe, York County; George A. Ruby, York County; Richard R. Rusher, York; Gordon D. Rutters, Hanover; Henry D. Rutters, York County; Robert A. Ryder, York County; William E. Ryder, York.

S

Ralph L. Sallada, Manchester; James L. Sawyer, York; Orrie A. Saylor, Red Lion; Robert L. Scantling, Wrightsville; John D. Schaeberle, York; George S. Schroyer, York County; George E. Schue, York County; Carl A. Schwab, York County; Charles M. Scott III, York County; Clair E. Sechrist, Hellam; Thomas P. Sechrist, Dallastown; Harold E. Seitz, Dallastown; Roy E. Selak, York; John A. Senft Jr., Spring Grove; Robert G. Serff, Hanover; Harold J. Shane, York; Calvin R.

KENNETH LEROY MINNICH
*Second Lieutenant, Pilot B-24 Bomber—
Army Air Corps*

Parents: Mr. and Mrs. Roy Minnich, 23 S. Franklin St. Born Nov. 17, 1922. *Service:* Nov. 21, 1940 to Aug. 21, 1943. *Basic Training:* Langley Field, Va. Assigned to 357th Bomb Squadron, 82nd Bomb Group. Sailed on *Empress of Scotland,* a British troop ship, July, 1943, from Newport News, Va. Arrived at Casablanca, French West Africa. Combat duty in North Africa, Libya and Italy. Citations: Purple Heart, Pre-Pearl Harbor and ETO Ribbons and Good Conduct Medal. *Type of Work:* Pilot. Killed in action over Italy Aug. 21, 1943. A letter from a surviving crew member stated while on a mission to bomb the Marshalling Yards at Cancello, Italy, at exactly 2 P.M., we dropped our bombs on the target—still battling swarms of fighters now attacking. A shell struck giving me a jolt, throwing me from my turret down on the cameraman who was already dead from a wound in the stomach. Lt. Minnich and Lt. Cook were still in the cockpit trying to level the plane now in a spin so we could jump. Lt. Minnich waved us all out with his right arm as he leveled the plane for a short time (control cables were all shattered by the direct hit of flak on the lower right side of the flight deck). Falling in mid-air, I pulled my rip-cord as my descent slowed I looked to see our shattered burning plane. I later learned only three survived the crash.

Red Lion's Kenneth Leroy Minnich, a B-24 pilot, lost his life in fighting over Italy in 1943.

Shaw, York County; Luther W. Shaw, Windsor; M. Heine Shear, York; James C.R. Sheets, York County; Carrie T. Sheetz, Newberry Township; Lloyd H. Sheldon, York County; J.M. Shellenberger Jr., York; Guy E. Shelley Jr., York; William C. Shelton, York; Paul E. Shenberger, York; John J. Shetrone, York; Robert L. Shipe, York; Lester L. Shoemaker, Hanover; Guy E. Shoff, Red Lion; Walter D. Shouck, York; William A. Showers, York; Clarence S. Shuler, Dallastown; Roy F. Shultz, York County; Richard A. Silar, York County; George E. Simmons, York; Warren H. Sipe, Mount Wolf; Thomas L. Sipling, Hanover; Kenneth E. Slenker, York County; Maurice S. Small, Hanover; Wayne S. Smeigh, York; Charles F. Smith, York County; Guy L. Smith, Windsor; Leon C. Smith, York; Lynnwood W. Smith, York County; Nevin K. Smith, Glen Rock; Paul A. Smith, York County; Willis C. Smith, York County; Orville E. Snell, York; Athey H. Sober, Jackson Township; Boyd E. Sower, York County; Kenneth L.

Sowers, York; Paul A. Sowers, York; Chalmer E. Spangler, York; Edwin L. Spangler Jr., York; George L. Spangler, York County; Paul J. Spangler, York County; Thomas L. Spoerer, Dover; Edwin E. Sprenkel, York; Denton N. Sprenkle, Red Lion; Wilbert E. Sprenkle, Fawn Grove; Ernest E. Spyker, Windsor; Kenneth G. Staab, York County; Harry L. Stabley, Red Lion; Charles J. Stambach, York; Edward J. Stambaugh, Thomasville; Harold E. Stambaugh, York County; Paul E. Stambaugh, Dillsburg; Henry P. Starr and Earl W. Staub, York County; Robert E. Stauffer Jr., York; Quinton R. Steidler, Mount Wolf; Paul A. Steinfelt, Red Lion; George M. Stermer, Red Lion; John H. Sterner, Spring Grove; Russell A. Sterner, Seven Valleys; Guy A. Stewart, York; Thomas E. Stine, Dallastown; Stewart Stokes, Red Lion; Edward E. Stover, York; Harry Z. Strine, Ployd E. Stump, John W. Sullenberger and Donald N. Suereth, York; Herbert L. Suereth Jr., William H. Swartz and John W. Swenson, York; Glenn

Sweigart and Jacob C. Sweigart, New Cumberland.

T

Bruce K. Taylor, York Haven; Kenneth Taylor, York; Richard H. Taylor, York; Frank W. Tharp, York County; Wilford C. Thoman, York County; Elmer H. Thomas, York County; Lawrence E. Thomas, York County; George W. Throne, York County; John Tittnick, York New Salem; Max H. Tomb, York County; Chester W. Tome, Laurel; Kenneth K. Tredway, York County; Charles H. Trimmer, York; Norman L. Trimmer, York; William E. Trout, York County; James A. Tyler, York County.

U-V

Walter D. Uffelman, York County; Millard G. Unger and Brimley Varchol, Hanover; John W. Varholla, Mount Pleasant.

W

Robert C. Wagaman, Hanover; Albert J. Wagman, Laurel; Richard H.

Wakefield, Wrightsville; Marvin L. Walker, Glen Rock; Glenn M. Wallace, Windsor; Quay C. Wallace, York County; Russell A. Wallick, Red Lion; N.B. Waltemyer Jr., York County; Wilbur C. Waltermyer, Stewartstown; John W. Walton, Walter L. Wampler Jr. and Francis D. Warner, all of York; Dennis L. Weaver, York County; Herbert A. Weldman Jr. and David S. Welsh, both York County; Irvin J. Wentz, Hanover; William T. Wentz, York; Harry W. Werry, York County; Edwin L. Wertz, Etters; Reynier S. Wertz and Bernell E. Wherley, both of York County; Cleo F. Wetzel, York; Frederick S. Whimert, Dallastown; Charles R. White and Charles E. Williams, both of York; John P. Willwert, Red Lion; Charles W. Wilson, Russell H. Wilson and Paul J. Winebrenner, all of York County; Walter E. Winemiller, York; Gerald E. Wire, Thomasville; Oliver P. Wire, York; Melvin L. Wise, Red Lion; George F. Wisenall, York; John W. Witta, Red Lion; Harold J. Wolf, York County; William R. Wolf, York; Rodger E. Wright, York County.

Y

Anthony Yaqunito, Washington Township; Robert H. Yeager, Wrightsville; Jack T. Yeaple, Raymond H. Yeaple and Robert C. Yingling, all of York; Russel J. Yoder and George L. Young, both of York County.

Z

Lawrence E. Zepp and Robert W. Zercher, both of York County; William M. Zinn Jr., York; Clarence E. Zorbaugh, York County; Andy H. Zuidema, Newberry Township; Gorman L. Zumbrum, York; Frank E. Zyak, New Salem.

366

died in other wars in 20th and 21st centuries

———

Hundreds from York County gave their lives in World War I, Korean War, Vietnam War, Persian Gulf War and Global War on Terrorism.

TRIBUTE TREES ON THE LINCOLN HIGHWAY
"THE ROAD OF REMEMBRANCE"

These blanks filled, to be used as a record, for men who died in the service during the World War.

Name in full *Wilton H. Abel*
Residence *Wrightsville, Pa.*
Dept. of service *Coast Artillery – 50th Reg. – Btn. B*
Rank *Private*
Where died *On high seas – on board transport "America".*

This card provides information on Wilton H. Abel, who died in World War I. The Wrightsville Presbyterian Sunday School sponsored a tree along the Lincoln Highway in memory of Abel. More than 6,000 county residents served in the Great War. One hundred and ninety-five lost their lives.

World War I roll of honor

A
Samuel C. Abel, Hallam; Howard W. Abel, Wrightsville; Wilton Abel, Wrightsville; Harry C. Ahrens, York; Bernard P. Althoff, Hanover; Paul J. Althoff, York; William C. Arnold, Dillsburg.

B
Chester H. Bair, Gatchelville; Harold H. Bair, Hanover; Harry E. Barnhart, Yoe; John H. Basehore, Goldsboro; Elias M. Baugher, Jefferson; William H. Beck, Conewago Twp.; George L. Becker, N. Codorus Twp.; Charles R. Berkholder, Muddy Creek Forks; George Ardey Billmeyer, York; Noah R. Bisker, Yoe; George H. Brenner, York; Harry W. Brown, York; Wilbur D. Buchmeyer, York; Charles W. Buie, Seven Valleys; George G. Burgess, York.

C
Calvin A. Carbaugh, Hanover; Walter H. Case, Hanover; Charles T. Cassett, Hanover.

D
James A. Danner, Cly; Warren B. Dietz, York; John A. Doll, York; Clarence E. Dolls, Hanover; Elmer Dunkle, Wrightsville.

E
Walter J. Ely, Hallam; George E. Evans, York.

F
William J. Feldman, York; John H. Ferree, York; Charles G. Fetrow, Newberry Twp.; Walter L. Fitzgerald, York; Edward H. Flory, Spry; James E. Folckomer, York; Harry P. Folkomer, York New Salem; George J. Frey, Long Level; Oscar Frey, Mount Wolf.

G
Wilson J. Gailey, New Park; Michael Gardner, York; Walter S. Garrett, York; William F. Geesey, Dallastown; William F. Gehring, Hanover; John W. Geiser, Thomasville; Elmer H. Gemmill, Brogue; Quentin M. Gerbrick, Glen Rock; Howard H. Gilbert, Craley; Howard L. Goodling, Loganville; Austin L. Grove, Glen Rock; Walter E. Grove, Red Lion.

H
Chester G.N. Hannigan, East Prospect; Earl G. Harman, York; Thomas W. Haubert, Spring Garden Twp.; Urias C. Hays, Violet Hill; Robert G. Hays, Newberry Twp.; Wesley Heffner, Chanceford; Harrison D. Heindel, York; Curvin H. Heiss, Dallastown; Edward D. Heiss, Dallastown; Joseph H. Hendrickson, York; Walter B. Herrman, Red Lion; Charles B. Hess, Franklintown; George B. Hoffman, York; Nevin O. Hoffman, Stony Brook; Quentin A. Hose, Dallastown; Albert S. Hunt, Spry; Monroe R. Hunter, Carroll Twp.

UNUSUAL MEMORIAL DAY CEREMONIES HERE AND IN COUNTY; LINCOLN TRIBUTE

THOUSANDS GATHER TO DEDICATE SHRINE AT NATION'S CAPITOL

President Harding Accepts Memorial in Behalf of American People

AMPLIFIERS SPREAD SPEECH FAR AND WIDE

Little of Military Splendor About Dedication Services

Washington, May 30 (By the Associated Press)—The homage of a people was poured out today at the shrine erected by a decade of patient labor to Abraham Lincoln. Under the thoughtful gaze of his marble likeness, dim in the shadowy background of the gleaming white temple his countrymen have raised to him, thousands of Americans were gathered.

Men great in the councils of the nation were there. The President came to accept in the nation's name the memorial reared at the river him. A former president came gladly to give accounting of his trust as head of the commission that saw the great work to its completion. None

JOKINGLY CALLS FOR HELP SEVERAL TIMES; DROWNED

Rochester, Pa., May 30.—Because he had jokingly called for help several times while swimming in the Ohio river near Monaca, today, Tony Dallas, of Rochester, failed to receive assistance later when he was attacked by cramps and drowned before other bathers could reach him.

SAY OWNERS HAVE FIXED PRICE ON COAL

Retail Dealers Associations Will File Protests With Secretary Hoover

WILL MEAN ADVANCE

Washington, May 30.—Declaring that coal producers who are here in preparation for a conference with Secretary Hoover tomorrow on coal prices held a preliminary meeting today and agreed upon a price program calling for a minimum of $3 a ton at the mines, representatives of retail dealers' associations prepared tonight to file protests with the department of commerce against official approval being given any such figure. The conference has been called for a discussion with bituminous coal operators with the view of preventing an advance in prices dur-

UNVEILING OF "ROAD TO REMEMBRANCE" TABLETS AN EPOCH

Great Crowds Witness Exercises at Abbottstown and Wrightsville

SOLEMN CEREMONIES AT PROSPECT HILL

Citizens Participate in Parade in York; Head Address by Charles F. Pass

Perfect weather, with a burning sun overhead, but a cool, refreshing breeze bringing relief, marked the first community observance of Memorial day in this city. All York put on its gayest of gala attire, many of the buildings in the center of the city being bedecked with large American flags and other elaborate buntings floating in the breeze. The unveiling of the "Road of Remembrance" tablets at Wrightsville and Abbottstown, the decoration of soldiers' graves, a mammoth parade in York at 1:30 o'clock, followed by ceremonies of a most solemn and impressive character at Prospect Hill cemetery, were the principal

In reporting on Memorial Day, 1922, activities, The Gazette and Daily highlighted the 'Road to Remembrance' program, observing the planting of 1,500 red oaks, elms, sugar maples and tulip trees along the Lincoln Highway between Wrightsville and Abbottstown. Five-foot-high monuments were erected in those two towns to commemorate those who served and those who died. The Women's Club of York helped fund the planting. The War Mothers Club supported a similar planting of sycamore trees along the Susquehanna Trail. Today, some trees remain along the roadways, but many have fallen victim to disease, neglect, wider roads and fast-moving cars.

J

Kerwin E. Jacoby, York; Malvin N. Jamison, Spring Grove.

K

Charles E. Kain, York; Millard Kearney, New Freedom; Albert J. Kinsell, Hanover; Henry L. Kinsey, Dover; Joseph E. Klinedinst, York; Clarence E. Knaub, Red Lion; Raymond F. Knighton, York; Charles R. Kohler, Stewartstown; Charles E. Kohr, Mount Wolf; Clarence Kopp, Penn Twp.; Stewart W. Krider, York; Cecil J. Krone, Warrington Twp.; Robert Krout, Springfield Twp.

L

John T. Lane, Peach Bottom; Paul E. Lau, Hanover; Clarence E. Leash, York; Sherman W. Leifer, York; George H. Leitheiser, Wrightsville; Sherman C. Leonard, York; George M. Lightner, York; John E. Lillich, York; Harry E. Loose, Menges Mills; Raymond A. Lowe, Hanover; Valentine K. Lutz, East Hopewell Twp.

M

Roy A. McClane, York; Clark R. McWilliams, Hanover; Clarence W. March, Mount Royal; Russell E. Markey, York; Samuel N. Markley, Cly;

Jacob Markline, Penn Twp.; Allen L. Meckley, Glenville; William H. Meckley, Hanover; David F. Miller, Red Lion; Ervin C. Miller, Hanover; Harry J. Miller, Lower Chanceford Twp.; Harry W. Miller, Dillsburg; Joseph M. Miller, Hanover; Robert B. Miller, Dillsburg; George R. Monroe, York; John F. Morton, York; David W. Mundis, West Manchester Twp.; Walter E. Myers, York; William H. Myers, York; John L. Mayer, York.

N

Aaron D. Neff, York; William M. Neff, York; Harold C. Nobel, York.

O

Howard B. Olewiler, Red Lion.

P

David E. Poff, Wrightsville; Rodney W. Polack, York.

R

Cletus F. Rebert, West Manheim Twp.; Edwin C. Rebert, York; Wilbert Reever, Mount Zion; Alvin T. Rehmeyer, Stewartstown; William R. Reisinger, Windsor Twp.; William T. Ringland, Lower Chanceford Twp.; Milton M. Rittenhouse, York County; Harry B. Rodes, York; Melvin A. Rohrbaugh, Marburg; Edward Roser, York; Homer N. Roth, Hanover; David Rupp III, York; Wilford Rupprecht, Hanover.

S

Erwin E. Sayers, York; Latimer Sayers, York; Charles Schroll, Cly; James F. Schuman, York; Joseph Sciortino, York; Sherman C. Scott, York; George H. Sechrist, Felton; Lawrence W. Seiberlick, Hanover; Sterling W. Seitz, Yoe; Norman Shaffer, West Manchester Twp.; Frank O.

Shauck Jr., New Freedom; Ervin O. Sheffer, York; Luther Shive, York; William M. Shive, York; Daniel Shroll, New Holland; Charles H. Sipe, York; Frank A. Sipe, York; Charles J. Slonaker, York; James F. Small, York; Granville Smith, Dover; Horatio Smith, Jefferson; Norman E. Smith, York; Peter J. Smith, York; Russell D. Smith, York; Samuel A. Smith, York; Charles S. Snydeman, York; Owen D. Sprenkle, Glen Rock; William A. Spurley, York; Chanceford Stambaugh, Spring Grove; George L. Stauffer, Dillsburg; Harry B. Stough, York; Harry C. Stover, Jackson Twp.; George E. Strausbaugh, Jackson Twp.; Augustus V. Strawbridge, Gatchelville; Harry E. Strayer, York; Lemon C. Stump, Heidelberg Twp.; Wilbur C. Suiter, York; Edward Swartzbaugh, Codorus; George S. Sweitzer, York.

T

George F. Thoman, York; Warren L. Thomas, York; Ernest C. Tipton, York; Herman P. Tresselt, York; Landis L. Trimmer, Washington Twp.; Chester Trone, Marburg.

U

John Urey, Laurel; Paul H. Utz, West Manheim Twp.

W

Clayton D. Warner, Seven Valleys; Parker W. Weaver, Dillsburg; Robert H. Weaver, Seitzland; Ralph E. Weiler, Hanover; Martin S. Weiser, York; Roy R. Whorley, Hanover; Allen H. Winter, Yorkana; Harry W. Withers, York; John D. Withers, York; John M. Wise, Bryansville; Charles Witmer, Dover; George A. Woods, York.

Y

Harry R. Yingling, Hanover.

Korean War roll of honor

A
Comer L. Altland, York.

B
Harry W. Baer, York; Roger Ballard, York; Dale G. Barnhart, Dover; George V. Baxley, Dallastown; Harold E. Beard Jr., Hanover; Harry S. Beltz Jr., York; Robert D. Blaebaum, York; Palmer C. Bortner, Dover; Rodney M. Briggs, York; Eugene B. Burkett, York.

C
Earl S. Clouser, Hanover; Walter Copenheaver, York; Henry J. Cornies Jr., Wrightsville.

D
Clyde M. Dittenhaffer, Manchester.

E
Ray E. Etter, Manchester.

F
Grant R. Fetrow, York; James L. Franklin, New Freedom.

G
Ralph E. Garner, York; Charles J. Garrett, Glen Rock; John E. Gladfelter, York; William P. Goodyear, Manchester; George G. Greenwell, York.

H
Ralph S. Hagarman Jr., York; Thomas R. Haldeman, York; Charles R. Hammer, Wrightsville; Edwin D. Hartlaub, Hanover; Robert W. Hawkins, York; Albert K. Hoover, York.

I
Paul J. Iddings Jr., Fawn Grove.

J
Francis R. Jenkins, York.

K
August F. Karst Jr., Hanover; John P. Kendig, York; Joseph T. Klinefelter, Red Lion; John Kyle, York.

L
Jack T. Lewis, York.

M
Earl H. Markle, York; Floyd A. Markle, York; Victor E. McMinn, York; William L. Meckley, York; John M. Miller, York; William D. Morris, York; Ronald K. Myers, York.

N
Dunnick N. Ness, York; Frank E. Neail III, Hanover; Richard Nonemaker, York.

P
Bruce K. Phillips, Stewartstown.

S
Joseph D. Sanko, York New Salem; Franklin R. Schleeter, York; Donald P. Schneider, York; Gordon R. Shertzer, York; Raymond A. Shortino, York; John P. Smith, Hanover; Levere E. Smith, York; William L. Smith, York; Michael D. Smyser, York; Charles S. Sparks, Delta; Charles W. Sprenkle, York; Richard Strickler, York; Harry L. Swartz, Spring Grove.

T
Martin L. Therit, Hanover.

W
Charles C. Wilhelm, York; Wilbur W. Wolgamuth, Manchester.

Vietnam War roll of honor

A
Walter L. Albright, York; John S. Almoney, York; Rodney E. Althoff, York; John H. Anderson Jr., Wellsville.

After World War II, workers at Bowen-McLaughlin's plant in West Manchester Township readied tanks for possible combat service in Korea and elsewhere. Here, workmen prepare a Sherman tank for assembly line modifications. Metal-working plants throughout York County contributed to the refurbishing project. Gen. Jacob L. Devers helped develop the Sherman during World War II. The Korean War was costly to York County. About 6,900 county residents served in the military during the war, and 63 died.

B
Jeffrey R. Beardsley, York; H. Austin Beaverson Jr., York; Joseph R. Beck Jr., York; Rodney E. Beck, Manchester; William D. Bell, Seven Valleys; Martin E. Bixler, Glen Rock; Thomas R. Bliss, York; Joseph M. Bowman, York; David E. Boyer, Hellam; Eckhard G. Brenker, York; Richard E. Brenneman, Dover; Emmett R. Brown, North Hills; James B. Brown, York; Robert E. Bubb, York; Bernard J. Burns Jr., York; Frank K. Bush, York; Robert K. Buss, York; William G. Butler Jr., Peach Bottom.

C
David J. Combs, York; Ronald C. Conley, Etters; Edward J. Corcoran, North Hills; Guy B. Creep Jr., York; James J. Criswell, Red Lion; Gary L. Crone, York.

D
John W. Dahr, Dillsburg; James A. Daugherty, York; Richard L. Davis, Red Lion; Wendell L. Day, York; Terry E. Diffenderfer, York; John M. Dudley, Glen Rock.

E
Barry L. Eichelberger, Lewisberry.

F
Duane K. Fisher, York; Roger L. Fraker, Hellam; William A. Frey, York; James M. Fuhrman, York; Fred S. Fullerton Jr., York.

G
Robert A. Gamber, York; Robert M. Gibbs, York; John B. Gingery, Lewisberry; Donald R. Gise, Spring Grove; Larry E. Gladfelter, Glen Rock; William A. Gleixner, Andersontown.

H
Charlotte J. Hall, Spring Grove; Roy A. Harbaugh

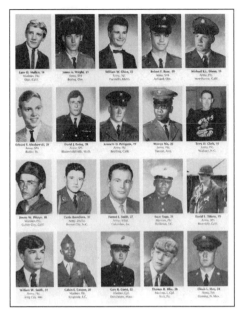

The toll of war hits home as two county men appear in 'Life' magazine's June 1969 roll call of those killed in the Vietnam War in one week. Thomas R. Bliss of York is pictured on the left page, bottom row, fourth from left. A photograph of Jeffery A. Richardson of Red Lion appears on the right page, second row from top, second from left. About 11,470 York County residents served in the military during the war. One hundred and one lost their lives.

Jr., Hanover; William E. Heilman, York; Ricky B. Henry, York; Robert C. Herman, York; Kenneth A. Hofe, Hanover; Kenneth L. Holder, Mount Wolf.

J

Paul H. Jackson Jr., Manchester; Robert N. Jones, Delta.

K

Lester S. Kinard, Seven Valleys; Barry E. Kincaid, York; Daniel M. Knight Jr., York.

L

Donald E. Laird, Dover; Michael A. Lauchman, Menges Mill; Lloyd C. Laugerman, Hanover; Paul A. Lecrone, Hanover; Lee F. Linch, Hanover.

M

Allan V. Merrifield, York; Jeffrey H. Miller, Hanover;

Larry Miller, York; Lonny L. Mitzel, Red Lion; George L. Mummert, Hanover; G. Edward Myers, Spring Grove.

N

Gary P. Neiman, York; Lester M. Ness, York.

O

Edwin J. Olmeda, York.

R

Calvin C. Rice Jr., York; Jeffrey A. Richardson, Red Lion; Dennis L. Riley, Hanover; Marshall L. Ritz, Delta; David B. Rodman, Hanover; John M. Rouscher, Manchester.

S

James C. Sager, Hanover; Larry G. Sandnes, New Cumberland; Thomas E. Sauble, York; Randy S. Schell, Mount Wolf; Gary L. Shank, Spring Grove;

Leslie F. Shenk, Holtwood; William H. Shireman, York; Charles E. Smeltzer III, York; Barry L. Smith, York; Harry C. Smith, York; Austin J. Snyder Jr., Red Lion; Stanley E. Spangler Jr., York; Dennis A. Sprenkle, York; Jay T. States, York.

T

James D. Talley Jr., York; Terry L. Taylor, York; Tyrone G. Thomas, Seven Valleys; Charles M. Thompson, New Freedom.

U

Ralph N. Unger, York.

W

Richard A. Wallick, York; Edgar W. Weitkamp Jr., York; John L. Wilhelm, East Berlin; William L. Young Jr., York.

Persian Gulf War roll of honor

Daniel J. McKinsey, York.

Global War on Terrorism roll of honor

Ryan G. Carlock, York; Michael Cohen, York County; Brian M. Kennedy, York; Martin W. Kondor, Hellam; Joseph B. Maglione, York; Neil C. Roberts, York; Nicholas J. Zangara, York.

The names that are part of the World War II roll of honor appear on tablets on the facade of the York County Courthouse, East Market Street, with the following additions: Glenn R. Bruaw, York Haven; Eugene B. Bubb, York; Homer H. Hildebrand, York; and William A. Showers, York. Paul W. Pottorf, York County, is spelled as such on the plaque, as is Henry Z. Strine of York County. Variant spellings appear in the Supreme Sacrifice Memorial Committee's booklet. Thomas W. Frutiger's name is misspelled in the booklet but has been corrected in the list above. Glen Leroy Baubilitz is spelled as such in "Service Record Book of Men and Women of New Freedom, Pa., and Community."

The names that are part of the Korean War roll of honor appear on the courthouse tablets, with the following additions that are not part of the Supreme Sacrifice booklet: Ray E. Etter, Manchester, and Frank E. Neail III, Hanover.

The Supreme Sacrifice booklet lists the spelling of Vietnam War honoree Jeffrey A. Richardson as such.

The names of the Global War on Terrorism roll of honor, all with connections to York County, come from the York County Veterans Affairs Office, effective March 31, 2005.

25

York Corporation military men pay ultimate price

This list is adapted from Shop News, York Corporation's newsletter, published on November-December 1945. The original was titled, "The Price of Victory, 1200 of Us Marched to War — 25 of Our Boys Gave Their Lives — Many Were Wounded. May We So Live That These Honored Dead Shall Not Have Died in Vain."

The price of victory

When the last beach was stormed and the final Jap gun silenced, twenty-five Gold Stars waved on the Yorkco service flag. Twenty-five Yorkco lads had given their lives for their country during World War II.*

Sixteen of these boys were killed in action while fighting on foreign soil. Of the nine who lost their lives during training in the States, six were killed in plane crashes. Only two made the supreme sacrifice while fighting the Japanese in the Pacific, and one over China.

Albert N. Bodine

Capt. Albert Bodine was killed in action in France on July 5, 1944. Albert was employed by the Philadelphia branch office shortly after his graduation from Virginia Polytechnic Institute. He then entered the Student Course here at York. Being a reserve officer, he was called to active duty on January 21, 1941. He is survived by his wife and infant child.

BODINE

Karl B. Boll

Cpl. Karl Boll died suddenly at Fairmount Army Air Field, Geneva, Nebraska. The Army reported his death due to a heart attack. Karl, who entered the air corps in November, 1942, was well known around the West York shops where he was employed as a trucker. His wife, Beatrice McCubbin Boll, is also employed at Yorkco.

BOLL

Walter L. Boyer

Private Walter L. Boyer was killed in action July 21, 1944, while fighting in France. Private Boyer, a well known West York athlete, was a member of the mechanized cavalry. He was inducted into the Army on July 4, 1943, and sailed overseas almost a year later. Walter was employed in the Grey Iron Foundry at Grantley.

BOYER

Durwood F. Brunk

Durwood Brunk died in Italy. The cause of his death is unknown. He participated in the Tunisian campaign and landed in Italy in October, 1943. He was with the first wave of troops that established the Anzio beachhead and held on tenaciously from January until June. Durwood worked on the night shift in the machine shop at West York.

BRUNK

George J. Devono

George Devono, pilot of a B-17, was killed in action over Germany, July 4, 1944. The young lieutenant was reported missing for almost a year before the War Department officially declared him as having been killed during a mission. George was in the service for three years at the time of his death and was stationed in France. He was employed in the Dispatching Department.

DEVONO

Frank C. Dunaway

Frank Dunaway, who was a file clerk in our Houston office, was killed in an airplane crash somewhere in Alaska. Frank was attached to the Weather Bureau of the U. S. Army Air Corps. He entered military service October 31, 1942. According to a letter received just before his death, Frank said that he was operating teletype machines and giving weather reports.

William D. Ensminger, Jr.

ENSMINGER

William Ensminger, Jr., was killed when the bomber, on which he served as top gunner, crashed during a regular training flight over Avon Park Bombing Range in Florida. The plane exploded in mid-air and the crash killed the entire six-man crew. "Bill," who was our first Gold Star, was a draftsman at West York.

George J. Ensslen, Jr.

ENSSLEN

George Ensslen, Jr., pilot of a P-38 fighter plane, was killed in aerial combat over enemy territory August 31, 1943. According to reports, George was fighting in the skies over China when he met his death. The young, flying lieutenant was commended for his courage in attacks upon Sardinia, Sicily and Pantelleria. He was employed in the Production Control Department.

Thomas W. Frutiger

FRUTIGER

Thomas Frutiger was killed December 15, 1944, while being transported on a Japanese vessel as a prisoner of war. "Tom" was a prisoner of the Japanese Army since the fall of Bataan Peninsula in 1942. According to the several communications received by his family during his imprisonment, "Tom" was in good health in spite of lengthy internment. He was a rate setter before being called to active service May 1, 1941.

Harold H. Garbrick

GARBRICK

Harold Garbrick was killed in action while fighting in Germany, November 21, 1944. As to how he met his death on the battlefields of Germany has not been revealed by the War Department. Harold was a well known baseball player in several county leagues. He was inducted April 30, 1941, and was employed in the Shipping Department.

William L. Glatfelter, II

GLATFELTER

Major William Glatfelter was one of six men killed in the crash of an Army transport plane near Horn Lake, Mississippi. Details of the crash were never given. "Bill" is the son of Philip H. Glatfelter, a member of our Board of Directors. He was employed in our Philadelphia office before entering the Army three years ago.

Harold R. Heilman

HEILMAN

Harold Heilman, a former Can Shop employee, was killed in action in Germany, February 28, 1945. He was a member of one of the Ninth Army's tank destroyer battalions and had been overseas sixteen months when he met his death on the German front. He was inducted into the service March 4, 1943. His dad, Sherman Heilman, is employed on the Drawing Room.

Paul C. March

MARCH

Paul March was killed in a plane crash at the Marianna Army Air Field in Florida six months after he had won his wings. Paul, who was employed in the Engineering Drafting Department, enlisted in the U. S. Army Air Corps in June of 1941. After graduation from Spence Field, Florida, he was assigned to the 57th fighter group as instructor.

Chester F. Marshall

MARSHALL

Chester F. Marshall lost his life in the North African area two months after he landed overseas. He was a class leader and barracks chief at Airplane Mechanics' School, Roosevelt Field, New York, before sailing for the battle front. Chester, an employee of the Grantley foundry, served in the Army of Occupation following World War I.

Charles J. Rotunda, Jr.

ROTUNDA

Charles Rotunda, Jr., was instantly killed when the automobile in which he was returning to Camp Philips, Kansas, from night maneuvers met with a fatal accident. A tire on the automobile blew out and the car rolled over several times, killing Rotunda who was asleep in the rear seat. The young Lieutenant was employed in our New York office.

*The predecessor to York Corporation sent 141 men to the service in World War I. Ninety-one saw action in France, and three were killed. Lt. George E. Evans, Lt. Wilbur C. Suiter and Sgt.-Major E. Clair Rebert were Gold Star military men.

James L. Sawyer

James Sawyer was accidentally killed while on maneuvers at Camp Sibert, Alabama. No details of his death have ever been released by the War Department.

SAWYER

Lieutenant Sawyer enlisted in the service September, 1942. He was assigned to the chemical warfare service immediately after he received his commission. James was employed as a chemist in the foundry laboratory at Grantley.

Robert G. Serff

Robert Serff, a bazooka gunner with General Patton's Third Army, was killed in action during the vicious tank battle below Nancy, France, in mid-September,

SERFF

1944. "Bob" was one of our York-Penn State cooperative engineering students, alternately working in the shops here at York and attending classes at Penn State.

Clark L. Sherman

Clark Sherman was a coremaker in the Grey Iron foundry at Grantley before induction into the Army, July 14, 1941. According to reports, Clark was fighting in

SHERMAN

Luxembourg. He had been overseas eleven months and had participated in many major battles in France before his death.

John J. Shetrone

John Shetrone was killed in action on Leyte, in the Philippines, during the first days of the invasion of that Jap-held island. John, who was attached to the Medical Corps, had been overseas

SHETRONE

almost a year when he was killed. He was a helper in the machine shop at West York before entering the Army.

Kenneth L. Sowers

Kenneth Sowers was killed in a training plane crash at Bainbridge Army Air Field, Bainbridge, Georgia. The Yorkco air cadet was flying in an attack formation when his plane

SOWERS

crashed to the ground, instantly killing its young pilot. "Ken" was employed as a dispatcher in our York shops.

William E. Trout

William Trout was killed in action while fighting somewhere in Germany. He was a member of a tank battalion. "Bill" entered the Army, February 24, 1942, and sailed overseas in July, 1944. He served in

TROUT

England, France, Luxembourg and Germany. He was employed in the Five Story Building.

Glenn M. Wallace

Glenn Wallace was killed during the May 23, 1944, battle in Italy. Glenn, who was employed in the Welding department before he entered the service, was induct-

WALLACE

ed May 1, 1943. He received his basic training at Camp Wheeler, Georgia.

John W. Walton

John Walton crashed to his death in an Army bomber near Beighbors, California. John was one of our machinist apprentices before he enlisted in the Army Air Corps,

WALTON

October 23, 1942. He was a gunner and assistant flight engineer of the bomber in which he met his death. John just turned twenty-one before the fatal crash.

Frederick S. Whimert

Frederick Whimert was killed in action in Italy, July 16, 1944. Private Whimert was in an infantry division with the Fifth Army and had received the infantry's combat

WHIMERT

pin, which is awarded to those who show outstanding ability in combat. Fred, who was employed in the Can Shop, was inducted into the Army, February 16, 1943.

Robert W. Zercher

Robert Zercher, former Test Plant employee, was killed on April 29, 1944, while on a bombing mission over Berlin. "Bob" was serving with the Eighth Air Force based in England. He was a gunner. He enlisted in the Air Corps Reserve and was later transferred to the Army Air Corps where he received his training as a gunner.

46

citizen soldiers of York and Adams counties

_____

Most of these brief biographies were first published in the York Daily Record's special report — "York County's Greatest Generation" on Nov. 23, 2000.

Service that changed lives

They came from farms, boroughs and cities. They served on the front lines, behind the lines or on the home front.

Whether they enlisted or answered the call of the draft, they all shared something in common: They called York and Adams counties home at some point in their lives.

These stories tell about some of the men and women who represented this area — or other Pennsylvania towns — during World War II. For many of them, the worst part of the war was not the bloodshed or the violence itself but the never-ending longing for their homes and their families.

Everette Leierer
Municipality: Dover
Where did you serve/work, and what was your job?
U.S. Marines, South Pacific, Guam, Okinawa, China — motor transit, first lieutenant.
What were the best/worst times during the war? Best: The occupation of China, Peiping and Tientsin.
Worst: Landing on Guam — heavy fire from Japanese — also Okinawa, after the landing. Kamikaze planes, snipers and rough terrain.
How did your experience change your life? Realized the seriousness of life in combat and importance of working together.

Harold Neibert
Municipality:
Springettsbury Township
Where did you serve/work, and what was your job?
Private infantry replacement in 5th squad, Company D, 101st Infantry, 26th Infantry Division attached to Patton's

NEIBERT

3rd Army. Became member of squad in 1944 in area of Nancy, France. Traveled with division. May 5, 1945, ended in Oberplan, Czechoslovakia. Put in charge of 80 captured horses from German surrender. Was in Austria for occupation until discharged March 1946.
What were the best/worst times during the war? Best: When the division was replaced and we got showers and clean clothes.

Worst: Trying to sleep in a foxhole full of water in France, the Bulge — went for 48 hours without food, very cold.
How did your experience change your life? "Became very mature because of it. Actually had best school grades ever post-Army. More dedicated."

William G. Clary Jr.
Municipality: Glen Rock
Where did you serve/work, and what was your job? South Pacific, Guadalcanal invasion, midshipman, Merchant Marine.
What were the best/worst times during the war? Best: Going to Japan after they surrendered.
Worst was the Guadalcanal invasion.
How did your experience change your life? "I became an officer in the U.S. Merchant Marine for 27 years and retired."

Voni B. Grimes
Municipality: York
Where did you serve/work, and what was your job? I served with the 246 Ordnance ammunition company in Guam and Saipan, working at headquarters typing, filing issuing and censoring mail.
What were the best/worst times during the war? Best: Not being directly in combat. However, I prayed for those who experienced combat.

GRIMES

Worst: I had a pup tent during a particularly bad monsoon, and I imagined combat soldiers elsewhere without anything for shelter.
How did your experience change your life? It made a man of me: Responsibility, service and to continue to serve God. Also, it taught respect for each other and to respect the cultures of others.

Myron Bird
Municipality: Lake Meade
Where did you serve/work, and what was your job? York, collecting scrap for salvage. Third- through sixth-graders were given the day off about once every two months to collect all kinds of scrap materials, which then were sorted in the school basement and sent to be used for raw materials in the war. "It wasn't unusual for us to collect 20 tons of scrap in one day."
What were the best/worst times during the war? "Being only 9 years old and not

having any close relative in the war, I was unaware of the real seriousness of the war. The worst experience I had was the night I went with my dad to the York Fairgrounds Grandstand to see a Civilian Defense demonstration. Part of the demonstration was a simulated air raid at night complete with exploding bombs. For months, I had nightmares about that demonstration.

The best time was playing with my friends and how we had to use our imaginations and our creativity for toys because there were so few available; metal wasn't available, and only a couple very poor plastics were being made. We shared what we had."

How did your experience change your life? Had to be creative and use imagination, became a more resourceful person. "I learned to appreciate whatever I had and took care of my possessions."

Harry J. Ilgenfritz
Municipality: Pine Grove
Where did you serve/work, and what was your job? Staff sergeant, European Theater/mostly infantry.

ILGENFRITZ

What were the best/worst times during the war? Best: Getting a little sleep and getting a little something to eat and drink. Had 16 vehicles and 33 men. Had to make sure men ate, slept, survived.

How did your experience change your life? Took training into civilian life as a father, grandfather, great-grandfather.

Vernon Black
Municipality: New Freedom
Where did you serve/work, and what was your job?
Started out as a private at Schofield, after a year private 1st class, corporal,

BLACK

sergeant, later at discharge, technical sergeant.

What were the best/worst times during the war? "No best or worst. You were patriotic and performed to the best of your ability. I suppose before the war started was the best."

How did your experience change your life? "It was an exciting experience and, for many, a tragic one. I consider myself lucky to be there."

George S. Deitz
Municipality: York
Where did you serve/work, and what was your job?
Quartermaster aboard USS LCS in the Philippines, one landing — delivering supplies.

DEITZ

What were the best/worst times during the war? Cruising with no lights and challenged by another ship, told to identify self; fortunately, it was a U.S. ship.

How did your experience change your life? "I saved my beloved America and saw parts of the world I otherwise would not get to see."

Charles C. Innerst
Municipality: Springettsbury Township
Where did you serve/work, and what was your job? Army, trained at Camp Edwards, Mass. Served in Central Pacific for two years. Joined in the invasion of Saipan and the Mariana Islands.

What were the best/worst times during the war? Best: Summer on Cape Cod 1943 and thrill of return to U.S. from Saipan.

Worst: Going over the side of troop ship and getting into a landing craft to land on island.

How did your experience change your life? "Enlarged my perspective of the world in which we live and profoundly increased my respect for the military as a part of our global society."

Kenneth Fritchman
Municipality: New Oxford
Where did you serve/work, and what was your job? Army field artillery.

What were the best/worst times during the war? Best was basic training in Ft. Sill, Okla., before being shipped to Europe.

Worst was the Battle of the Bulge at Malmedy. Outfit B Battery was murdered.

How did your experience change your life? "I never could ask for forgiveness to God because it was kill or be killed. The same night I asked to return to base, and the next morning the complete area was wiped out, including my foxhole area... . My life is now dedicated to abolishing war."

Jack Bentivegna
Municipality: Springettsbury Township
Where did you serve/work, and what was your job? Fought with the Marines at Guadalcanal, Guam and Iwo Jima in the 3rd Tank Battalion, Co. "C" as platoon sergeant.

BENTIVEGNA

What were the best/worst times during the war? Best: When as a young man passed Marine fitness test.

Worst: Engaging Japanese forces in Pacific, hit by kamikaze plane, almost sinking LST 477 and all tanks aboard.

How did your experience change your life? "Made me realize that there is a God and that there is a book up there that tells when you die. Why else would I still be here and so many Marines died? My page has not come up yet. I was born to come back and have a beautiful family and grandchildren."

Frances W. McCabe
Municipality: York
Where did you serve/work, and what was your job? WAAC and WAC First Army, East Coast, personnel administration.

What were the best/worst times during the war? Best: The fun and camaraderie and differences in people, train travel.

Worst: Standing at reveille in sub-zero weather.

How did your experience change your life? Learned discipline and respect for authority. Was one of the first WACs from York County, entered as a basic trainer, was discharged as first lieutenant.

Ralph E. Murray Sr.

Municipality: York Township

Where did you serve/work, and what was your job?

Graduated from mechanics school, assisted in training of other Army recruits, primarily a transportation company, trained in automatic weapons as Coast Artillery Corps, anti-aircraft gunners. Landed in England Jan. 2, 1945, Omaha Beach in February and started trek through France, Holland and into Germany.

What were the best/worst times during the war? Was assigned to protect bridge across Rhine River. There about two weeks until pontoon bridges could be built. Soon after crossing Rhine River, was hit with pneumonia and hospitalized. By the time of return to action, the war in Europe was over.

How did your experience change your life? "April 5, 1946, I was discharged from Ft. Dix, N.J., and sent home."

Jesse L. Miller

Municipality: York

Where did you serve/work, and what was your job? Combat engineer sergeant and squad leader. Building bridges, laying mines, acting as infantry if needed.

What were the best/worst times during the war? Remembers running onto Utah Beach. Long column of vehicles were lined up and could not advance. He was told to go up the road and find a place that needed a bridge to move the vehicles. "As luck would have it, there was a truck in the column that had bridge material. ...We used the treadway to make a bridge. ...The use of this bridge was the primary exit from Utah Beach and had been destroyed by the Germans."

How did your experience change your life? "I grew up fast in the next few years, but I am also very proud to have been able to serve my coun-

try and to be a member of a fine group of men, the 238th Combat Battalion. Having met every year since 1946, the members of our association are like family."

James W. Williams

Municipality: Jackson Township

Where did you serve/work, and what was your job?

Staff sergeant, served in Europe, military police and prisoner of war work.

WILLIAMS

What were the best/worst times during the war? The worst came during a tour of France when he had to disarm and search throngs of German prisoners. In Germany, he rounded up residents to dig out burned bodies of mostly Polish prisoners who had been herded into a barn that was set afire.

How did your experience change your life? "Without the GI Bill I might not have been able to finish my college education and attain my bachelor of science in civil engineering and pursue my vocation as a graduate engineer. Upon graduation, my first large project was with P.H. Glatfelter in 1954."

Leo Ruvolis

Municipality: Dover Township

Where did you serve/work, and what was your job?

Airplane mechanic, aerial gunner, flight engineer, served 18 months in the North Atlantic

RUVOLIS

German submarine campaign. Air Force bomber pilot, flew combat missions with 8th Air Force and on D-Day. Shot down in aerial combat with German fighter planes. POW for a year in Germany. Held ranks of private to major.

What were the best/worst times during the war? Best: Receiving Air Force pilot wings, liberation from POW camp.

Worst: Getting shot down over Germany with four crewmen killed, one lost a leg, four held POW.

How did your experience change your life? "Military experience gave me the confidence and the maturity needed and the GI Bill gave me the educational opportunities needed to develop a successful professional career as director of the computer center and as an associate professor at York College."

Walter Eisele

Municipality: Hallam

Where did you serve/work, and what was your job? Pacific Theater, airborne radar operator, precision navigation, bombing, etc.

What were the best/worst times during the war? Best: Too embarrassing.

Worst: Too many episodes to describe and eight months hospitalization, four months in full body cast.

How did your experience change your life? "Profoundly — healthwise, socially and financially."

Ives Wahrman

Municipality: Springettsbury Township

Where did you serve/work, and what was your job? Air Force, lead navigator, 8th Air Force in England, 446th Bomb Group, 704th Squadron.

WAHRMAN

What were the best/worst times during the war? Led three squadrons in mission to bomb railroad yards and bridge in Salzburg, Austria, a 10-hour flight, mostly over enemy territory with lots of anti-aircraft guns and enemy fighter planes. Just 30 minutes from target, had to abandon dangerous and harrowing mission due to severe icing and cloud layers over the target.

How did your experience change your life? "The lesson learned from aerial combat is that there is a lot of luck, chance, fortune and discipline in life. And I've been lucky to have some of each."

Fred Auchey
Municipality: Spring Garden Township
Where did you serve/work, and what was your job? Private, Ft. Howard, 8th Infantry Division, Ft. Jackson, S.C.

AUCHEY

What were the best/worst times during the war? Worst: Fought in France from June 1944 until captured on Dec. 18. Held in a German camp until April 1945.

Best: Returned to states for a 60-day furlough, two weeks at Atlantic City. "Milton Berle did a stand-up routine there; he was so rotten, we walked out."

How did your experience change your life? "I wasn't religious, but I was smart enough to realize I didn't get through all that on my own. I now go to church regularly, thanking the Lord. I have written my autobiography for my grandchildren."

Norman H. Miller
Municipality: Springettsbury Township
Where did you serve/work, and what was your job? European Theater, parts man in maintenance and bridge builder.

MILLER

What were the best/worst times during the war? Best: Weekend passes to town and stateside.

Worst: Buzz bombs, strafing from low airplanes and standing guard alone at night.

How did your experience change your life? "This was an altogether different life, since I was out of the Army I realized how nice civilian life is, and it made me a man to accept my responsibilities."

Donald E. McCreary
Municipality: York
Where did you serve/work, and what was your job? Air Force, 70 combat missions as tail gunner.

European Theater 9th Air Force, 391st Bomb Group, 572 Squadron.
What were the best/worst times during the war? Best was when the war ended.

Worst was Dec. 15, 1944, when 16 of the Martin Marauder Bombers out of 32 from 391st bomb group were shot down by German fighters.

How did your experience change your life? "The discipline that I was taught benefited me throughout the rest of my life."

Kenneth Wheat
Municipality: Springfield Township
Where did you serve/work, and what was your job? Army Signal Corp Pfc. radar.

WHEAT

What were the best/worst times during the war? "We could tell the enemy planes from our planes. We took our planes over to destroy. We reported the enemy planes to our Air Force so they could be up there shooting them down. They tried to bomb us so we could not tell the enemy was coming."

How did your experience change your life? "I was happy to serve my country. I was 19 years old. I was in the Army 3 years, 2 years overseas. I was so happy to get home."

Jack Pritchard
Municipality: Springettsbury Township
Where did you serve/work, and what was your job? Glenn L. Martin aircraft factory, Middle River, Md. Ground and flight

PRITCHARD

mechanic. Navy petty officer 2nd class Guam and Pearl Harbor.
What were the best/worst times during the war? Best: When the war was over, coming under the Golden Gate Bridge.

Worst: Leaving Pearl Harbor and

not knowing what was ahead.
How did your experience change your life? "I was sure the war changed my life. If the war never happened, I never would have come to Baltimore and on to Pennsylvania and gotten married and had six children and 13 grandchildren."

Claude W. Davis
Municipality: Shrewsbury Township
Where did you serve/work, and what was your job? Army Air Force, bombardier, B-17.

DAVIS

What were the best/worst times during the war? Best: Having a wife devoted enough to follow wherever he went.

Worst: All that training and the war ended before he got to go overseas.

How did your experience change your life? "It is unbelievable the hell you went through for a whole year to become a pilot." He still flies a small plane today, at the age of 80.

John Harms
Municipality: New Freedom
Where did you serve/work, and what was your job? Battle of the Bulge, infantry machine gunner, promoted to battalion intelligence, noncommissioned staff sergeant.

What were the best/worst times during the war? The best was preparing to invade Japan, Truman dropping the bomb.

Seeing friends killed in combat was the worst.

How did your experience change your life? "Learned humility. The great value of life. Learned to show friendship to all people and thank the Lord for getting through WWII, but always wonder how I got through without injury. It wasn't just luck."

Chalmers W. Bahn

Municipality: York Township

Where did you serve/work, and what was your job? Seaman 2nd Class aboard USS Beatty, sailed to Sicily to partici-pate in the inva-sion.

BAHN

In 1944, he was aboard the USS Rhind as Torpedo Mate Third Class, running convoys into Mediterranean and the Atlantic. Escorted aircraft carriers in the Pacific.

What were the best/worst times during the war? The best time was when the surrender was signed or when they would pick up pilots who had crashed into the ocean.

The worst was the sinking of the USS Beatty in the North Atlantic and the German planes in the Mediterranean.

Charles W. Lippy

Municipality: Seven Valleys

Where did you serve/work, and what was your job? Served on USS Missouri.

What were the best/worst times during the war? Saw signing of peace treaty, went on goodwill tour around the world after war. Many stories, made many lifelong friends.

How did your experience change your life? "My father enlisted shortly after myself. He served in Aleutian Islands on a seagoing tug. My broth-er Robert served on the Yorktown. My brother Jack served in the Merchant Marine."

Hassel Cartwright

Municipality: York

Where did you serve/work, and what was your job? Served in Europe with Co. "A" Regiment of the 90th Infantry Division of the 3rd Army, machine gunner and 60mm mortar gunner.

What were the best/worst times during the war? Best: Seeing his brother for 30 minutes at Falaise Gap, sleeping in a bed and getting a back rub in a hospital in Paris, and when the Germans gave up. Also, receiving letters from a woman who later became his wife. Now married 54 years. His belief in God made even the worst situations tolerable.

Worst: Friends killed or wounded, nights without sleep, seven days with-out food across the Saar River, one shower in 5 months, being cold and wet for days, sleeping in a foxhole or on the ground every night for months. Also, the prospect of being killed or wounded at any time and three to four weeks to get mail from home.

How did your experience change your life? "I learned early in life to take anything a politician might say with a grain of salt. FDR said 'No American boy will fight on foreign soil' and 'we have nothing to fear... .' I thought of those two statements when we were in some very tough fighting in Normandy. It was foreign soil, and it was fighting. Nine months after graduation from high school, I was in the Army, so my life was just beginning, and therefore there was nothing to change. I did see a great deal of the world that I probably would not have seen."

Dean Wantland

Municipality: York

Where did you serve/work, and what was your job? Army infantry — Italy, France, Germany.

What were the best/worst times during the war? The best

WANTLAND

was when he ran into his brother in Paris.

The worst was going to the front line, also when "our tanks were shooting their cannons and were falling short onto us."

How did your experience change your life? "I was 17 when I enlisted, and it made me grow up very fast. I didn't shave until I went into basic training."

Harry F. Becker

Municipality: York

Where did you serve/work, and what was your job? Africa, Sicily, Italy, Corsica, France, Germany, all in the artillery.

BECKER

What were the best/worst times during the war? Invasion of Italy in 1943 and the protection of deep water at the Port of Naples, Italy, October to March, then leaving to go up through the mud, etc., of Italy.

How did your experience change your life? "Made me think that every-thing isn't free."

Earl Drennen Jr.

Municipality: Hellam Township

Where did you serve/work, and what was your job? Navy for 6 years, sea duty, USS Nashville, USS Hane, USS Waters, USS Prairie, USS Dixie

DRENNEN

and USS Piedmont. Was a radar operator, battle station was a 6-inch gunner.

What were the best/worst times during the war? Best time was pulling into port and going on liberty.

Worst were when in action against the Japanese.

How did your experience change your life? "That is rather hard to answer. ... When my six years were up, I joined the reserves for four years. I lost sev-eral of my friends and best friend one night when we were bombarded. They were Marines. The men who were killed we buried at sea. The other men who were burned severely were transferred off the ship."

Murray D. Friedman

Municipality: Manchester Township

Where did you serve/work, and what was your job? Army Air Corps. Flew in 8th Air Force (England) as bombardier-navigator.

FRIEDMAN

What were the best/worst times during the war? Best: Meeting such great people who were so reliable. Best day was when he flew his last combat mission.

Worst: Coming back to air base and his best friend was shot down.

How did your experience change your life? "I became more aware of people and activities around me. It made me want to help people and my community."

S.R. Shelley

Municipality: Dover

Where did you serve/work, and what was your job?

Navy as a gunner on merchant vessel USS Woodrow Wilson, Europe.

What were the best/worst times during the war? Best: V-E Day in Times Square and the day he was discharged.

Worst: Long watches on trips back and forth across Atlantic, general quarters for hours at a time.

How did your experience change your life? "Camaraderie built up as we lived in close quarters. Makes you think about future and how to grow up fast. How great our country is and freedom we have."

Gerald F. Snyder

Municipality: York

Where did you serve/work, and what was your job? 737th Railroad Operating Battalion.

What were the best/worst times during the war? No worst times. Was in background and only called on a few times to set up transit and point

SNYDER

out difficulties in "bump" sections of the track in the Philippine Islands — Luzon. Could hear fighting in background. Never got into battle.

How did your experience change your life? "This was the first time Erma and I were separated (26 months). Army life was not difficult, but changed locations as we progressed toward victory over Japan. In Japan, the emperor gave orders to the people to receive us peacefully, and they did."

Leonard Warner

Municipality: Dover Township

Where did you serve/work, and what was your job? U.S. Army, 65th Division, assigned to 3rd Army in Europe. Soldier first, then company clerk.

WARNER

What were the best/worst times during the war? Came through the war without injury. The worst time was seeing the liberation of a German concentration camp. His division flag is on display at the Holocaust Museum in Washington, D.C.

How did your experience change your life? "I went in at age 19 in 1943 and was discharged as a technician fourth grade in April 1946. I went from a kid to a man in those 3 years."

Samuel S. Spicer

Municipality: New Freedom

Where did you serve/work, and what was your job? 108th Infantry, Hawaii, Guadalcanal, Philippines, Korea, other places.

What were the best/worst times during the war? Was away from home for 37 months.

How did your experience change your life? "I was married Jan. 3, 1942. Left for service Oct. 22, 1942. Discharged Nov. 27, 1945. If that didn't change your life, don't know what would."

Jeannene Tylee

Municipality: Fawn Grove

Where did you serve/work, and what was your job?

Aircraft spotter volunteer in Clarks Summit. Every Saturday morning her father would drive her to the fire tower, where she kept watch. "We didn't see action, not even one plane with a red circle on its side or a black swastika, but we did an important job — we were the eyes and ears along flight paths."

What were the best/worst times during the war? Best: The feeling that she was helping her big brother by watching the sky over Pennsylvania.

Worst: Worrying about the safety of brother and his friends.

How did your experience change your life? "My experience made me mature quicker than I would have in our little town had I not taken my spotting job."

Bill Hinton

Municipality: Springettsbury Township

Where did you serve/work, and what was your job? Staff driver 28th Division Headquarters, 109th Infantry 28th — was runner for regiment.

HINTON

What were the best/worst times during the war?

Drove Gen. Eisenhower for tour one day and got stuck in mud. "Ike said, 'Soldier, this is one day you won't forget.' "

Worst: Saw and felt the hardships. No plumbing, day and night out on the ground, summer and winter.

How did your experience change your life?

"I learned what your body goes through facing death. What it can do, and how tired you can get . . . Today each day is a lifetime."

Norman Callahan Jr.

Municipality: West Manchester Township

Where did you serve/work, and what was your job? The Atlantic Fleet Amphibious Force. Responsible for all activities in Mediterranean Sea in

1942 and English Channel in 1943. Gunnery officer, first lieutenant and executive officer of the ship.

What were the best/worst times during the war? Best was when he returned to the states. Didn't beach on D-Day. Present watching the battles during D-Day.

How did your experience change your life? "I came back home a different person than I left. Having that much responsibility is a lot for a young man. I went in a smiling young man and came out as a grizzled military officer."

Robert Gotwalt Sr.

Municipality: East Manchester Township

Where did you serve/work, and what was your job? Served in European Theater of Operations. Point scout in a reconnaissance troop, 83rd Infantry Division.

What were the best/worst times during the war? Best: When he knew he was coming home in 1945.

Worst: When he lost his best friend in Normandy and was wounded a third time in Germany.

How did your experience change your life? "Made me grow up. I was only 18 years old when I went into the Army in 1942."

W.C. Moore

Municipality: York

Where did you serve/work, and what was your job? Worked for the constructing quartermaster of the Army at Camp Livingston as a draftsman, then in 1941 was civilian sanitary engineer at Dale Mabry Field near Tallahassee, Fla., then chemical engineer for Union Carbide at Oak Ridge, Tenn.

What were the best/worst times during the war?

Inspected cleanliness of piping components for Gaseous Diffusion plant for separation of uranium isotopes. "At first I had no idea why this was required, but after my security clearance had been obtained, I learned that we were engaged in a project to develop the atomic bomb."

How did your experience change your life? "In retrospect, this was a great once-in-a-lifetime opportunity. I am glad that I could and did help end the war with Japan. It was this experience that led even-

tually to my moving to York, Pa., in 1962 as vice president for engineering and research with the York Division of Borg Warner."

Robert L. Keller

Municipality: York Township

Where did you serve/work, and what was your job? Infantryman at Iwo Jima, front line Marine.

What were the best/worst times during the war? The only good experience was getting off the island. The worst was crawling over my fallen fellow Marines.

How did your experience change your life? "The experience helped me understand that life is full of risks."

Clair E. Frey

Municipality: Conewago Township

Where did you serve/work, and what was your job? South Pacific, fueled planes.

What were the best/worst times during the war? Was in a

FREY

typhoon in the Pacific on the way to the Philippines Dec. 17, 1944. There were 14 ships in the task force. Three destroyers rolled over (Hull, Spence, Monaghan), 790 officers and men lost overboard.

How did your experience change your life? "War is a very terrible, tragic event, with many shipmates killed and injured and pilots going down at sea."

William Kapp

Municipality: Glen Rock

Where did you serve/work, and what was your job?

Served in the weapons platoon of "A" Co. Battalion 5th Marine regiment.

What were the best/worst times during the war? When he learned that "A" Co. would be the assault company to lead the Marines ashore at Guadalcanal in 1942. Also, Oct. 12, 1944 when Japanese bombers unloaded on "A" Co. and killed men and many more wounded.

How did your experience change your life? "In civilian life after dis-

charge, I returned to my job at Peoples Bank of Glen Rock."

C.W. Schaeffer

Municipality: Springettsbury Township

Where did you serve/work, and what was your job? European Theater platoon leader Combat Bridge Co., followed infantry and built bridges for heavy equipment.

What were the best/worst times during the war? First year as an officer with my wife at Camp Polk, La., was best.

Worst was immediately after D-Day.

How did your experience change your life?

"Not aware of anything."

Robert R. Merritt

Municipality: Manchester Township

Where did you serve/work, and what was your job? European Theater: In three campaigns, Ardennes, Rhineland and

MERRITT

Central Germany. Served as platoon sergeant and forward observer, seeking out the enemy in order to attack them with artillery fire.

What were the best/worst times during the war?

Best times: When the shooting stopped, and Germany surrendered. Also, crossing the Rhine River in the Ruhr pocket, one of the turning points of the war. Later, receiving the Combat Infantry Badge.

Worst times: Helping wounded buddies, or ones that had been killed. War is hell.

How did your experience change your life? In seeing the importance of freedom, the price it cost, and those who were in slave labor or concentration camps. I was overwhelmed with the reality and joy that I was truly a free man.

25

lists of

World War II

achievers

———

More than 20,000 York County men and women served in uniform and thousands of others patrolled the home front. These lists provide but a sampling of those who served.

During the day, Jack Hespenheide instructed the William Penn High School boys — prospective civilian or military pilots — at York Airport. Posing here, front row, from left: H. Bonneville, J. Ort, C. Miller. Second row: R. Fair, J. Gingerich, P. Hirschfield. Standing: Jack Hespenheide, E. Thieme, C. Anstadt Jr., J. Binkley. 'The trainees completing this course are privileged to voluntarily enlist in any branch of our armed forces,' The Tattler, William Penn's yearbook, stated in 1943. At night, instructor Oscar L. Hostetter taught ground school three hours each evening, three evenings each week.

List of defense lists

1. Jacobus-area Geiselmans who served (Jacobus was named after Jacob Geiselman.)

- Preston E. Geiselman
- Ralph J. Geiselman
- Richard L. Geiselman
- Clark E. Geiselman
— more than 140 others from the Jacobus area served in uniform.

2. Sons of Henry H. and Geraldine Williams of York who served

- Charles E., killed in action.
- Samuel I., Army
- Harvey E., Army
- Curvin J., Army
- Roscoe B., Navy
- Gordon E., Navy

3. Women in first welding class, York Corporation

- Henrietta Stare
- Bernice Robinson
- Emma Sheffer
- Helen Fickes
- Beatrice Gladfelter
- Jane May Sanders
- Josephine Dise
- Helena Kefauver

4. Felton-area Groves who served

- Clayton S. Grove
- Glenn F. Grove
- J. Richard Grove
- Luther E. Grove
- Paul L. Grove
- Richard E. Grove
- Robert L. Grove
- William F. Grove
- Charles H. Grove
— more than 50 other Felton-area residents served, including Eugene Heffner, who died in uniform.

5. County fighting men serving in post-war Berlin occupying force

- Harry J. Crimmins
- Kenneth R. McAfee
- Erwin W. Hoff
- Samuel H. Kocher
- Robert E. Rife
- Robert J. Druck
- Raymond J. Glatfelter
- Lester H. Grim
- Milton U. Kressler

6. Servicemen from New Freedom-Glen Rock area who died

- Reed Donald Allison
- Glen Leroy Baublitz
- Richard L. Black
- Harold Thomas Bose
- Horace J. Cooper
- Maynard P. Fuhrman
- Leo Pershing Getz
- Joseph Edward Horn
- Norman H. Parrish
- Benjamin S. Hunt Jr.
— about 10 others died

7. A sampling of servicemen from Hanover area who died

- Charles Robert Miller
- Lawrence E. Zepp
- Charles Edward Rohrbaugh
- Ralph R. Miller
- Cletus Henry Bortner
- Walter Leroy Crowl
- Donald J. Gallagher
- Lawrence E. Duncan
- Ralph R. Miller
- Russell Wentz Hartman
— more than 30 others died

8. Executive Committee, York County USO, 1945

- Walter I. Anderson, chairman
- Paul Murphy, treasurer
- Margaret Swartz, secretary
- Ruth Seymour
- Mildred Chapman
- Mrs. Robert A. Angelo
- Jason Snyder
- Adjutant Ronald Irwin
- Mose Leibowitz
- Minnie B. Hatton

9. Delta-area military men and women who served

- James E. Atkin
- Reginald T. Beattie
- Alfred B. Cooper
- Charles E. Glackin
- Laura Heaps Hamilton
- Neal Johnson Kilgore
- Edmund Jarrett Watkins
- Vallie F. Williams
- Doris Jean Wentz Wolfe
- Carrol Barton
— about 600 others from the Delta area served

10. Ten Seven Valleys-area men and women who served

- Vivian LaMaster
- Harvey Lau
- Loretta Spies
- Charles Burkhart
- Lavern Gladfelter
- Dean Henry
- Eugene Rohrbaugh
- John Toomey
- John Taylor
- Charles Sanders
— about 40 others served

11. Officers and directors Manufacturers' Association of York, York Plan organizers, 1941

- Robert P. Turner, chairman and president
- Charles B. Wolf, vice president and director
- Robert E. Gephart, secretary
- Walter B. Liggit, treasurer and asst. secretary
- Charles F. Sioberg
- F.A. Hespenheide
- W.S. McClellan
- George S. Schmidt
- E.J. Fitzgerald
- E.A. Kleinschmidt
- Herbert W. Stone

12. American Red Cross, Nurse's Aide Corps, Hanover, 1943

- Jeune Gobrecht
- Pearl H. Gelwicks
- Pearl E. Heagy
- Catherine Knippel
- Pearl Knippel
- Nancy W. Nace
- Helen Overbaugh
- Elizabeth R. Smith
- Thelma Stavely
- Evelyn Elizabeth Topper
- Iva Grace Wildasin
- (Miss O.A. Green, instructor)

13. Dillsburg Council of Defense, officers

- Alton B. Zerby, chairman
- Harold Starry, secretary
- H.H. Spoerlein, secretary
- Mrs. Marietta Lehmer, secretary
- R.L. Krall, chief, air raid warden
- Donald K. Fry, chief, auxiliary police
- Robert P. McClure, Sr., chief, auxiliary police
- John Cross, chief, auxiliary firemen
- Dr. M. L. Bailey, chief, medical auxiliary
- Kathryn Smith, control center telephone operator
- J. Ernest Hartman, chief, messenger corps
- Mrs. H.H. Spoerlein, liaison, control center and medical auxiliary

This roll of honor, appearing in The York-High Weekly in May 1943, shows the military reached deep into high schools to fill its fighting units.

14. Rohrbaugh family, Jefferson, in the military

- Alton Rohrbaugh
- Carroll Rohrbaugh
- Clyde D. Rohrbaugh
- Earle C. Rohrbaugh
- Emanuel Rohrbaugh
- Glenn Rohrbaugh
- Harvey E. Rohrbaugh
- Laverne Rohrbaugh
- Mark A. Rohrbaugh
- Mark L. Rohrbaugh
- Marlen L. Rohrbaugh
- William F. Rohrbaugh
— more than 140 other Jefferson-area residents served, including Woodrow Baugher, William Trout and Elmer Kelbaugh, who died in uniform.

15. York City-County Council of Defense, 1943

- George S. Love, chairman
- Hon. Harvey N. Werner
- Ralph H. Lookingbill, executive director
- Robert P. Turner
- William S. Shipley
- A. M. Squair
- Henry D. Schmidt
- W.F.O. Rosenmiller
- Chester M. Hartman
- Arthur Thomas
- Alan Ross
- Col. William H. Beckner
- Henry Butler

16. York County Chapter American Red Cross goals met

- 1942 goal: $125,000; raised: $127,233
- 1943 goal: $135,000; raised: $155,622
- 1944 goal: $235,000; raised: $247,782
- 1945 goal: $235,110; raised: $261,000 (est.)

17. War bond drives — More than $100 million was raised in York County

1st, 1942: goal, $13 million; raised, $14 million
2nd, 1942: goal, $16.4 million; raised, $17.8 million
3rd, 1943: goal, $16.4 million; raised, $21.5 million
4th, 1944: goal, $16.9 million; raised, $18.6 million
5th, 1944: goal, $17.5 million; raised, $23.1 million
6th, 1944: goal, $15.1 million; raised, $21.9 million
7th, 1945: goal, $11.7 million; raised, N/A

18. Etters Council of Defense, officers

- Clyde B. Shelly, chairman
- Earl E. Bashore, air raid wardens
- John R. Rhoads, director of emergency defense
- Arden Aughenbaugh, police
- A.A. Zeigler, fire
- George Yinger, drivers
- Mervin A. Bowles, medical corps
- John Souders, nurses aides
- Paul Sturgen, messengers
- Miles Brubaker, rescue squads
- N.B. Wilson, food and housing
- J. H. Shickle, decontamination corps
- Charles S. Willis, demolition, repair & clearance
- George Beshore, road repair crew

19. Servicewomen from New Freedom-Glen Rock area

- Virginia Kelbough Bennett, WAVE
- Myra Gerbrick Clark, WAC
- Roxie R. Curry, WAVE
- Marion E. Gemmill, Navy Nurse Corps
- Margie Flynn Goodfellow, WAC
- Mildred B. Kirchner, Coast Guard, Women's Reserve
- Anna Louise Sweitzer Nonemaker, Navy Nurse Corps
- Bernice Fells Pitts, WAC, Army Air Force
- Catherine Shaver Wilborn, Navy
- Rosalie Skelly Smith, Navy
- Margaret E. Stabler, WAC
- Kathryn I. Stabler, WAC, Army Air Corps
- Mary E. Stermer, WAC, Medical Department
- Grace E. Trout, Army Nurse Corps
- Ruth Ann Young, Army Nurse Corps

20. Wrightsville Council of Defense, air raid wardens

- Guy Wakefield
- Kenneth Smith
- Morton Nauss
- Jacob Hevner
- Harold Crumling
- Elwood Burg
- Harry Williams
- Clifton Shutter
- R. Andrew Hoover
- Arthur E. Warfield
- James D. Turner
- Austin Smeltzer
- William T. Samis
- Leroy E. Miller
- Harris B. Martin

21. Recipients, Army-Navy "E" Award

- York Safe and Lock Co.
- York-Hoover Corporation
- American Chain & Cable's:
  — Wright-Manley Division
  — Electric Welding Plant
  —York Malleable Foundry
- A.B. Farquhar Co.
- Century Ribbons Mills
- General Electric Co.
- Read Machinery Co.
- York Corporation
- International Chain & Manufacturing Co.
- York-Shipley Inc.
- H.J. Freezer Co.
- S. Morgan Smith Co.
- York Corrugating Co.
- American Foundry Machine Co. – Glen Rock
- New York Wire Cloth Co.
- The Pennsylvania Tool & Manufacturing Co.
- Blaw-Knox Co., U.S. Naval Ordnance Plant

WORLD WAR II · RED LION, PA.   199

EDWARD FIFE HOLLAND
Stewards Mate First Class—Merchant Seaman
Parents: Dr. and Mrs. H. H. Holland, E. Broadway. Service: Sept. 5, 1945, to date. Basic Training: Sheepshead Bay, N. Y. Assigned as Merchant Seaman to a tanker and Esso Fleet.

NED ROGER KINARD
Messman—Maritime Service
Parents: Mr. and Mrs. Ivan Kinard, 244 First Ave. Service: Aug. 20, 1945, to date. Basic Training: Sheepshead Bay, N. Y. Now serving on a tanker. Type of Work: Messman.

THOMAS ARTHUR LLOYD, JR.
Maritime Service
Parents: Mr. and Mrs. Thomas Lloyd, 337 Maple St. Service: Began duty 1943. Basic Training: Sheepshead Bay, N. Y. Assigned to SS Thomas Clyde, SS Trojan, SS James Kerney and SS Richard Stockdon. Sea duty in the North Atlantic, Atlantic, Mediterranean, Asiatic and Pacific. Type of Work: Able-bodied seaman and bowswain.

DUKE RICHARD MARKEY
Seaman—Maritime Service
Parents: Mr. and Mrs. Clarke Markey, 118 N. Main St. Service: Sept. 14, 1945, to date. Basic Training: Sheepshead Bay, N. Y. Assigned to James L. Richards, a coastwise ship. Type of Work: Deck hand.

Red Lion's 'Those Who Served,' published in 1946, also honored the Maritime Service, responsible for supplying a global Allied Army of several million men as well as transporting servicemen. 'Delivering the goods through mined waters, being the target for enemy submarines and running the gauntlet of enemy aircraft was often the experience of those who service our merchant fleet,' the publication stated.

22. Red Lion-area men in Maritime Service

- Wayne Cyril Fake
- Eugene Leon Ferree
- George Andrew Grove
- Gladston Charles Harris
- Edward Fife Holland
- Richard W. Keller
- Ned Roger Kinard
- Thomas Arthur Lloyd, Jr.
- Duke Richard Markey
- Cecil Vinton Matthews
- Richard Seth Minnich
- Arthur Elwood Oberlander
- Charles Milwen Oberlander
- Paul Charles Raub
- James Garfield Sheffer
- Henry Edmund Shive
- Bruce Clay Smith
- George Warren Taylor
- William Clair Thompson
- Irwin H. Trout

23. Penn Township Council of Defense volunteers, medical auxiliary members

- Mrs. William Crook
- Mrs. Bruce Moller
- Mrs. John Sheeley
- Mrs. Laura Bowman
- Marie Scheivert
- Mrs. Violet Yingling
- Anna Raubenstine
- Mrs. Velare Bair
- Mrs. Bernice Brenneman
- Eileen Kline
- Lottie Kraft
- Virginia Stahl
- Alta Koontz
- Mrs. Florence Wise
— plus about 20 others

24. York City-County Council of Defense committee chairmen, 1943

- Col. William H. Beckner
- C. Kenneth Shanaman
- Horace Keesey
- Mrs. Jay B. Arnold
- William J. Fisher
- Edwin C. Resser
- Arthur Thomas
- Mrs. C.B. Heinly
- Dr. Raymond M. Lauer
- John L. Snyder
- Mrs. Edythe Brenneman
- J.C. Huntting

25. Dover Council of Defense volunteers, auxiliary firemen

- Harry Neiman
- Ray Nagle
- Earl Lehigh
- Nelson Baughman
- Charles H. Spangler
- G.O. Gross
- Arthur Krone
- Raymond E. Miller
- William Mummert
- W.N. Gentzler
- John Yost
- Raymond Leas
- Clark Dallheimer
- William Swartz
- Emory Eisenhooth
- Blain Yost
- Earl Paulis
- C.E. Snellbaker
- Curvin Gettys
- Charles Goodwin Jr.
- S.T. Strayer
- Earl Sloat
- J. William Strayer
- J. William Klepper
- Curvin Shaffer

Thousands of Americans die in major wars

War	Numbers engaged	Battle deaths	Other deaths	Total deaths	Non-mortal wounds
Revolutionary War	Not available	4,435	Not available	Not available	6,188
War of 1812	286,730	2,260	Not available	Not available	4,505
Mexican War	78,718	1,733	Not available	Not available	4,152
Civil War	3,867,500	184,594	373,458	558,052	412,175
Union	2,803,300	110,070	249,458	359,528	275,175
Confederate	1,064,200	74,524	124,000	198,524	137,000
Spanish-American War	306,760	385	2,061	2,446	1,662
World War I	4,734,991	53,402	63,114	116,516	204,002
World War II	16,112,566	291,557	113,842	405,399	670,846
Korean War	5,720,000	33,652	3,262	36,914	103,284
War in Southeast Asia	8,744,000	47,366	10,801	58,167	153,303

Note: Numbers should be considered estimates

York County by the numbers

5th — Rank among state's oldest counties
1st — Rank west of the Susquehanna River

Notable early dates:
1741 — York's founding date
1749 — County separated from Lancaster County
1763-1767 — Mason and Dixon surveyed Pennsylvania-Maryland boundary line
1777 (Sept. 30) - 1778 (June 27) — Continental Congress' American Revolution visit
1787 — Incorporation of York as a borough
1800 — Adams County, with Gettysburg as county seat, separated from York County
1838 — Northern Central Railway reached York
1847 — Telegraph reached York
1887 — Incorporation of York as a city

Population:	1880	1940	1950
York City	13,979	56,712	59,704
York County	87,841	178,022	202,737

Geography:
1,400 square miles — Approximate county size before 1800
905 square miles — Approximate size after 1800
48 miles — Eastern boundary along Susquehanna River
40 miles — Southern boundary, Mason-Dixon Line
39 degrees 44 minutes — Latitude, Mason-Dixon Line
76 degrees 15 minutes west — Longitude, Susquehanna River
109 feet — Lowest county elevation (Susquehanna River near Peach Bottom)
392.975 feet — York's elevation (above sea level):
1,384 feet — Highest county elevation (Stone Head, near Dillsburg)

15

York Plan objectives

—

These are excerpts from William S. Shipley's speech "The York Plan," delivered on Feb. 10, 1941, at the 35th annual meeting of the Manufacturers' Association of York.

This cover photo from the York Ice Machinery Corporation newsletter for September 1941 shows executives from several York companies poring over drawings for 6-inch Barbette gun carriages, designed for harbor defense. Yorkco had just received a $2 million contract for the guns and sought to pool other companies in their production. W.S. Shipley, Yorkco board chairman, is at the head of the table, face resting on hand. Representatives from Brandt-Warner Manufacturing Co., S. Morgan Smith Co., Read Machinery Co. and A.B. Farquhar Co. also study the drawings.

'To do what we can ...'

The basic principles of the (York) Plan are as old as time itself, and it may be for this reason that the Plan stands out. Taking advice and helping each other is nothing new. So long as people have existed, they have been doing that. One of the outstanding reasons, I believe, for the development and growth of our country has been this very principle. I still say that our group claims no right of discovery. All we do claim, if we can claim anything, is putting back into harness these homely principles.

This Plan consists of 15 objectives, as follows:

1. To make use of our present facilities in regards to tools.

2. To get idle tools and idle men working.

3. To make a survey of the tools outside the metal trades.

4. To study types of work we could do, with the facilities at our command.

5. To make a decided effort to explain and sell the Defense Plan to the community.

6. To assist in educational work as it pertained to educating new employees.

7. To study housing.

8. To study workers' health.

9. To establish the costs of the sub-contractor to the prime contractor.

10. To study deliveries of sub-contractors so that the material would be supplied to the prime contractor as needed.

11. To impress on the minds of the sub-contractors the necessity for accuracy of work so as to assure Federal acceptance of the parts being furnished to the prime contractor.

12. To study supplying needed labor if and when working three shifts.

13. To study labor potentials in York.

14. To take steps to supply this additional labor when and where needed.

15. To enter into all local activities that dealt either directly or indirectly with the present emergency.

Having decided on our objective, we adopted as a slogan, and one that we have tried to live up to — TO DO WHAT WE CAN WITH WHAT WE HAVE. If we can follow this slogan, we know that we will be doing our country a great service.

Works consulted

Writers of history must depend on others who have provided scholarship in specific areas. This work is indebted to the following writers, whose material was used directly or indirectly. Many of these works are available at the York County Heritage Trust Historical Society Archives and Library.

York County/World War II history

Bloomfield, Charles Arthur. "The Great Depression in York County, Pennsylvania." Master's thesis. Millersville State College, 1973.

Gates, Norma Bear. "WW II Years ... The Way Life Was, As Told By Those Who Were There." York, Pa.: Norma Bear Gates, 2001.

Hatch, Carl E. and Joseph B. Hicks, eds. "World War I, York, Pennsylvania's Response." York, Pa.: Strine Publishing Co., 1972.

Hatch, Carl E., Joseph B. Hicks, Richard E. Kohler. "York, Pa. in the Roaring '20's." York, Pa.: Strine Publishing Co., 1973.

Hatch, Carl E., Joseph B. Hicks, Richard E. Kohler, Gordon W. Bailey. "York, Pa. in the Depression 1930's." York, Pa.: Strine Publishing Co., 1974.

Markey, Michael. "Jake, The General From West York Avenue." York, Pa.: York County Heritage Trust, 1998.

Mellander, G.A. and Carl E. Hatch. "The York Dispatch Index. The War Torn 1940s." York, Pa.: The Strine Publishing Co., n.d.

Rentzel, Bradley. "A History of Mount Wolf." Mount Wolf, Pa.: Mount Wolf Borough Council, 1978.

Rudisill, James. "York Since 1741." York, Pa.: York Graphic Services, Inc., 1991.

Schaefer, Thomas L. "York County at 250: Patterns of Our Past." York, Pa.: York County 250th Anniversary Commission, 1999.

Sheets, Georg R. "York County, To the Setting of the Sun, An Illustrated History." Sun Valley, Calif.: American Historical Press, 2002.

— "Made in York, A Survey of the Agricultural & Industrial Heritage of York County, Pennsylvania." York, Pa.: Agricultural & Industrial Museum of York County, 1991.

— "Children of the Circuit Riders: The Story of Asbury United Methodist Church." York, Pa.: Asbury United Methodist Church, 1985.

General History/World War II

Associated Press. "World War II, A 50th Anniversary History." New York: Henry Holt and Co., 1989.

Cooper, Patricia A., "Once A

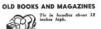

Standard Rag and Paper Co. provides wartime instructions on saving valuable waste paper in this 1942 advertisement.

Cigarmaker." Chicago: University of Illinois Press, 1992.

Dear, I.C.B., Gen. Ed., "The Oxford Companion to World War II." Oxford: Oxford University Press, 2001.

Kurzman, Dan. "No Greater Glory, The Four Immortal Chaplains and the Sinking of the Dorchester in World War II." New York: Random House, 2004.

Lawton, Manny. "Some Survived." Chapel Hill, N.C.: Algonquin Books, 2004.

McCullough, David. "Truman." New York: Simon & Schuster, 1992.

Morton, Lewis. "The Fall of the Philippines." Washington, D.C.: Center of Military History, U.S. Army, 1989.

"Pennsylvania's First Year at War." Harrisburg, Pa.: Pennsylvania Historical and Museum Commission, 1943.

"Pennsylvania's Second Year at War." Harrisburg, Pa.: Pennsylvania Historical and Museum Commission, 1945.

"Pennsylvania At War, 1941-1945." Harrisburg, Pa.: Pennsylvania Historical and Museum Commission, 1946.

Whiting, Charles. "America's Forgotten Army: The Story of the U.S. 7th." New York: St. Martin's Paperbacks, 1999.

Wright, Mike. "What They Didn't Teach You About World War II." New York: Ballantine Books, 1998.

General History/York County

"A History of West Manchester Township, York County, 1799-1999." York, Pa.: West Manchester Township Board of Supervisors, 1999.

"Centennial Celebration, 1899-1999, Felton, Pennsylvania." Felton, Pa.: History Book Committee, 1999.

"Commemorating the 100th Year of the Incorporation of New Freedom, Pennsylvania, 1873-1973." York, Pa.: Mehl Ad-Associates, 1973.

Curtis, James W., ed. "Yesterday's Hanover." Shippensburg, Pa.: Curtis & Co. and The Friends of the Hanover Public Library, 1994.

Drawbaugh, Charles C., ed. "A History of Dover Township, York County Pennsylvania, 1740s-1990s." Dover, Pa.: Dover Township Board of Supervisors, 1994.

Eberly, Philip K. "Susquehanna Radio, The First Fifty Years." York, Pa.: Susquehanna Radio Co., 1992.

Garrett, Elizabeth S., ed. "Greater Dover Bicentennial Celebration, 1764-1964." Dover, Pa.: No publisher, 1964.

Gates, Elizabeth Phillips. "The Life & Times of Goldsboro." Goldsboro, Pa.: Goldsboro Historical Association, 1976.

Gayman, Robert F. "History of Dillsburg, Pa., From Hitching Post to Drive-in Theater, 1901-1950." Dillsburg, Pa.: Northern York County Historical and Preservation Society, 2001.

Geiselman, John. "Commencing the 150th Year of the Founding of the Borough of Jacobus, York County, Pennsylvania, 1837-1987." York, Pa.: Mehl Ad-Associates, 1987.

Gladfelter, Armand. "Das Siebenthal, A History of Seven Valleys." York, Pa.: Mehl Ad-Associates, 1978.

Glatfelter, Charles. "The Story of Jefferson Codorus, Pennsylvania." Codorus, Pa.: Jefferson Community Centennial, Inc., 1966.

Grove, June R. and Richard K. Konkel. "A History of Chanceford Township, York County, Pennsylvania, 1747-1997." Brogue, Pa.: Brogue Community Lions Club, 1997.

Saving and collecting scrap to provide scarce metals and other resources for military use became a way of life in World War II. Here, Ammon R. Smith Auto Co. officials scour a York warehouse to find eight tons of material during a 1942 scrap drive. The used car sign, left, weighed several tons. The Smith warehouse also yielded several truckloads of junk material.

Hall, Clifford J. and John P. Lehr. "York County and the World War, 1914-1919." York, Pa.: Clifford J. Hall, John P. Lehr, 1920.

Hall, Joseph S., compiler. "Stewartstown, Pennsylvania, Then and Now, A Pictorial History of the Changing Faces of our Town." Stewartstown, Pa.: Stewartstown Historical Society, 2001.

Hatch, Carl E., Richard E. Kohler, and John F. Rauhauser, Jr. "Essays on York County History, 1776-1976." York, Pa.: Strine Publishing Co., 1976.

Hatch, Carl E., Richard E. Kohler, and Robert H. Terry. "Bicentennial Essays on York, Pa." York, Pa.: Strine Publishing Co., 1976.

"History of New Salem Borough, York County, Pa." York, Pa.: Mehl Ad-Associates, 1976.

Hubley, Jim. "Off the Record: York County Life Through a Newsman's Eyes." York, Pa.: York Graphic Services, 1994.

Jones, Molly K. "York City: 250 Years, 1741-1991." York, Pa.: Campbell, Harrington & Brear, Inc., 1991.

Kurowski, Sandra S., ed. "The Spring Grove Years." Spring Grove, Pa.: Spring Grove Centennial Publications Committee, 1982.

Lipper, Mark. "Paper, People, Progress. The Story of P.H. Glatfelter Company of Spring Grove, Pa." Englewood Cliffs, N.J.: Prentice Hall, Inc., 1980.

McClure, James. "Never to be Forgotten." York, Pa.: York Daily Record, 1999.

— "Murals of York," York, Pa.: York Daily Record, 2000.

— "Nine Months in York Town," York, Pa.: York Daily Record, 2001.

— "Almost Forgotten," York, Pa.: York Daily Record, 2002.

— "East of Gettysburg," York, Pa.: York Daily Record, 2003.

McGinnis, J. Ross. "Trials of Hex." York, Pa.: J. Ross McInnis, 2000.

Olson, McKinley C., ed. "J.W. Gitt's Sweet Land of Liberty." New York: Jerome S. Ozer, Publisher, 1975.

Peckham, Betty. "The Story of a Dynamic Community, York, Pa." York, Pa.: York Chamber of Commerce, 1946.

Rodengen, Jeffrey L. "The Legend of York International." Fort Lauderdale, Fla.: Write Stuff Syndicate, Inc., 1997.

Taub, Lynn Smolens. "Greater York in Action." York, Pa.: The York Area Chamber of Commerce, 1968.

Wilson, Roger B., Donald C. Robinson, James L. Morris, David B. Glenn. "The River and the Ridge, 300 Years of Local History, Peach Bottom Township and Delta, Pennsylvania, Cardiff and Whiteford, Maryland." Delta, Pa.: Old Line Museum, 2003.

All of us can Serve

PRAISE THE LORD!

Praise the Lord,
And get your scrap a-scrappin';
Praise the Lord,
For anything can happen;
Praise the Lord,
And get your scrap a-scrappin'
And we'll all be free.

Praise the Lord, the iron and steel is needed;
Praise the Lord, and let the call be heeded;
Praise the Lord, the iron and steel is needed
From you and me.

So go through the basement
And go through the attic
Get every piece of scrap you can see. Oh—oh,
Praise the Lord,
And get your scrap a-scrappin';
Praise the Lord, don't let them catch you
nappin';
Praise the Lord, and get your scrap a-scrappin'
For Vic-to-ry.

York City and County Council of Defense
SALVAGE COMMITTEE

County defense officials did what they could in 1943, including publishing verse, to raise awareness about the need for residents to search their basements and attics for scrap that could be turned into military materiel.

"1866-1966, 100 Years of Growth, Dallastown, Pennsylvania." York, Pa.: York, Pennsylvania Press Inc., undated.

Newspapers

The Associated Press

The Evening Sun, Hanover

The Gazette and Daily

The Gettysburg Times

The Sun, Baltimore

York Daily Record

The York Dispatch/York Sunday News

Publications, pamphlets, unpublished works

"Back to York." York Corp., undated.

Becker, Thomas, producer. "Vegetables for Victory, Spring 1943-1995." York, Pa.: Penn State Cooperative Extension, 1995.

"Cold Magic," "Shop News," publications of York Corp., 1939-1946.

Ferguson, Arthur W., compiler. "Annual Report of the York Public Schools, 1941-42 — 1954-5."

"Hello, Washington – York, Pa., Calling." The Saturday Evening Post, Oct. 25, 1941.

"Heroes of Hanover." Hanover, Pa.: Hanover Evening Sun, 1997.

Kling, Barbara. "The Homefront." Undated.

LeCates, Byron H. "The U.S.S. Indianapolis Tragedy." Paper read to the YsJs at York College, Nov. 27, 2000.

Misc. papers, World War II manuscript file 740.001-740.033, York County Heritage Trust Library and Archives.

"Polk's York City Directory, 1945-46." Boston: R.L. Polk & Co., Inc., Publishers, 1946.

"Red Lion Echoes, For the Boys in the Service." Red Lion, Pa.: Citizens of Red Lion, Penna., 1944-45.

"Red Lion Hilltop." Red Lion High School, Oct. 24, 1941.

Shipley, Bill III. "Shipley Shape, Essays on the Occasion of our 75th Anniversary," 2004.

"The Tattler." William Penn High School, 1943.

"The York-High Weekly." York, Pa., 1942-1944.

"The York Plan: Addresses delivered at the Thirty-Fifth Annual Meeting of the Association." Feb. 10, 1941.

"Those Who Served in World War II, Red Lion, Pennsylvania." Red Lion, Pa.: Citizens Committee of Red Lion, Pa., 1946.

Wolfe, John F. M., compiler. "Profile of Aviation, York County, Pennsylvania, 1925-1998." York, Pa.: Wolf Printing, 1998.

"World War II, Through the YCI-YCA Looking Glass." The Heritage Society, Fourth Annual Dinner, 1995.

Interviews and private collections

Orin Stambaugh, correspondence with the author.

Robert Frutiger, Red Lion

Papers of Anne Frutiger, Red Lion.

Robert N. and Ethel Senft, York.

World Wide Web

'America from the Great Depression to World War II," http://memory.loc.gov/ammen/fsahtml/fahome.html.

"Blue and White Devils: The Story of the 3rd Infantry Division," www.lonesentry.com/, 2005

"Bravest of Four Minute Men: Volunteer Speeches During World War I," www.historymatters.gmu.edu, 2005.

"Company overview," www.glatfelter.com/, 2005.

"Evelyn Sharp," http://www.wpafb.af.mil/museum/history/wasp/wasp29.htm, 2005.

"Grandson improves on Pearl Harbor vet's burial request," http://starbulletin.com/2003/08/31/news/story4.html, 2005

"Powers of Persuasion — Posters from World War II," National Archives and Records Administration, www.archives.gov/exhibit_hall/, 2005.

"Produce For Victory, Posters on the American Home Front (1941-45)," Museum of American History www.americanhistory.si.edu/victory/, 2005.

"Shipley's History," www.shipleyenergy.com, 2005.

"The Bravest of the Brave," "The Medal of Honor." www.medalofhonor.com/, 2005.

"A summons to comradeship," University of Minnesota Libraries, http://digital.lib.umn.edu/war-posters/, 2005.

"War Posters Collection," Enoch Pratt Free Library, www.epfl.net/exhibits/warposters/, 2005.

"World War II Poster Collection, Northwestern University Library, http://www.library.northwestern.edu/govpub/collections/wwii-posters/, 2005.

Index

Farm Security Administration-Office of War Information representatives visited York County in 1942 to document war mobilization efforts. Here, a government photographer captures a York Safe and Lock worker making 37 mm guns and gun mounts.

By February 1942, Floorola's York plant had almost completed conversion of equipment to accommodate defense work. In this Office of War Information photograph, a worker operates a five-spindle drill press, previously used to make floor-waxing machines, equipped with a special chuck and drill for production of anti-aircraft guns.

C

D

Gerald Smith, 28, assembles 37 mm gun mounts at York Safe and Lock Company. The work of Farm Security Administration-Office of War Information photographers is important in the history of documentary photography. The work initially portrayed Americans in rural areas, emphasizing the era of the Great Depression. The program evolved to capture the buildup in U.S. defense plants, which brought America out of the Depression. Government photographers took 160,000 black-and-white images and 1,600 color photographs from 1935-1945.

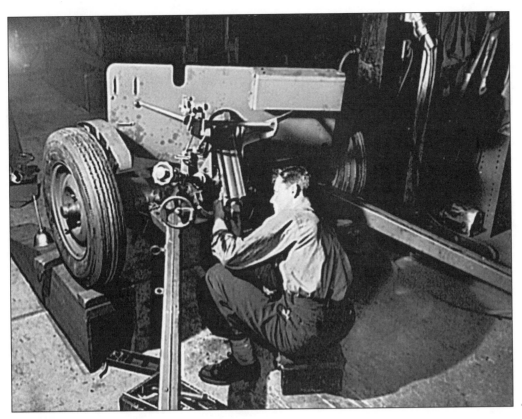

An Office of War Information photographer captures Gerald Smith on film with the caption, 'Assembling weapons for Victory to be used by the armed forces.'

This York Safe and Lock worker, an auto mechanic for 16 years, assembles 37 mm gun mounts.

Twenty children initially attended a nursery school sponsored by the York City and County Council of Defense. The council created the school to aid children whose parents were working in defense plants, away in uniform or both. Pictured having an afternoon snack in this Gazette and Daily photo, from left: Nancy Ann Myers, Bonita Lambert, Freddie Miller, Lynn Douglas, Jeanne Shutter and Barbara Ann Ernst. The school operated at Visiting Nurse Association headquarters from 6:30 a.m.-6:30 p.m., 6 days a week. Priscilla Ilgenfritz was in charge of the students.

Many women were compelled to enter the manufacturing workplace after the attack on Pearl Harbor. Men formerly on shop floors were called to war, thus creating a strong demand. Many women had to work because the military pay afforded their husbands or family breadwinner could not cover family expenses. Here, in a photograph from York County Heritage Trust, young women work on an assembly line at a York defense plant.

This young woman handles the controls at a York defense plant, circa 1942, in this York County Heritage Trust photograph.

JAMES McCLURE

James McClure is editor of the York Daily Record/Sunday News. He earned a master's degree in American studies from Penn State Harrisburg. He is past president of the Pennsylvania Associated Press Managing Editors and the Pennsylvania Society of Newspaper Editors. His previous historical publications include four books: "Never to be Forgotten, A Year-By-Year Look at York County's Past"; "Nine Months in York Town, American Revolutionaries Labor on Pennsylvania's Frontier"; "Almost Forgotten, A Glimpse at Black History in York County, Pa."; and "East of Gettysburg, A Gray Shadow Crosses York County, Pa." He served as general editor of the three-volume "250th Chronicles," published during York County's bisesquicentennial in 1999.

Editors

KIM STRONG

Kim Strong, assistant managing editor for The Patriot-News, Harrisburg, served as the primary content editor of this work. She earned a bachelor of arts degree from Penn State University and later served as adviser to the Daily Collegian at Penn State and editorial page editor and writing coach for the York Daily Record. She is a frequent presenter at regional and national newspaper writing workshops.

DEBORAH L. HUMMEL

Deborah L. Hummel, Daily Record/Sunday News copy editor, edited this work. She earned a bachelor of arts degree in English from Millersville University, a master's of education degree in reading and the language arts from the same university, and holds elementary education and reading specialist certifications.

Designers

TED SICKLER

Ted Sickler, assistant managing editor for the Daily Record/Sunday News, coordinated photographs and served as principal designer for this work. He is a doctoral candidate in American history at the University of Delaware. He earned a master's degree in American studies from Penn State Harrisburg and serves as an adjunct instructor in American studies at Lebanon Valley College.

TRACEY BISHER CULLEN

Tracey Bisher Cullen, Daily Record/Sunday News graphic artist, designed the cover and other pages. She earned a bachelor of fine arts degree from Kutztown University.

SAMANTHA K. DELLINGER

Samantha K, Dellinger, Daily Record/Sunday News graphic artist, designed the maps and other pages. She earned an associate's degree in graphic design at the Pennsylvania School of Art and Design.

The June 1943 issue of Shop News shows York Corporation's service pennant bearing one Gold Star and the number of Yorkco employees then in the Armed Services. The Gold Star recognized the death of gunner William D. Ensminger Jr., who died when his bomber crashed in a training exercise in Florida.

This flag at York Corporation's West York plant shows that 24 Gold-Star employees lost their lives in World War II through V-E Day, and 1,148 served in the military. News about Thomas W. Frutiger's death after a lengthy imprisonment in the Philippines reached the community in July 1945, upping the company's Gold Star total to 25. The company placed the final number served at 1,200.

FLO SNYDER

Flo's SCRAPBOOK

A VISION

How long does it take to live a
    dream?
  Renew once more a forgotten way,
To count the bands of sunlight beams,
  Or wait for night to turn to day?

At dusk I climb upon a hill
  Where I can almost touch a star,
To pray and hope with all my fill
  And recount every blissful hour.

I press my ear unto the earth
  Sure that I may hear some sound,
Of him who from his land of birth
  Is fighting on some foreign ground.

I lift my head upward to pray
  Then humbly lower it instead.
To Thee, dear God, I want to say
  My soul hungers, it must be fed.

The things I want, they are not great,
  In fact they're very small.
To Thee my weary heart I bring
  For Thee to remedy all.

I want a house in which to rest,
  Some happy children, too.
True friends that prove they are the
    best,
  A land that's bright and new.

I want to see the level plains,
  The mountains, rivers, lakes.
The smell of Nature's fresh clean
    rain,
  All beauty that God makes.

I want to see the fearless men
  With peace lights in their eyes,
Who build our Nation up again
  Through guidance from the skies.

Then last, O God, I want to see
  My love and all return,
Back to their land of liberty
  Where flames of hope forever burn.

Written by
Flo Snyder
Manufacturing-Accounting Dept.

York Corporation's Flo Snyder's "A Vision" summed up the dreams of many during the darkest days of the war. It appeared in the June 1943 edition of Shop News.